Women and the National Experience

Primary Sources in American History

Ellen Skinner
Pace University

Executive Editor: Bruce Borland
Supplements Editor: Jessica Bayne
Page Design and Layout: Judith Anderson
Cover Design: Kay Petronio
Manufacturing and Production: Rohnda Barnes

Ellen Skinner, *Women and the National Experience: Primary Sources in American History*.

ISBN: 0-673-99297-7

98 99 00 9 8 7 6 5 4

Contents

Preface

This collection, *Women and the National Experience: Primary Sources in American History*, brings together a diverse selection of women's voices from the American past. Read together, these sources underline the historical significance of women's lives and the role of women in molding the national experience. Covering a wide range of experiences and including the voices of women from different class, ethnic, racial and regional backgrounds, the sources enhance a holistic understanding of the nation's development. The documentary record provides dramatic evidence that outspoken women attained a public voice and participated in the development of national events and policies long before they gained the vote, legal rights, or equal educational opportunity.

Although social and cultural norms limited women to private lives and banned them from public speaking, women from diverse backgrounds spoke out and embarked on a crusade for political and legal rights. In the 1830s, the abolitionist Sarah Grimké responded to male outrage over her "ostentatious" and "intrusive" public speaking by claiming that women possessed the same right as men to express their conscience in public. Told that such a public display was unnatural behavior for a woman, she responded "all I ask of our brethren is that they take their feet off our necks and permit us to stand upright." Women such as Elizabeth Cady Stanton, Lucy Stone and Susan B. Anthony spent a lifetime writing and lecturing about the need for legal equity and the right to vote. Other women such as Emma Willard and M. Carey Thomas devoted their lives to securing educational opportunity for women. African-American women faced an enormous challenge of overcoming racist and sexist assumptions and led lives limited, in most cases, by poverty. Yet, Harriet Tubman, Sojourner Truth, and Ida Wells-Barnett struggled to liberate others. Defiant and courageous, their lives testified to the superficiality of the stereotypes that described women as submissive and weak.

Despite attempts to limit them to the home, women participated in humanitarian and social reforms. Both white and African-American women organized benevolent associations and launched community-based charity work. Women such as Dorothea Dix played a central role in securing better treatment for the mentally ill. Still without the vote, between the 1880s and World War I, nationwide networks of women's clubs promoted government reform that linked the concerns of the home to the well-being of the nation. During the Progressive era, Jane Addams and Florence Kelley were among the nation's foremost advocates of protective legislation for women and children.

Although women were assumed to be domestic beings, they provided the nation with its first major source of industrial labor. At Lowell, Massachusetts, women factory workers like Sarah Bagley asserted their right to better working conditions and, despite the fact that women had no political voice, spoke before the Massachusetts state legislature on the need for a ten-hour work day. Some, like Ellen Munroe, demanded not only better conditions but equal pay.

Both the domestic and public aspects of women's lives were vital to the development of the nation, yet, until recently neither role was considered significant for historical study. The exclusion of women from the historical record expressed deeply entrenched and widely held cultural beliefs that women's work and women's lives were too inconsequential and insignificant for historical study. Yet women were never at the margins of history. Affirming women's patriotism during the American Revolution, Esther de Berdt Reed noted how some would censure women from even knowing about their past. Denying women's history has served to reinforce women's subordinate status. It is only when gendered assumptions are accepted as historical fact that women's lives appear secondary to those of men.

Throughout the nation's history, gender differentiation has helped determine appropriate male and female behavior. Between the colonial period and the present, vast changes in gender roles and the relationship between men and women have occurred. As a society, it is no longer acceptable for husbands to beat or have sexual control over their wives. We are dismayed by Emily Collins' reminiscences that before the Civil War it was considered "right and proper" in rural areas for husbands to beat their wives. From an 1840s lament about unwanted pregnancy ("Unwelcome Child") to the letters written to Margaret Sanger demanding birth control information, we are reminded that husbands all too often exercised their ownership of their wives' bodies. Only recently have state laws begun to acknowledge marital rape.

For generations, women were denied a public voice. Church and political leaders repeatedly informed women that they should confine themselves to the home. It took more than seventy years of protest before the vote was gained in 1920. Now women frequently run for public office. In *Bradwell* v. *Illinois* (1869), the Supreme Court found "the natural and proper timidity and delicacy which belongs to the female sex evidently unfits it for many of the occupations of civil life." This included the practice of law. Now women occupy seats on the Supreme Court.

The founding fathers wove the subordination of women into the fabric of the new nation. John Adams dismissed his wife Abigail's plea for a more equitable distribution of power despite his commitment to liberty. He ignored her warning that "All men would be tyrants if they could." Incorporated in the nation's political and social system was the legal tradition that denied married women an identity separate from that of their husbands. In this tradition, known as *femme covert*, men had complete claim to their spouses' property and body.

During the nineteenth century, assertions about the differences between men and women crystallized into an elaborate, full-blown ideology of separate spheres. Commentary about appropriate female behavior flowed into popular journals, prescriptive literature and sermons. It was asserted that "true" womanhood depended on women being full-time wives and mothers. Advocates depicted women as naturally sympathetic, emotional, caring, pious and virtuous, qualities that ideally suited them to motherhood, but made them poor choices for commercial and political life. Within their sphere, women gained respect as mothers but grew increasingly dependent on their husbands. Paid employment for married women was considered inappropriate. Husbands alone were to be responsible for their family's support. From the advice books of John S. C. Abbott to the words of former President Grover Cleveland, women were tied to cultural norms of domesticity and motherhood. Women who departed from this role were described as unnatural, unfeminine, and a threat to social stability and national well-being.

Although the majority of families still lived on farms and in rural towns, emphasis on female dependency reflected the decline of the urban middle-class home as a unit of shared economic production. Responding to new commercial opportunities, husbands left their wives with full responsibility for child and home care. Household work no longer included spinning and weaving, but still involved everything from canning fruit and vegetables, to baking and cleaning. Even with the help of domestics, housework was unending and exhausting before the development of labor saving technology. Unpaid, housework confirmed the belief that "real work"— paid labor outside the home—belonged to men.

The division between the work roles of men and women cut across class barriers and influenced the structure of the workplace. Most unions excluded women. Within the professions of medicine and law, men vigilantly protected themselves from female intrusion. Dr. Edward Clark of Harvard University offered (supposedly) clinical evidence to prove that college education weakened women's minds and destroyed their reproductive organs. Working-class men agitated for a family wage that would make it unnecessary for wives to work outside their homes. Employers used these assumptions about women's domestic role to keep their pay at approximately half of what men received. After all, a "true" woman had a husband to support her and only needed a supplementary wage. Even Leonora Barry, who organized women for membership in the Knights of Labor during the late nineteenth century, wrote that the family wage was a preferable alternative to women working. Yet, women such as Caroline Dall and Rose Schneiderman cried out for empowerment and workplace equity. Their defiant emphasis on women's fundamental economic rights offset those who fostered women's dependency.

During the Depression in the 1930s, the issue of married women working became part of a national debate. Ruth Shallcross wrote that most Americans thought married women should not work. Only at times of national emergency were gender roles relaxed. World Wars I and II created a labor shortage, and women were hired for nontraditional work in large numbers. After both wars women were displaced by men, even though many claimed they needed to work for their economic survival.

Women responded to the construction of gender roles in different ways. Some women, like the late nineteenth-century anti-suffragist Amelia Barr, internalized the belief that women were vastly different from men and in need of male protection. Such women found fulfillment within their separate sphere and promoted women's identity as caregivers and housewives. In contrast, feminists like Elizabeth Cady Stanton, Lucy Stone, and Lucretia Mott held men responsible for the constraints that narrowed women's life choices. They shared the belief that women's social, economic, and political subordination arose not as a result of biology but because men imposed limitations on women that expressed and reinforced male power.

Pioneer feminists labeled women's dependency on men degrading. They argued for women's right to self-definition. The first-generation feminists recognized that women's authority and security within their private sphere was more an illusion than reality, since women remained financially dependent on their husbands and lacked the right to control their own bodies. In an 1855 letter, Lucy Stone noted "Has a woman a right to herself? It is very little to me to have the right to vote, to own property, etc., if I may not keep my body and its uses in my absolute right. Not one wife in a thousand can do that now."

The Seneca Falls Declaration of Sentiments (1848) can be read as a cry for autonomy. Feminists argued that women should be allowed to find their own sphere of activity; to work, to enter the professions; or, if they chose, to be wives and mothers. Although women's rights advocates were generally also mothers, they sought to dismantle the notion that "true" womanhood depended only on the roles of wife and mother. To women like Elizabeth Cady Stanton, a woman was a human being, a citizen, an individual, and her identity as a wife and mother were incidental. This was a direct challenge to the conventional assumptions succinctly expressed by a male critic of women's rights: "A woman is nothing. A wife is everything. . . [their] rights are as Wives, Belles, Virgins, and Mothers, and not as women."

Not as militant as the pioneer feminists, other women accommodated themselves to the cultural assumption that linked women to the domestic realm, but infused domesticity with activist zeal. They carried their maternal mission from the home to the community and ultimately to the nation. Rooted in women's benevolent associations of the early 1800s, white and African-American women carved out reforms that helped promote government's assumption of social responsibility. Twentieth-century suffragists repeatedly argued that women's maternal interests and sympathetic natures entitled them to the public participation that would "protect the home" and benefit the nation.

The resurgence of feminism in the 1960s gave new prominence to issues of gender. In its first organizational statement (1966) the National Organization for Women called upon men and women to restructure gender roles. Only then would women be able to combine motherhood and career without a dual burden or an impossible choice. Women's liberationists spoke of sexism, and alleged that male abuse of power was at the root of rape and other forms of violence toward women. They affirmed a women's right to control her own body. Although they promoted a women's right to a safe abortion, in contrast to the pioneer feminists' argument for "voluntary motherhood" and sexual abstinence, the issue of self-determination was the same.

Although gendered beliefs and institutions confront all women, they have not applied equally to women of different class, ethnic, and racial groups. African-American women encountered the intersection of race and gender bias. As enslaved women they were vulnerable to sexual abuse and exploitation. With emancipation they continued to encounter racism. Mary Church Terrell, whose fight for civil rights stretched from the 1880s to the 1950s, described what it was like to be a black woman in Washington D.C. at the turn of the century. She recounts the indignity of sitting behind a screen in a restaurant and being denied entry into a theater. Doors open to her white "sisters" were shut in her face. While some women, like the antebellum abolitionists, sought to develop a sisterhood that cut across racial lines, twentieth-century white women's clubs and suffrage groups refused membership to African-American women. Many African-American women have promoted racial solidarity with black men. Yet, at times, racial identity clashed with gender identity for African-American women, as can be seen in the recent sexual harassment allegations of Anita Hill against Clarence Thomas. Similar complexities of identity have confronted Mexican and Native American women. The Native American Kate Shanley relates the struggle to balance feminist objectives with ethnic identity and tribal concerns.

Thus, gender separated women from men and contributed to women's personal and social identities, but neither guaranteed the development of an inclusive sisterhood, nor unanimity about whether to uphold, modify, or dismantle traditional gender roles. Still, generations of women in the United States have struggled for empowerment. The lengthy crusade to obtain gender equity is an essential part of the narrative of American history.

This collection of primary sources contributes to the growing field of gender studies and women's history and underscores the inadequacy of studying the nation's past from a male perspective.

I would like to acknowledge several outside reviewers for their thoughtful critiques and suggestions, especially Judith Parsons of Sul Ross State University; Ardis Cameron of the University of Southern Maine; and Rebecca Sharpless of Baylor University. At HarperCollins, I am especially indebted to Jessica Bayne whose intelligence and imagination contributed greatly to this book.

1

Gender Patterns in the Colonial Era

In colonial America and in Europe, people commonly believed that women were the "weaker vessel"—morally and mentally deficient and physically inferior to men. As the "weaker sex," women were subordinate to men, and subject to male authority—first to their fathers' and then to their husbands'. Within the family and society, men were the "head," the "governing body" to which women were expected to be obedient. Women were expected to be wives and mothers and to lead quiet, unassuming private lives, like the exemplary Anne Bradstreet whose literary gifts remained hidden within the confines of her family. Women who violated the boundaries of acceptable behavior—and, like Anne Hutchinson developed a public identity—risked communal censure and punishment.

At marriage, a colonial woman's legal identity was erased and became subsumed under that of her husband, in a tradition referred to as femme covert, from the French, meaning "covered" woman. This tradition ensured that married women could not own or control property, obtain guardianship over their children, or sue or be sued in court. Husbands had complete authority over their wives and children; however, they were expected to be benevolent patriarchs. Clergymen, like Benjamin Wadsworth, counseled husbands to rule their wives with love and kindness.

For most wives household production, frequent pregnancies and the care of large families molded daily existence. Women were expected to bear many children. Pain, suffering and even death in childbirth were considered part of female destiny. In a society characterized by frequent births, midwives played a critical role. Colonial women actively participated in the production of food and goods on which family survival depended. Women sustained their families by spinning cloth, churning butter, making soap and candles and tending chicken and cows. Gender specified tasks, but household production was a family venture, and women were expected to have both physical strength and multiple skills. Wives also helped their husbands in shoemaking, innkeeping and producing flour. Some widows and single women ran small businesses and taverns. Although their contribution to economic survival was vital, women's social status remained secondary and supplemental to that of men. Moreover, because women were assumed to be destined at birth for maternal and domestic roles, education was not considered necessary, so very few colonial women were literate.

Only in religion did women receive some degree of equality. The Puritans considered the conversion experience possible for both men and women, and Anne Bradstreet's poetry testifies to the centrality of religious beliefs. Yet, Puritan men strictly enforced the ban on women speaking in public or assuming religious leadership. A more genuine expression of gender equity occurred within the Quaker religion. Women shared spiritual authority with men and the right to speak at religious meetings.

A division of labor and authority by gender also prevailed among Native Americans. Yet, in many significant ways, as Mary Jemison's narrative of her life among the Seneca reveals, Native American women's life experiences were different from those of European women. Native American women left no written testimony. The primary documents that survive are mainly observations of European explorers, missionaries and male colonists. Because these writers, like Chrestien Le Clercq, lacked familiarity with the indigenous people, much of their interpretations were biased and reflect European, rather than indigenous, cultural preoccupations. Despite these documentary limitations, the available evidence indicates that indigenous women possessed more power and authority than their colonial counterparts. But neither women's authority nor that of Native American men could prevent the displacement, death and tribal destruction that accompanied colonial settlement.

Within colonial society, social relationships reflected a complex set of distinctions—the intertwined identities of race, class, and gender. Thus, although women were, in general, subordinate to men, elite white women shared with men certain privileges based on their race and class. Indentured servants and African-American slaves were at the bottom of the social hierarchy, and their lives were limited by their oppression. Statutes in Virginia and Maryland outlawed interracial unions, and penalized the children of these unions with enslavement. Both indentured servants and enslaved women were vulnerable to sexual exploitation, and had no defense against unwanted sexual advances. Indentured servants who became pregnant were subject to extended terms of servitude.

Anne Hutchinson, *Trial* (1638)

Anne Hutchinson (1591–1643) arrived in the Puritan colony of Massachusetts Bay in 1634, and soon began to serve as a midwife and a religious advisor. She challenged both orthodox religious tenets and male authority. The following document is from her 1637 trial where she was found guilty of holding unacceptable religious beliefs. She was banished from the colony. Her punishment reflected more than orthodox outrage at her religious practices—it expressed disapproval of her transgression of gender roles. As a religious instructor, she violated the ban against women speaking in public, and her mixed audiences were considered "promiscuous." What evidence did the court offer that Hutchinson's behavior was inappropriate and threatened family stability? What defense did Hutchinson provide?[*]

One Mistris Hutchinson, the wife of Mr. William Hutchinson of Boston (a very honest and peaceable man of good estate) and the daughter of Mr. Marbury, sometimes a Preacher in Lincolnshire, after of London [was] a woman of haughty and fierce carriage, of a nimble wit and active spirit, and a very voluble tongue, more bold then a man, though in understanding and judgment, inferior to many women. This woman had learned her skill in England, and had discovered some of her opinions in the Ship, as she came over, which has caused some jealousie of her, which gave occasion of some delay of her admission, when she cunningly dissembled and coloured her opinions; as she soon got over that block, and was admitted into the Church, then she began to go to work, and became a woman very helpfull in the times of child-birth, and other occasions of bodily infirmities, and well furnished with means for those purposes, she easily insinuated her selfe into the affections of many. . . . But when she had thus prepared the way by such wholesome truths, then she begins to set forth her own stuffe, and taught that no sanctification was nay evidence of a good estate, except their justification were first cleared up to them by the immediate witnesse of the Spirit, and that to see any work of grace (either faith or repentance, &c.) before this immediate witnesse, was a Covenant of works: whereupon many good soules, that had been of long approved godlinesse, were brought to renounce all the work of grace in them, and to wait for this immediate revelation. . . . Indeed it was a wonder upon what a sudden the whole Church of Boston (some few excepted) were become her new converts, and infected with her opinions, and many also out of the Church, and of other Churches also, yea, many profane persons became of her opinion, for it was a

---

[*] From John Winthrop, *The Short Story of the Rise, Reign and Ruin of the Antinomians of New England* (London, 1644).

very easie, and acceptable way to heaven, to see nothing, to have nothing, but waite for Christ to do all; so that after she had thus prevailed, and had drawn some of eminent place and parts to her party (whereof some profited so well, as in a few months they outwent their teacher) then she kept open house for all comers, and set up two Lecture dayes in the week, when they usually met at her house, threescore or fourescore persons, the pretense was to repeate Sermons, but when that was done, she would comment upon the Doctrines, and interpret all passages at her pleasure . . .

COURT: What say you to your weekly publick meetings? can you shew a warrant for them?

HUTCH: I will shew you how I took it up, there were such meetings in use before I came, and because I went to none of them, this was the speciall reason of my taking up this course, wee began it but with five or six, and though it grew to more in future time, yet being tolerated at the first, I knew not why it might not continue.

COURT: There were private meetings indeed, and arte still in many places, of some few neighbours, but not so publick and frequent as yours, and are of use for increase of love, and mutuall edification, but yours are of another nature, if they had been such as yours they had been evill, and therefore no good warrant to justifie yours; but answer by what authority, or rule, you uphold them.

HUTCH: By Tit. 2 where the elder women are to teach the younger.

COURT: So wee allow you to do, as the Apostle there meanes, privately, and upon occasion, but that gives no warrant of such set meetings for that purpose; and besides, you take upon you to teach many that are elder than your selfe, neither do you teach them that which the Apostle commands, *viz*, to keep at home.

HUTCH: Will you please to give mee a rule against it, and I will yield?

COURT: You must have a rule for it, or else you cannot do it in faith, yet you have a plaine rule against it; I permit not a woman to teach.

HUTCH: That is meant of teaching me.

COURT: If a man in distresse of conscience or other temptation, &c. should come and ask your counsell in private, might you not teach him?

HUTCH: Yes.

COURT: Then it is cleare, that it is not meant of teaching men, but of teaching in publick.

HUTCH: It is said, I will poure my Spirit upon your Daughters, and they shall prophesie, &c. If God give mee a gift of Prophecy, I may use it . . .

COURT: Yes, you are the woman of most note, and of best abilities, and if some other take upon them the like, it is by your teaching and example, but you shew not in all this, by what authority you take upon you to bee such a publick instructor: (after shee had stood a short time, the Court gave her leave to sit downe, for her countenance discovered some bodily infirmity.)

HUTCH: Here is my authority, Aquila and Priscilla, tooke upon them to instruct Apollo, more perfectly, yet he was a man of good parts, but they being better instructed might teach him.

COURT: See how your argument stands, Priscilla with her husband, tooke Apollo home and instruct him privately, therefore Mistris Hutchinson without her husband may teach sixty or eighty.

HUTCH: I call them not, but if they come to me, I may instruct them.

COURT: Yet you shew us not a rule.

HUTCH: I have given you two places of Scripture.

COURT: But neither of them will sute your practise.

HUTCH: Must I shew my name written therein?

COURT: You must shew that which must be equivalent, seeing your Ministry is publicke, you would have them receive your instruction, as coming from such an Ordinance.

HUTCH: They must not take it as it comes from me, but as it comes from the Lord Jesus Christ, and if I tooke upon me a publick Ministry, I should breake a rule, but not in exercising a gift of Prophecy, and I would see a rule to turne away them that come to me.

COURT: It is your exercise which drawes them, and by occasion thereof, many families are neglected, and much time lost, and a great damage comes to the Common-Wealth thereby, which wee that are be trusted with, as the Fathers of the Common-Wealth, are not to suffer . . .

    Forasmuch as you, Mrs. Huchison, have highly transgressed & offended, & forasmuch as yow have soe many ways troubled the Church with yor Errors & *have drawen away many a poor soule & have* upheld yor Revelations: *& forasmuch as* you have made a Lye, *&c. Therefore in the name of our Lord Je: Ch: & in the name of the Church I doe not only pronounce you worthy to be cast owt, but* I doe cast yow out & *in the name of Ch. I doe deliver you up to Satan, that yow may learne no more to blaspheme, to seduce & to lye, & I doe account yow from this time forth to be a Hethen & a Publican & soe to be held of all the Bretheren & Sisters, of this Congregation, & of others: therefor* I command yow *in the name of Ch: Je: & of this Church* as a Leper to withdraw yor selfe owt of the Congregation; *that as formerly yow have dispised & contemned the*

Holy Ordinances of God, & turned yor Backe on them, soe yow may now have no part in them nor benefit by them . . .

Then God himselfe was pleased to step in with his casting voice, and bring in his owne vote and suffrage from heaven, by testifying his displeasure against their opinions and practices, as clearly as if he had pointed with his finger, in causing the two fomenting women in the time of the height of the Opinions to produce out of their wombs, as before they had out of their braines, such monstrous births as no Chronicle (I thinke) hardly ever recorded the life. Mistris Dier brought forth her birth of a woman child, a fist, a beast, and a fowle, all woven together in one, and without an head . . .

Anne Bradstreet, *Before the Birth of One of Her Children* (c. 1650)

Although Ann Bradstreet (1612–1672) is now considered the seventeenth century's leading colonial poet, she did not write for publication. She wrote privately, for her family, in part because Puritan culture limited women to the home and family. In the following poem, Bradstreet addressed the possibility that she might die in childbirth. During the colonial era, death during childbirth was frequent. What did Bradstreet mean by the plea that her "babes" be protected from "stepdam's injury?" For whom is the poem written?[*]

All things within this fading world have end.
Adversity doth still our joys attend;
No ties so strong, no friends so dear and sweet,
But with death's parting blow are sure to meet.
The sentence passed is most irrevocable,
A common thing, yet, oh, inevitable.
How soon, my dear, death may my steps attend,
How soon it may be thy lot to lose thy friend,
We both are ignorant; yet love bids me
These farewell lines to recommend to three,
That when that knot's untied that made us one
I may seem thine who in effect am none.
And if I see not half my days that are due,

---

[*] From Anne Bradstreet, *The Poems of Mrs. Anne Bradstreet* (Boston, 1758).

What nature would God grant to yours and you.
The many faults that well you know I have
Let be interred in my oblivion's grave;
If any worth or virtue were in me,
Let that live freshly in thy memory,
And when thou feelest no grief, as I no harms,
Yet love thy dead, who long lay in thine arms;
And when thy loss shall be repaid with gains
Look to my little babes, my dear remains,
And if thou love thyself, or lovedst me,
These oh protect from stepdam's injury.
And if chance to thine eyes shall bring this verse,
With some sad sighs honor my absent hearse;
And kiss this paper for thy love's dear sake,
Who with salt tears this last farewell did take.

Cotton Mather, *The Wonders of the Invisible World: Trial of Susanna Martin* (1692)

A series of witchcraft trials were held in Salem, Massachusetts, during 1692. The highly influential Puritan minister Cotton Mather recorded the proceedings described in this document. As alleged witches and accusers, women played a major role in the Salem witch trials. The assumption that women were morally weak and easily seduced by the devil had deep roots in European history, and the allegation of witchcraft frequently resulted in death. What particular manifestations of "She-Devil" behavior did Susanna Martin exhibit?*

I. Susanna Martin, pleading Not Guilty to the Indictment of Witchcraft brought in against her, there were produced the evidences of many persons very sensibly and grievously Bewitched; who all complained of the prisoner at the Bar, as the person whom they Believed the cause of their Miseries. And now, as well as in the other Trials, there was an extraordinary endeavor by Witchcrafts, with Cruel and Frequent Fits, to hinder the poor sufferers from giving in their complaints; which the Court was forced with much patience to obtain, by much waiting and watching for it . . .

---

* From *Narratives of the Witchcraft Cases, 1648–1706*, ed. George Lincoln Burr, (New York: Barnes and Noble, Inc., 1946), 229–36.

IV. John Atkinson Testify'd, That he Exchanged a Cow with a Son of Susanna Martins's, whereat she muttered, and was unwilling he should have it. Going to Receive this Cow, tho' he Hamstring'd her, and Halter'd her, she of a Tame Creature grew so mad, that they could scarce get her along. She broke all the Ropes that were fastened unto her, and though she was Ty'd fast unto a Tree, yet she made her Escape, and gave them such further Trouble, as they could ascribe to no cause by Witchcraft.

V. Bernard testify'd, That being in Bed on a Lords-day Night, he heard a scrabbling at the Window, whereat he then saw Susanna Martin come in, and jump down upon the Floor. She took hold of this Deponents Feet, and drawing his Body up into a Heap, she lay upon him near Two Hours; in all which time he could neither speak nor stir. At length, when he could begin to move, he laid hold on her Hand, and pulling it up to his mouth, he bit three of the Fingers, as he judged unto the Bone. Whereupon she went from the Chamber, down the Stairs, out at the Door. This Deponent thereupon called unto the people of the House, to advise them of what passed; and he himself did follow her. The people saw her not; but there being a Bucket at the Left-hand of the Door, there was a drop of Blood found on it; and several more drops of Blood upon the Snow newly falled abroad. There was likewise the print of her tow feet just without the Threshold; but no more sign of any Footing further off . . .

VI. Robert Downer testifyed, That this Prisoner being some years ago prosecuted at Court for a Witch, he then said unto her, He believed she was a Witch. Whereat she being dissatisfied, said, That some She-Devil would Shortly fetch him away! Which words were heard by others, as well as himself. The night following, as he lay in his Bed, there came in at the Window the likeness of a Cat, which Flew upon him, took fast hold of his Throat, lay on him a considerable while, and almost killed him. At length he remembered what Susanna Martin had threatened the Day before; and with must striving he cryed out, "Avoid, though She-Devil! In the Name of God the Father, the Son, and the Holy Ghost, Avoid!" Whereupon it left him, leap'd on the Floor, and Flew out the Window.

And there also came in several Testimonies, that before ever Downer spoke a word of this Accident, Susanna Martin and her Family had related, How this Downer had been Handled! . . .

VIII. William Brown testify'd, that Heaven having blessed him with a most Pious and prudent wife, this wife of his one day mett with Susanna Martin; but when she approch'd just unto her, Martin vanished out of sight, and left her extremely affrighted. After which time, the said Martin often appear'd unto her, giving her no little trouble; and when she did come, she was visited with Birds that sorely peck'd and Prick'd her; and sometimes a Bunch, like a pullets egg, would Rise in her throat, ready to Choak her, till she cry'd out, "Witch, you shan't choak me!" While this good woman was in this Extremity, the Church appointed a Day of Prayer, on her behalf; whereupon her Trouble ceas'd; she saw not Martin as formerly; and the Church, instead of their Fast, gave Thanks for her Deliverance. But a considerable while after, she begin Summoned to give in some Evidence at the Court, against this Martin, quickly thereupon this Martin came behind her, while she was Milking her Cow, and said unto her "For thy defaming me at Court, I'll make thee the miserablest Creature in the World." Soon after which, she fell into a strange kind of Distemper, and became horribly Frantick, and uncapable of any Reasonable Action; the Physicians declaring, that her Distemper was preternatural, and that some Devil had certainly Bewitched her; and in that Condition she now remained. . . .

Note, This Woman was one of the most Impugned, Scurrilous, wicked creates in the world; and she did now throughout her whole Trial discover herself to be such a one. Yet when she was asked, what she had to say for herself? her Cheef Plea was, That she had Led a most virtuous and Holy Life!

Antenuptual Contract (1653) and Femme Sole Trader Act (1718)

Marriage contracts document how women gained some control over the property they brought into marriage. Femme Sole Trader Acts were legal exemptions to the tradition of femme covert granted to widows or wives deserted by their spouses. However, the Femme Sole Trader Acts reflected a need for labor and an effort to provide widows with a means of self-support, lest they become a burden to the community. The legislation was not intended to create more flexible opportunities. In this Femme Sole Trader Act what evidence exists that its major objective is to prevent women and children from becoming a financial burden to the community?*

Articles of agreement, dated Apr. 30, 1653, between Joseph Jewett of Rowley, merchant, and Ann, late wife to Cpt. Bozoon Allen, deceased . . .; Joseph Jewett, in consideration of a marriage shortly to be solemnized between him and Ann, widow of said Allen, and with receipt of her thirds and 600li, the children's portions, agreed in case of his death to leave the 600li to his wife, and also agreed that his wife might dispose of 100li during her life to her children by said Allen; that the eldest son should be brought up to learning, kept at a good school, found in diet, apparel and books until he should be fitted for the University, and to be there maintained; that the other children should be brought up to learning and be supported until the age of twenty-one or marriage; that said Anne might give away to any of her children, a

---

* From Records and Files of the Quarterly Court of Essex County, Massachusetts, 1672–1674 (Salem: Essex Institute, 1916), 5:394–95 and from Laws of the Commonwealth of Pennsylvania, Philadelphia, Penna: 1810), I: 99-101.

feather bed, bolster and pillow, with a bedstead, covering, pair of blankets, pair of fine sheets, five pillow beers, curtains and wrought valance, livery cupboard and cupboard cloth of needle work suitable for the valance, two wrought cushions, two tables, one chair, two wrought stools, two trunks, two chests, two cases with glasses, one silver tankard, one silver bowl, six silver spoons, two gold rings, one silver dram cup, with the childbed linen in the trunk; that Joseph agreed to pay to Priscilla, the eldest daughter of said Anne 20£. over and above her portion; also that the mares which Captain Allen left, mentioned in the inventory, be allowed to run with their increase as the profit of that part of the double portion of John Allen until he came of age, and that said Joseph pay to John, Priscilla, Ann, Deborah, Isaac, and Bozoon Allen the portions their father left them in corn or cattle, when they become of age or are married, etc. Wit: Thomas Broughton, Thomas Buttolph, and Tho. Roberts. Acknowledged, 1 : 8 : 1653, before William Hibbins. Recorded, Feb 3, 1653, by Edward Rawson, recorder. Copy made by Isa. Addington, cleric.

An Act Concerning Femme Sole Traders, 1718 [Pennsylvania]

Whereas it often happens that mariners and others, whose circumstances as well as vocations oblige them to go to sea, leave their wives in a way of shopkeeping: and such of them as are industrious, and take due care to pay the merchants they gain so much credit with, as to be well supplied with shop-goods from time to time, whereby they get a competent maintenance for themselves and children, and have been enabled to discharge considerable debts, left unpaid by their husbands at their going away; but some of those husbands, having so far lost sight of their duty to their wives and tender children, that their affections are turned to those, who, in all probability, will put them upon measures, not only to waste what they may get abroad, but misapply such effects as they leave in this province: for preventing whereof, and to the end that the estates belonging to such absent husbands may be secured for the maintenance of their wives and children, and that the goods and effects which such wives acquire, or are entrusted to sell in their husband's absence, may be preserved for satisfying of those who so entrust them, *Be it enacted*, that where any mariners or others are gone, or hereafter shall go, to sea, leaving their wives at shop-keeping, or to work for their livelihood at any other trade in this province, all such wives shall be deemed, adjudged and taken, and are hereby declared to be, as femme-sole traders, and shall have ability and are by this act enabled, to sue and be sued, pleased and be impleaded at law, in any court or courts in this province, during their husbands' natural lives, without naming their husbands in such suits, pleas or actions: and when judgments are given against such wives for any debts contracted, or sums of money due from them, since their husbands left them, executions shall be awarded against the goods and chattels in the possession of such wives, or in the hands or possession of others in trust for them, and not against the goods and chattels of their husbands; unless it may appear to the court where those executions are returnable, that such wives have, out of their separate stock or profit of their trade, paid debts which were contracted by their husbands, or laid out money for the necessary support and maintenance of themselves and children; then, and in such case, executions shall be levied on the estate, real and personal, of such husbands, to the value so paid or laid out, and no more.

II. *And be it further enacted*, That if any of the said absent husbands, being owners of lands, tenements, or other estate in this province, have aliened, or hereafter shall give, grant, mortgage or alienate, from his wife and children, any of his said lands, tenements or estate, without making an equivalent provision for their maintenance, in lieu thereof, every such gift, grant, mortgage or alienation, shall be deemed, adjudged and taken to be null and void.

III. *Provided nevertheless,* That if such absent husband shall happen to suffer shipwreck, or be by sickness or other casualty disabled to maintain himself, then, and in such case, and not otherwise, it shall be lawful for such distressed husband to sell or mortgage so much of his said estate, as shall be necessary to relieve him, and bring him home again to his family, any thing herein contained to the contrary notwithstanding.

IV. But if such absent husband, having his health and liberty, stays away so long from his wife and children, without making such provision for their maintenance before or after his going away, till they are like to become chargeable to the town or place where they inhabit; or in case such husband doth live or shall live in adultery, or cohabit unlawfully with another woman, and refuses or neglects, within seven years next after his going to sea, or departing this province, to return to his wife, and cohabit with her again; then, and in every such case, the lands, tenements and estate, belonging to such husbands, shall be and are hereby made liable and subject to be seized and taken in execution, to satisfy any sum or sums of money, which the wives of such husbands, or guardians of their children, shall necessarily expend or lay out for their support and maintenance; which execution shall be founded upon process of attachment against such estate, wherein the absent husband shall be made defendant; any law or usage to the contrary in any wise notwithstanding.

Benjamin Wadsworth, *A Well-Ordered Family* (1712)

Within the Puritan community, the clergy provided most advice on family governance. A Congregational clergyman, Benjamin Wadsworth emphasized that the husband was the "head" ordained by God to "rule and govern." Harmony between husbands and wives and family stability were considered essential to social order. How did Wadsworth try to enforce this? What particular advice did he offer husbands?[*]

---

[*] From Benjamin Wadsworth, *A Well-Ordered Family,* 2d ed. (Boston, 1719), 4–5; 22–59.

About the Duties of Husbands and Wives

Concerning the duties of this relation we may assert a few things. *It is their duty to dwell together with one another.* Surely they should dwell together; if one house cannot hold them, surely they are not affected to each other as they should be. They should have a very great and tender love and affection to one another. This is plainly commanded by God. This duty of love is mutual; it should be performed by each, to each of them. When, therefore, they quarrel or disagree, then they do the Devil's work; he is pleased at it, glad of it. But such contention provokes God; it dishonors Him; it is a vile example before inferiors in the family; it tends to prevent family prayer.

As to outward things. If the one is sick, troubled or distressed, the other should manifest care, tenderness, pity, and compassion, and afford all possible relief and succor. They should likewise unite their prudent counsels and endeavor comfortably to maintain themselves and the family under their joint care.

Husband and wife should be patient toward another. If both are truly pious, yet neither of them is perfectly holy, in such cases a patient, forgiving, forbearing spirit is very needful. You, therefore, that are husbands or wives, do not aggravate every error or mistake, every wrong or hasty word, every wry step as though it were a willfully designed intolerable crime; for this would soon break all to pieces: but rather put the best construction on things, and bear with and forgive one another's failings.

The husband's government ought to be gentle and easy, and the wife's obedience ready and cheerful. The husband is called the head of the woman. It belongs to the head to rule and govern. Wives are part of the house and family, and ought to be under the husband's government. Yet his government should not be with rigor, haughtiness, harshness, severity, but with the greatest love, gentleness, kindness, tenderness that may be. Though he governs her, he must not treat her as a servant, but as his own flesh; he must love her as himself.

Those husbands are much to blame who do not carry it lovingly and kindly to their wives. O Man, if your wife is not so young, beautiful, healthy, well-tempered, and qualified as you would wish; if she did not bring a large estate to you, or cannot do so much for you, as some other women have done for their husbands; yet she is your wife, and the great God commands you to love her, be not bitter, but kind to her. What can be more plain and expressive than that?

Those wives are much to blame who do not carry it lovingly and obediently to their own husbands. O woman, if your husband is not as young, beautiful, healthy, so well-tempered, and qualified as you could wish; if he has not such abilities, riches, honors, as some others have; yet he is your husband, and the great God commands you to love, honor and obey him. Yea, though possibly you have greater abilities of mind than he has, are of some high birth, and he of a more common birth, or did bring more estate, yet since he is your husband, God has made him your head, and set him above you, and made it your duty to love and revere him.

Parents should act wisely and prudently in the matching of their children. They should endeavor that they may marry someone who is most proper for them, most likely to bring blessings to them.

Chrestien Le Clercq, *The Customs and Religion of the Indians* (c.1700)

Written by a Christian missionary, this document provides an example of how gender roles are culturally constructed. Accustomed to European assumptions about male superiority, LeClercq expressed shock that Indians endowed women with spiritual authority, a role Europeans reserved for men. What evidence does Le Clercq offer about the women "meddling" with the role of "patriarch?"*

As our Indians perceive that much honour is accorded to the missionaries, and that they have given themselves in respect and reverence the title of Patriarch, some of these barbarians have often been seen meddling with, and affecting to perform, the office and functions of missionary, even to hearing confession, like us, from their fellow countrymen. So therefore, when persons of this kind wish to give authority to that which they say, and to set themselves up as patriarchs, they make our Gaspesians [Micmacs] believe that they have received some particular gift from heaven, as in the case of one from Kenebec [Maine], who said that he had received an image from heaven. This was, however, only a picture which had been given him when he was trading with our French.

It is a surprising fact that this ambition to act the patriarch does not only prevail among the men, but even the women meddle therewith. These, in usurping the duality and the name of *religieuses*, say certain prayers in their own fashion, and affect a manner of living more reserved than that of the commonalty of Indians, who allow themselves to be dazzled by the glamour of a false and ridiculous devotion. They look upon these women as extraordinary persons, whom they believe to hold converse, to speak familiarly, and to hold communication with the sun, which they have all adored as their divinity. Not long ago, we had a famous one of them who, by her extravagant superstitions, encouraged the same in these poor Indians. I had an extreme desire to see her, but she died in the woods without the baptism that I had the intention to give her, if I had been so happy as to render her worthy of it. This aged woman, who counted more than a hundred and fourteen years since her birth, had as the basis for all her ridiculous and superstitious devotions, some beads of jet, which were the remains of an unthreaded rosary. These she carefully preserved, and gave them only to those who were her friends, protesting to them, meanwhile, that the gift which she gave them had come originally from heaven, which was always continuing to give her the same favour just so many times as she, in order to worship the sun, went out from

---

* From Father Chrestien Le Clercq, *New Relation of Gaspesia With the Customs and Religion of the Gaspesian Indians*, ed. and trans. William F. Ganong (Toronto: The Champlain Society, 1910), 229–30.

her wigwam and rendered it her homage and adoration. "I have only, then," said she to them, "to hold up my hand and to open it, in order to bring down from heaven these mysterious beads which have the power and the property not only of succoring the Indians in their sicknesses and all their most pressing necessities, but also of preserving them from surprise, from persecution, and from the fury of their enemies." It can truly be said that if some one of these people would devote himself wholly to goodness, and would take care to instruct the others, he could accomplish prodigies among them, since they would easily believe everything that a man of their nation would tell them. This imposture, then, that the rosary beads came from heaven, was so well received by those who gloried in possessing some of them, that such persons preserved them as they did the things which they held most dear in the world; and it angered these persons beyond endurance to contradict them in a foolishness which passed in their esteem for something divine and sacred.

Mary Jemison, *A Narrative of the Life of Mrs. Mary Jemison* (1724)

Captured by Indians when she was fifteen, Mary Jemison (1743–1833) subsequently chose to live most of her life among the Seneca of New York. Unable to write, oral interviews formed the basis of her autobiography. Her long years among Native Americans make her testimony an important corrective to the Eurocentric views of male missionaries who supplied most of the written evidence about Native American customs. What does Jemison's phrase "treated like a real sister" mean?[*]

The night was spent in gloomy foreboding. What the result of our captivity would be, it was out of our power to determine, or even imagine. At times, we could almost realize the approach of our masters to butcher and scalp us; again, we could nearly see the pile of wood kindling on which we were to be roasted; and then we would imagine ourselves at liberty, alone and defenseless in the forest, surrounded by wild beasts that were ready to devour us. The anxiety of our minds drove sleep from our eyelids; and it was with a dreadful hope and painful impatience that we waited for the morning to determine our fate.

---

[*] From James E. Seaver, *A Narrative of the Life of Mary Jemison; Deh-He-Wa-Mis*, 4th ed. (New York: Miller, Orton, and Mulligan, 1856), 52, 55–63, 67–70, 72–74.

The morning at length arrived, and our masters came early and let us out of the house, and gave the young man and boy to the French, who immediately took them away. Their fate I never learned, as I have not seen or heard of them since.

I was now left alone in the fort, deprived of my former companions, and of every thing that was near or dear to me but life. But it was not long before I was in some measure relieved by the appearance of two pleasant-looking squaws, of the Seneca tribe, who came and examined me attentively for a short time, and then went out. After a few minutes' absence, they returned in company with my former masters, who gave me to the squaws to dispose of as they pleased.

The Indians by whom I was taken were a party of Shawnees, if I remember right, that lived, when at home, a long distance down the Ohio. . . .

It was my happy lot to be accepted for adoption. At the time of the ceremony I was received by the two squaws to supply the place of their brother in the family; and I was even considered and treated by them as a real sister, the same as though I had been born of their mother. During the ceremony of my adoption, I sat motionless, nearly terrified to death at the appearance and actions of the company, expecting every moment to feel their vengeance, and suffer death on the spot. I was, however, happily disappointed; when at the close of the ceremony the company retired, and my sisters commenced employing every means for my consolation and comfort.

Being now settled and provided with a home, I was employed in nursing the children, and doing light work about the house. Occasionally, I was sent out with the Indian hunters, when they went but a short distance, to help them carry their game. My situation was easy; I had no particular hardships to endure. But still, the recollection of my parents, my brothers and sisters, my home and my own captivity, destroyed my happiness, and made me constantly solitary, lonesome, and gloomy.

My sisters would not allow me to speak English in their hearing; but remembering the charge that my dear mother gave me at the time I left her, whenever I chanced to be alone I made a business of repeating my prayer, catechism, or something I had learned, in order that I might not forget my own language. By practicing it that way, I retained it till I came to Genesee flats, where I soon became acquainted with English people, with whom I have been almost daily in the habit of conversing.

My sisters were very diligent in teaching me their language; and to their great satisfaction, I soon learned so that I could understand it readily, and speak it fluently. I was very fortunate in falling into their hands; for they were kind good-natured women; peaceable and mild in their dispositions; temperate and decent in their habits, and very tender and gentle toward me. I have great reason to respect them, though they have been dead a great number of years. . . .

In the second summer of my living at Wiishto, I had a child, at the time that the kernels of corn first appeared on the cob. When I was taken sick, Sheninjee was absent, and I was sent to a small shed on the bank of the river, which was made of boughs, where I was obliged to stay till my husband returned. My two sisters, who were my only companions, attended me; and on the second day of my confinement my child was born; but it lived only two days. It was a girl; and notwithstanding the shortness of time that I possessed it, it was a great grief to me to lose it.

After the birth of my child I was very sick, but was not allowed to go into the house for two weeks; when, to my great joy, Sheninjee returned, and I was taken in, and as comfortably provided for as our situation would admit. My disease continued to increase for a number of days; and I became so far reduced that my recovery was despaired of by my friends, and I concluded that my troubles would soon be finished. At length, however, my complaint took a favorable turn, and by the time the corn was ripe I was able to get about. I continued to gain my health, and in the fall was able to go to our winter quarters, on the Saratoga, with the Indians.

Elizabeth Sprigs, *Letter from an Indentured Servant* (1756)

Europeans too poor to pay their own passage to America often became indentured servants. Elizabeth Sprig's letter is one of the few primary sources that describe the conditions of female indentured servants. As can be seen from Sprig's letter, servitude and poverty molded a miserable and precarious existence. What evidence does Sprig give of her own helplessness?[*]

Maryland, Sept'r 22'd 1756

Honred Father

My being for ever banished from your sight, will I hope pardon the Boldness I now take of troubling you with these, my long silence has been purely owning to my undutifullness to you, and well knowing I had offended in the highest Degree, put a tie to my tongue and pen, for fear I should be extinct from your good Graces and add a further Trouble to you, but too well knowing your care and tenderness for me so long as I retain'd my Duty to you, induced me once again to endeavor if possible, to kindle up that flame again. O Dear Father, believe what I am going to relate the words of truth and sincerity, and Balance my former bad Conduct my sufferings here, and then I am sure you'll pity your Destress Daughter, What we unfortunate English People suffer here is beyond the probability of you in England to Conceive, let it suffice that I one of the unhappy Number, am toiling almost Day and Night, and very often in the Horses drudgery, with only this comfort that you Bitch you do not halfe enough, and then tied up and whipp'd to that Degree that you'd not serve an Animal, scarce any thing but Indian Corn and Salt to eat and that even begrudged nay many Negroes are better used, almost naked no shoes nor stockings to wear, and the comfort after slaving during Masters pleasure, what rest we can get is to rap ourselves up in a Blanket and ly upon the Ground, this is the deplorable Condition your poor Betty

---

[*] From Elizabeth Sprigs, "Letter to Mr. John Sprigs in White Cross Street near Cripple Gate, London," September 22, 1756. Reprinted by permission of the Connecticut Chapter of the National Society of Colonial Dames of America.

endures, and now I beg if you have any Bowels of Compassion left show it by sending me some Relief, Clothing is the principal thing wanting, which if you should condiscend to, may easily send them to me by any of the ships bound to Baltimore Town Patapsco River Maryland, and give me leave to conclude in Duty to you and Uncles and Aunts, and Respect to all Friends

Honored Father
Your undutifull and Disobedient Child
Elizabeth Sprigs

State of Virginia, *Statute Outlawing Interracial Unions* (1691)

This statute tells us as much about the definition of race as it does about the process of enslavement. Passed to end the development of an interracially free community, the legislation reflects the power whites assumed over people of color. In pinning the stigma of thirty years of bondage on interracial children, what objective did the statute seek to accomplish? What do terms such as "abominable mixture" and "spurious issue" tell us about racial assumptions? *

[1691] . . . for prevention of that abominable mixture and spurious issue which hereafter may encrease in this dominion, as well as by negroes, mulattos, and Indians intermarrying with English, or other white women, as by their unlawfull accompanying with one another, *Be it enacted* . . . that . . . whatsoever English or other white man or woman being free, shall intermarry with a negro, mulatto or Indian man or woman bond or free shall within three months after such marriage be banished and removed from this dominion forever. . . .

And be it further enacted . . . That if any English woman being free shall have a bastard child by any negro or mulatto, she pay the sum of fifteen pounds sterling, within one month after such bastard child shall be born, to the Church wardens of the parish . . . and in default of such payment she shall be taken into the possession of the said Church wardens and disposed of for five yeares, and the said fine of fifteen pounds, or whatever the woman shall be disposed of for, shall be paid, one third part

---

* From the Assembly of Virginia, Act XVI, April 1691, in William Waller Henning, *The Statutes at Large: Being a Collection of All the Laws of Virginia, from the First Session of the Legislature, in the Year 1619*, 13 vols. (New York: 1823), 3: 86–87; and Assembly of Virginia, chap. XLIX, sec. XX, October 1705, in Henning, 3: 453.

to their majesties . . . and one other third part to the use of the parish . . . and the other third part to the informer, and that such bastard child be bound out as a servant by the said Church wardens until he or she shall attain the age of thirty yeares, and in case such English woman that shall have such bastard child be a servant, she shall be sold by the said church wardens (after her time is expired that she ought by law serve her master), for five yeares, and the money she shall be sold for divided as if before appointed, and the child to serve as aforesaid.

[1705] *And be it further enacted*, That no minister of the church of England, or other minister, or person whatsoever, within this colony and dominion, shall hereafter wittingly presume to marry a white man with a negro or mulatto woman; or to marry a white woman with a negro or mulatto man, upon paid of forfeiting or paying, for every such marriage the sum of ten thousand pounds of tobacco; one half to our sovereign lady the Queen . . . and the other half to the informer.

Judith Cocks, *Letter to James Hillhouse* (1795)

Documents concerning the enslaved female experience reveal the deep anguish felt by women who experienced the sale of their children to other plantations. Mothers struggled to keep their families intact and developed deep bonds with their children. This particular letter to a former master describes a mother's effort to protect her son from his new owners. Why was the mother separated from her son? What did she hope to achieve?*

Judith Cocks to James Hillhouse

Marietta, 8th March 1795

Sir

I have been so unhappy at Mrs. Woodbridges that I was obliged to leeve thare by the consent of Mrs. Woodbridge who gave up my Indentures and has offen said that had she known that I was so sickly and expensive she would not have brought me to this Country but all this is the least of my trouble and I can truly say sir had I nothing else or no one but myself I am sure I should make any complaint to you But my Little son Jupiter who is now with Mrs. Woodbridge is my greatest care and from what she says and from the usage he meets with there is so trying to me that I am all most

---

* From the Hillhouse Family Papers. Letter from Judith Cocks to James Hillhouse dated March 8, 1795. From the Hillhouse Family Papers, Manuscripts and Archives, Yale University Library. Reprinted by permission.

distracted therefore if you will be so kind as to write me how Long Jupiter is to remain with them as she tells me he is to live with her untill he is twenty five years of age this is something that I had no idea of I all ways thought that he was to return with me to new england or at Longest only ten years these are matters I must beg of you sir to let me know as quick as you can make it convenient I hope you will excuse me of troubling you which I think you will do when you think that I am here in A strange country without one Friend to advise me [. . . .] I remain the greatest humility you Humble servant

Judith Cocks

please [don't] show this to Mrs. Woodbridge

2

From Revolution to Republic: Moral Motherhood and Civic Mission

---

The American Revolution transformed the lives of many women. They participated in crowd action, circulated petitions, and joined in the boycott of British goods. For some, like Sally Wister, homefront and battlefield merged, and war enveloped domestic life. Other women raised funds and produced supplies for soldiers. Esther deBerdt Reed defended women's equal claim to liberty and the right to participate in public events. She led women in a massive fundraising drive and under her leadership countless women produced homespun and sewed the shirts desperately needed by Washington's inadequately provisioned soldiers. Dressed in male clothing, Deborah Sampson completely crossed the boundary of prescribed roles and joined the revolutionary troops. Although the surviving documents are mainly the voices of an educated elite, women's contributions to the Revolution bridged class divisions and blurred the distinction between public and private life.

The involvement of women in revolutionary events did not redefine assumptions about women's domestic natures and the need to maintain male authority. Although some women, like Abigail Adams, hoped that the men who were constructing the new nation would "remember the ladies," the founding fathers did not extend political rights to women. The common-law tradition of *femme covert* became part of the legal foundation of the new nation. The power and authority men possessed in the public realm also governed the private realm, and created unequal relations between men and women. Husbands continued to own their wives' property and wages; they had a legal right to their wives' bodies, and although some states made wife-beating illegal, the law was poorly enforced and the practice continued. Although revolutionary events and the rhetoric of equality heightened a consciousness among women of their own worth, what benefits they derived from inclusion in a republican nation occurred not within the framework of equal rights, but as Republican wives and mothers. The new republic assigned to mothers the moral instruction of the nation's future male citizens. The concept of republican motherhood endowed maternity with a civic and patriotic mission that linked the personal and private responsibilities of mothers to national well-being.

Prompted by ministers like John Abbot, many middle-class women joined clergymen in promoting moral motherhood. The new emphasis on maternal guidance increased the significance of the domestic sphere, and served to confine and insulate women within the home. Yet, it also provided the rationale for public participation. During the early 1800s, moral motherhood developed a community dimension. In towns and urban centers throughout the young republic, countless women organized charitable and moral reform societies. Their associational activities and community involvement gave a public dimension to their domestic roles. Other women, like Emma Willard, founded schools for girls. Over time, women supplied the nation with the majority of its grammar-school teachers; however, once elementary education became perceived as a female occupation, the pay scale dropped, and career advancement for women became unlikely.

For the majority of African-American slaves, the revolutionary era did not lead to freedom. After the war the northern states developed emancipation schedules ranging from immediate to gradual freedom for slaves. Voluntary emancipation was a rarity in the South, where slavery was highly profitable and part of a patriarchal system of race and gender control. Nor was emancipation in the North accompanied by racial equality. Race and gender oppression damaged the lives and narrowed opportunities for free black women. Despite formidable barriers, African-American women still took charge of their lives. Like their white counterparts, they became involved in associational activity. Although generally poor themselves, they managed to administer charity to their communities.

Esther DeBerdt Reed, *Sentiments of an American Woman* (1780)

Esther DeBerdt Reed (1746–1780) arrived in the colonies in 1770 and died ten years later. During that brief time she gave birth to seven children and played a key role in recruiting women to support the patriotic effort. This document was written to mobilize women to provide the army with homespun clothing. Because the war curtailed the importation of British cloth, female production of homespun became a major priority. Reed's references to heroic women from the Old Testament and antiquity expressed an early effort to find alternative role models that would offset the belief that patriotism was a quality that belonged to men not women. What did DeBerdt Reed mean by the phrase "Born for Liberty?" What evidence does she give that women are denied knowledge of their own history? What social purpose would such denial serve?

On the commencement of actual war, the Women of America manifested a firm resolution to contribute as much as could depend on them, to the deliverance of their country. Animated by the purest patriotism, they are sensible of sorrow at this day, in not offering more than barren wishes for the success of so glorious a Revolution. They aspire to render themselves more really useful; and this sentiment is universal from the north to the south of the Thirteen United States. Our ambition is kindled by the fame of those heroines of antiquity, who have rendered their sex illustrious, and have proved to the universe, that, if the weakness of our Constitution, if opinion and manners did not forbid us to march to glory by the same paths as the Men, we should at least equal, and sometimes surpass them in our love for the public good. I glory in all that which my sex has done great and commendable. I call to mind with enthusiasm and with admiration, all those acts of courage, of constancy and patriotism, which history has transmitted to us: The people favoured by Heaven, preserved from destruction by the virtues, the zeal and the revolution of Deborah, of Judith, of Esther! The fortitude of the mother of the Machabees, in giving up her sons to die before her eyes: Rome saved from the fury of a victorious enemy by the efforts of Volumnia, and other Roman Ladies: So my famous siegers were the Women who have been seen forgetting the weakness of their sex, building new walls, digging trenches with their feeble hands, furnishing arms to their defenders, they themselves darting the missile weapons on the enemy, resigning the ornaments of their apparel and their fortune to fill the public treasury, and to hasten the deliverance of their country; burying themselves under its ruins; throwing themselves into the flames rather than submitt to the disgrace before a proud enemy.

Born for liberty, disdaining to bear the irons of a tyrannic Government, we associate ourselves to the grandeur of those Sovereigns, cherished and revered, who have held with so much splendor the scepter of the greatest States; the Matildas, the Elizabeths, the Maries, the Catherines, who have extended the empire of liberty, and contented to reign by sweetness and justice, have broken the chains of slavery, forged by tyrants in the times of ignorance and barbarity. The Spanish Women, do they not make, at this moment, the most patriotic sacrifices, to increase the means of victory in the hands of their Sovereign. He is a friend to the French Nation. They are our allies. We call to mind, doubly interested, that it was a French Maid who kindled up amongst her fellow-citizens, the flame of patriotism buried under long misfortunes: it was the Maid of Orleans who drove from the kingdom of France the ancestors of those same British, whose odious yoke we have just shaken off; and whom it is necessary that we drive from the Continent.

But I must limit myself to the recollection of this small number of achievements. Who knows if persons disposed to censure, and sometimes too severely with regard to us, may not disapprove our appearing acquainted even with the actions of which our sex boasts? We are at least certain, that he cannot be a good citizen who will not applaud our efforts for the relief of the armies which defend our lives, our possessions, our liberty? The situation of our soldiery has been represented to me; the evils inseparable from war, and the firm and generous spirit which has enabled them to support these. But it has been said, that they may apprehend, that, in the course of a long war, the view of their distresses may be lost, and their services be forgotten.

Forgotten! Never; I can answer in the name of all my sex. Brave Americans, your disinterestedness, your courage, and your constancy will always be dear to America, as long as she shall preserve her virtue.

We know that at a distance from the theatre of war, if we enjoy any tranquillity it is the fruit of your watchings, your labours, your dangers. If I live happy in the midst of my family; if my husband cultivates his field and reaps his harvest in peace; if, surrounded with my children, I myself nourish the youngest, and press it to my bosom, without being afraid of seeing myself separated from it, by a ferocious enemy; if the house in which we dwell; if our barns, our orchards are safe at the present time from the hands of those incendiaries, it is to you that we owe it. And shall we hesitate to evidence to you our gratitude? Shall we hesitate to wear a clothing more simple; hair dressed less elegant, while at the price of this small privation, we shall deserve your benedictions. Who, amongst us, will not renounce with the highest pleasure, those vain ornaments, when she shall consider that the valiant defenders of America will be able to draw some advantage from the money which she may have laid out in these; that they will be better defended from the rigors of the seasons, that after their painful toils, they will receive some extraordinary and unexpected relief; that these presents will perhaps be valued by them at a greater price, when they will have it in their power to say: *this is the offering of the Ladies.* The time is arrived to display the same sentiments which animated us at the beginning of the Revolution, when we renounced the use of teas, however agreeable to our taste, rather than receive them from our persecutors; when we made it appear to them that we placed former necessaries in the rank of superfluities, when our liberty was interested; when our republican and laborious hands spun the flax, prepared the linen intended for the use of our soldiers; when as exiles and fugitives we supported with courage all the evils which are the concomitants of war. Let us not lose a moment; let us be engaged to offer the homage of our gratitude at the altar of military valor, and you, our brave deliverers, while mercenary slaves combat to cause you to share with them the irons with which they are loaded, receive with a free hand our offering, the purest which can be presented to your virtue,

By an American Woman.

Sally Wister, *Revolutionary War Diary* (1777)

Fifteen-year-old Sally Wister moved with her family to the countryside after the British occupied Philadelphia. Wister's first-hand observations of the Revolution show how wartime events blurred the distinction between battlefield and home front, and awakened among women an awareness of political developments considered important only to men. In what ways did the dramatic unfolding of revolutionary events transform Wister's daily life?*

25 September 1777

Yesterday, which was the 24th of September, two Virginia officers called at our house, and informed us that the British army had crossed the Schuylkill. Presently, another person stopped, and confirmed what they had said, and that General Washington and army were near Pottsgrove. Well, they may be sure we were sufficiently scared; however, the road was very still till evening. About seven o'clock we heard a great noise. To the door we all went. A large number of wagons, with about three hundred of the Philadelphia militia. They begged for drink and several pushed into the house. One of those that entered was a little tipsy, and had a mind to be saucy. I then thought it time for me to retreat; so figure me (mightily scared, as not having presence of mind enough to face so many of the military) running in at one door, and out at another, all in a shake with fear; but after a little, seeing the officers appear gentlemanly and the soldiers civil, I called reason to my aid. My fears were in some measure dispelled, tho' my teeth rattled, and my hand shook like an aspen leaf. They did not offer to take their quarters with us; so, with many blessings, and as many adieus, they marched off. . . .

Fifth Day, September 26th

We were unusually silent all the morning; no passengers came by the house, except to the mill, and we don't place much dependence on mill news. About 12 o'clock, cousin Jesse heard that heard that General Howe's army had moved down toward Philadelphia. Then, my dear, our hopes and fears were engaged for you. However, my advice is, summon up all your resolution, call Fortitude to your aid, don't suffer your spirits to sink, my dear; there's nothing like courage; 'tis what I stand in need of myself, but unfortunately have but little of it in my composition. I was standing in the kitchen about 12, when somebody came to me in a hurry, screaming, "Sally, Sally, here are the light horse!" This was by far the greatest fright I had endured; fear tack'd wings to my feet; I was at the house in a moment; at the porch I stop't, and it really was the light horse. I ran immediately to the western door, where the family were assembled, anxiously waiting for the event. They rode up to the door and halted, inquired if we had horses to sell; he answered negatively. "Have not you, sir," to my father, "two black horses?"—"Yes, but have no mind to dispose of them." My terror had by this time nearly subsided. The officer and men behaved perfectly civil; they first drank two glasses of wine, rode away, bidding his men to follow, which, after adieus in number, they did. The officer was Lieutenant Lindsay, of

---

* From "Sally Wisters's Revolutionary War-Time Diary, September 1777." Reprinted in The Pennsylvania Magazine of History and Biography, Vol. 9, pps. 319–24, 326–27, 332–333, published by The Historical Society of Pennsylvania.

Bland's regiment, Lee's troop. The men, to our great joy, were Americans, and but four in all. What made us imagine them British, they wore blue and red, which with us is not common. It has rained all this afternoon, and, to present appearances, will all night. In all probability the English will take possession of the city tomorrow or next day. What a change it will be!. . . .

Nothing worth relating has occurred this afternoon. Now for trifles. I have set a stocking on the needles, and intend to be mighty industrious. This evening our folks heard a very heavy cannon. We suppose it to be fired by the English. The report seem'd to come from Philadelphia. We hear the American army will be within five miles of us tonight. The uncertainty of our position engrosses me quite. Perhaps to be in the midst of war, and ruin, and the clang of arms. But we must hope the best. . . .

Molly Wallace, *The Young Ladies' Academy of Philadelphia* (1790)

The Philadelphia Academy, founded by a group of wealthy men was one of the nation's first schools for girls. Academic objectives expressed the increased status attained by affluent white women during the postrevolutionary era. Wallace's argument for the right of women to speak in public represents an early example of the effort of educated women to surmount this taboo. What does Wallace's statement about the need to speak before a "select", not a "promiscuous" audience tell you about the status of women in postrevolutionary America?[*]

The silent and solemn attention of a respectable audience, has often, at the beginning of discourses intimidated even veterans in the art of public elocution. What then must my situation be, when my sex, my youth and inexperience all conspire to make me tremble at the task which I have undertaken? But the friendly encouragement, which I behold in almost every countenance, enables me to overcome difficulties, that would otherwise be insurmountable. With some, however, it has been made a question, whether we ought *ever* to appear in so public a manner. Our natural timidity, the domestic situation to which, by nature and custom we seem destined, as urged as arguments against what we have undertaken—many sarcastical observations have been handed out against female oratory: but to what do they amount? Do they not plainly inform us, that, because we are females, we ought therefore to be deprived of

---

[*] From Molly Wallace, *The Rise and Progress of the Young Ladies, Academy of Philadelphia.* (Philadelphia: Stewart and Cochran, 1794), pp. 212–13.

what is perhaps the most effectual means of acquiring a just, natural and graceful delivery? No one will pretend to deny that we should be taught to read in the best manner. And if to read, why not to speak? . . .

But yet it may be asked, what, has a female character to do with declamation? That she should harangue at the head of an Army, in the Senate, or before a popular Assembly, is not pretended, neither is it requested that she ought to be an adept in the stormy and contentious eloquence of the air, or in the abstract and subtle reasoning of the Senate—we look not for a female Pitt, Cicero, or Demothenes. . . .

Why is a boy diligently and carefully taught the Latin, the Greek, or the Hebrew language, in which he will seldom have occasion either to write or converse? Why is he taught to demonstrate the propositions of Euclid, when during his whole life, he will not perhaps make use of one of them? Are we taught to dance merely for the sake of becoming dancers? No, certainly. These things are commonly studied, more on account of the habits, which the learning of them establishes, than on account of any important advantages which the mere knowledge of them can afford. So a young lady, from the exercise of speaking before a properly selected audience, may acquire some valuable habits, which, otherwise she can obtain from no examples, and that no precept can give. But, this exercise can with propriety be performed only before a select audience: a promiscuous and indiscriminate one, for obvious reasons, would be absolutely unsuitable, and should always be carefully avoided.

Abigail Adams, *Letters to John Adams and His Reply* (1776)

Abigail Adams' (1744–1818) plea that her husband "remember the ladies" was an initial appeal for a more equitable distribution of power. Feminists of a later era would spell out in detail Adams' statement on the potential of male tyranny. On what basis do you think Adams alleged that "all Men would be tyrants if they could?" How did the revolutionary spirit influence her request and the argument of her May 7th letter? How did John Adams deal with the situation? What did he mean by the statement "we know better than to repeal our masculine systems"?*

* From *Adams Family Correspondence* ed. L.H. Butterfield, (Cambridge Mass.: Harvard University Press, 1963), 76–402.

Abigail Adams to John Adams

Braintree March 31 1776

—I long to hear that you have declared an independency—and by the way in the new Code of Laws which I suppose it will be necessary for you to make, I desire you would Remember the Ladies, and be more generous and favourable to them than your ancestors. Do not put such unlimited power into the hands of the Husbands. Remember all Men would be tyrants if they could. If particular care and attention is not paid to the Ladies we are determined to foment a Rebellion, and will not hold ourselves bound by any Laws in which we have no voice, or Representation.

That your Sex are Naturally Tyrannical is a Truth also thoroughly established as to admit of no dispute, but such of you as wish to be happy willingly give up the harsh title of Master for the more tender and endearing one of Friend. Why then, not put it out of the power of the vicious and the Lawless to use us with cruelty and indignity with impunity. Men of Sense in all Ages abhor those customs which treat us only as the vassals of your Sex. Regard us then as Being placed by providence under your protection and in imitation of the Supreme Being make use of that power only for our happiness.

John Adams to Abigail Adams

Ap. 14 1776

As to Declarations of Independency, be patient. Read our Privateering Laws, and our Commercial Laws. What signifies a Word.

As to your extraordinary Code of Laws, I cannot but laugh. We have been told that our Struggle has loosened the bands of Government everywhere. That Children and Apprentices were disobedient—that schools and Colleges were grown turbulent—that Indians slighted their Guardians and Negroes grew insolent to their Masters. But your Letter was the first Intimation that another Tribe more numerous and powerful than all the rest were grown discontented.—This is rather too coarse a Compliment but you are so saucy, I wont blot it out.

Depend upon it, We know better than to repeal our Masculine systems. Altho they are in full Force, you know they are little more than Theory. We dare not exert our Power in its full Latitude. We are obliged to go fair, and softly, and in Practice you know We are the subjects. We have only the Name of Masters, and rather than give up this, which would compleatly subject Us to the Despotism of the Petticoat, I hope General Washington, and all our brave Heroes would fight. I am sure every good Politician would plot, as long as he would against Despotism, Empire, Monarchy, Aristocracy, Oligarchy, or Ochlocracy.

Abigail Adams to John Adams

B[raintree]e May 7 1776

I can not say that I think you are very generous to the Ladies, for whilst you are proclaiming peace and good will to Men, Emancipating all Nations, you insist upon retaining an absolute power over Wives. But you must remember that Arbitrary power is like other things which are very hard, very liable to be broken—and notwithstanding all your wise Laws and Maxims we have it in our power not only to free ourselves but to subdue our Masters, and without violence throw both your natural and legal authority at our feet —

"Charm by accepting, by submitting sway
Yet have our Humour most when we obey."

Ladies Society of New York, *Constitution* (1800)

Benevolent societies were an early form of female association. This ladies' society specifically dealt with the relief of poor widows and small children. In cooperation with Protestant clergymen, women worked under clerical leadership and did not seek a new role as independent women. Still, involvement in visiting the poor, and in missionary and charity work brought women outside of their homes, literally, and into a wide range of activities. Not all poor widows were entitled to aid. The Ladies Society granted help only to those they considered morally respectable. To receive aid, what specific qualifications were necessary?[*]

Constitution

Among the many humane institutions in this city, there is none for the particular assistance of a large class of sufferers, who have peculiar claims on the public beneficence, viz. POOR WIDOWS WITH SMALL CHILDREN.

---

[*] From *Constitution of the Ladies Society, established in New York, for the Relief of Poor Widows with Small Children* (New York: James Oram, 1800); *Bylaws and Regulations of the Society for the Relief of Poor Widows with Small Children* (New York: Printed for the Society, J. Seymour, 1811). Courtesy of the New York Historical Society.

Commiserating their situation, and persuaded that none can be relieved with happier effect, a number of Ladies have formed, for their exclusive aid, a Society upon the following

Plan

the name of the society SHALL BE, The Society for the Relief of Poor Widows with Small Children . . .

By-laws and Regulations

Every Manager shall insert in a book the name, place of abode, and circumstances of every widow whom she relieves; the ages of her children; and the kind and amount of the relief granted to each family. . . .

Relief shall be given in necessaries, never in money, but by special vote of the Board.

It shall be the duty of the Manager to report to the Board from time to time, such widows under her care as have children of age to be bound to trades, or put out to service.

Every Manager shall confine her expenditures within the sum allowed, except in cases of sickness. . . .

Any poor widow of fair character, having two children under ten years of age, may, on application, be entitled to the attention and bounty of this society.

If any widow be seen begging publicly, either by means of a petition or otherwise, after having been cautioned against it by her Manager; her name shall be erased from the books of the Society.

Any women applying to the society for relief on account of the supposed death of her husband, must satisfy the Manager that he has not been heard of for twelve months and of the probability of his death. . . .

No widow shall be assisted, who, having a child fit for service, will not consent to its being put out to trade or service to a suitable person, if such can be found, unless special reasons being given to the contrary.

No widow shall be deprived of, or suspended from receiving, the society's bounty, either by the Directress or Managers, except by vote of the Board.

Relief shall not be granted any applicant, till she be listed at her dwelling by one of the Managers, and particular inquiry made into her character and circumstances. Immorality excludes from the patronage of the society.

No widow who possesses property, the interest of which is sufficient to pay her house-rent, shall be entitled to relief from this society.

No widow who sells spirituous liquors shall be relieved by this society.

A widow with one child under ten years of ago, and who is charged with an aged parent, entirely incapable of maintaining him or herself, or who has a child having any natural infirmity, so as to prevent it from being put out to a trade or service, shall be assisted. . . .

Colored Female Religious and Moral Society of Salem, Massachusetts, *Constitution* (1818)

Free black women also developed benevolent associations and societies. Because of the limited employment opportunities for African-Americans, problems of poverty were widespread; and black women made a major social contribution in providing aid to the poor and the sick. What evidence informs us that, like their white counterparts, African-American women also made moral behavior a requirement for assistance?*

Constitution

of the Colored Female Religious and Moral Society of Salem

Article I.—At the weekly meeting of the Society, when the appointed hour arrives, and a number are convened, the exercises shall begin by reading in some profitable book, till all have come in who are expected.

Art. II—A prayer shall then be made by one of the members, and after that, a chapter in the Bible shall be read, and religious conversation be attended to, as time will allow.

Art. III—Four quarterly days in the year, in January, April, July and October, beginning on the first day of every January, to be observed as a day of solemn fasting and prayer.

Art. IV—We promise not to ridicule or divulge the supposed or apparent infirmities of any fellow member; but to keep secret all things relating to the Society, the discovery of which might tend to do hurt to the Society or any individual.

Art. IV—We resolve to be charitably watchful over each other; to advise, caution and admonish where we may judge there is occasion, and that it may be useful; and we

---

* From the Constitution of the Female Anti-Slavery Society of Salem, Massachusetts. Reprinted in Sterling, Dorothy, *We are Your Sisters: Black Women in the Nineteenth Century*, (New York: Norton, 1984), 280–81.

promise not to resent, but kindly and thankfully receive such friendly advice or reproof from any one of our members.

Art. VI—Any female can become a member of this Society by conforming to the Constitution, and paying in fifty two cents per year.

Ar. VII—This Society is formed for the benefit of the sick and destitute of those members belonging to the Society.

Art. VIII—If any member commit any scandalous sin, or walk unruly, and after proper reproof continue manifestly impenitent, she shall be excluded from us, until she give evidence of her repentance.

Emma Willard, *Plan for Female Education* (1819)

Emma Willard (1787–1870) established one of the pre-Civil War's best known schools for women in Troy, New York. In her effort to obtain funding from the New York legislature, Willard linked women's education to the well-being of government. Willard's references to frivolity and idleness were addressed to privileged women. They would have little relevance to the harsh, work-filled lives of poor women. How does Willard relate "housewifery" to her educational objectives? What emphasis is placed on the maternal role?[*]

The inquiry to which these remarks have conducted us is this: what is offered by the plan of female education here proposed, which may teach or preserve, among females of wealthy families, that purity of manners which is allowed to be so essential to national prosperity, and so necessary to the existence of republican government.

1. Females, by having their understandings cultivated, their reasoning powers developed and strengthened, may be expected to act more from the dictates of reason and less from those of fashion or caprice.

2. With minds thus strengthened they would be taught systems of morality, enforced by the sanctions of religion; and they might be expected to acquire juster and more enlarged views of their duty, and stronger and higher motives to its performance.

---

[*] From *An Address to the Public; Particularly to the Members of the Legislation of New York, Proposing a Plan for Improving Female Education* (1819); in John Lord, *The Life of Emma Willard* (New York: Appelton, 1873), 76–84.

3. This plan of education offers all that can be done to preserve female youth from a contempt of useful labor. The pupils would become accustomed to it, in conjunction with the high objects of literature and the elegant pursuits of the fine arts; and it is so to be hoped that, both from habit and association, they might in future life regard it as respectable.

4. To this it may be added that, if housewifery could be raised to a regular art and taught upon philosophical principles, it would become a higher and more interesting occupation; and ladies of fortune, like wealthy agriculturists, might find that to regulate their business was an agreeable employment.

5. The pupils might be expected to acquire a taste for moral and intellectual pleasures, which would buoy them above a passion for show and parade, and which would make them seek to gratify the natural love of superiority, by endeavoring to excel others in intrinsic merit, rather than in the extrinsic frivolities of dress, furniture, and equipage.

6. By being enlightened in moral philosophy, and in that which teaches the operations of the mind, females would be enabled to perceive the nature and extent of that influence which they possess over their children, and the obligation which this lays them under, to watch the formation of their characters with unceasing violence, to become their instructors, to devise plans for their improvement, to weed out the vices from their minds, and to implant and foster the virtues. And surely there is that in the maternal bosom which, when its pleadings shall be aided by education, will overcome the seductions of wealth and fashion, and will lead the mother to seek her happiness in communing with her children and promoting their welfare, rather than in heartless intercourse with the votaries of pleasure: especially when, with an expanded mind, she extends her views to futurity, and sees her care to her offspring rewarded by peace of conscience, the blessings of her family, the prosperity of her country, and finally with everlasting pleasure to herself and them.

John S. C. Abbott, *The Mother at Home* (1833)

Ministers became a major force in the exaltation of motherhood. Protestant ministers such as John S.C. Abbott (1805-1870) constructed and publicized the concept of virtuous motherhood through child rearing manuals. Abbot assigned mothers the sole responsibility for the moral instruction of their young sons. Earlier Christian tradition linked Eve's fall to women's sinful natures, but nineteenth century ministers such as Abbott endowed motherhood with the moral redemption of the nation's sons. Abbott linked the failure of mothers to provide moral education for their children with the misery of the human race. What social purposes would it serve to endow motherhood with such awesome responsibility? In what ways would a mother's influence differ from political power? How would this description of maternal influence relate to the ideology of separate spheres?*

Mothers have as powerful an influence over the welfare of future generations, as all other earthly causes combined. Thus far the history of the world has been composed of the narrations of oppression and blood. War has scattered its unnumbered woes. The cry of the oppressed has unceasingly ascended to heaven. Where are we to look for the influence which shall change this scene, and fill the earth with the fruits of peace and benevolence? It is to the power of divine truth, to Christianity, as taught from a mother's lips. In a vast majority of cases the first six or seven years decide the character of the man. If the boy leave the paternal roof uncontrolled, turbulent, and vicious, he will, in all probability, rush on in the mad career of self-indulgence. There are exceptions; but these exceptions are rare. If, on the other hand, your son goes from home accustomed to control himself, he will probably retain that habit through life. If he has been taught to make sacrifices of his own enjoyment that he may promote the happiness of those around him, it may be expected that he will continue to practice benevolence, and consequently will be respected, and useful, and happy. If he has adopted firm resolutions to be faithful in all the relations of life, he, in all probability, will be a virtuous man and an estimable citizen, and a benefactor of his race.

When our land is filled with pious and patriotic mothers, then will it be filled with virtuous and patriotic men. The world's redeeming influence, under the blessing of the Holy Spirit, must come from a mother's lips. She who was first in the transgression, must be yet the principal earthly instrument in the restoration. Other causes may greatly aid. Other influences must be ready to receive the mind as it comes from the mother's hand, and carry it onward in its improvement. But the mothers of our race must be the chief instruments in its redemption. This sentiment will bear examining; and the more it is examined, the more manifestly true will it appear. It is alike the dictate of philosophy and experience. The mother who is neglecting personal effort, and relying upon other influences from the formation of virtuous character in her children, will find, when it is too late, that she has fatally erred. The patriot, who hopes that schools, and lyceums, and the general diffusion of knowledge, will promote the good order and happiness of the community, while family government is neglected, will find that he is attempting to purify the streams which are flowing from a corrupt foundation. It is maternal influence, after all, which must be the great agent, in the hands of God, in bringing back our guilty race to duty and happiness. O that mothers could feel this responsibility as they ought! Then would the world assume a

---

* From John S. C. Abbott, *The Mother at Home; or the Principles of Maternal Duty, Familiarly Illustrated* (New York: The American Tract Society, 1833), 159–61.

different aspect. Then should we less frequently behold unhappy families and brokenhearted parents. A new race of men would enter upon the busy scene of life, and cruelty and crime would pass away. O mothers! Reflect upon the power your Maker has placed in your hands! There is no earthly influence to be compared with yours. There is no combination of causes so powerful in promoting the happiness or the misery of our race, as the instructions of home. In a most peculiar sense God has constituted you the guardians and the controllers of the human family.

3

Emerging Industrialization: Sister Operatives and Homebound Workers

Although the majority of Americans still worked on farms, industrial growth began in the 1800s. Early factory owners hired women. In fact, female operatives, mainly from New England farms, provided the nation with a major source of factory laborers. This recruitment exposed the class limitations in domestic sphere ideology. Middle-class women could afford to stay in a woman's "proper place" at home. Poorer women needed paid employment, and Lowell textile factory owners bypassed the growing emphasis on female domesticity in order to recruit a labor force. Although the factory system eventually grew to major proportions, it co-existed with pre-industrial labor patterns in which women worked at home. New England's female shoe workers were part of a male-centered crafts tradition that viewed women's work as supplemental to that of men. Women who juggled child and home care with paid work faced a pervasive belief system that demeaned woman's work, whether domestic or home production, as non-burdensome chores. Even the meager wages they received for home manufacture legally belonged to their husbands, and their subordinate status within the family unit strengthened employer's resolve to keep women's wages low.

Faced with few employment options, native-born farm women chose factory work as a welcome alternative to domestic service. At first thankful for an opportunity to earn money, women at Lowell, like Harriet Robinson, soon confronted their employers over issues of low pay, long hours, and poor working conditions. Proud and assertive, the first generation of textile workers claimed their republican heritage, and as daughters of "Freemen" they struggled for greater control over the workplace. They organized labor associations, participated in strikes, and some, like Sarah Bagley, spoke out before a state investigative committee about poor factory conditions and the need for a ten-hour day.

During this period, organized women's activity took many forms. At Lowell, women workers lived in a close-knit community, and their labor protests expressed their collective bond as "sister operatives." Years before middle-class women met at Seneca Falls to mobilize for woman's rights, working-class women overcame the expectation of womanly submission and directly challenged male authority.

Harriet Hanson Robinson, *Lowell Textile Workers* (1898)

Harriet Hanson Robinson (1825-1911) began to work in Lowell as a child and left in the 1840s to get married. An advocate of women's rights, Hanson, in her memoir, describes conditions in the Lowell mills during the early years when poor farm women flocked to the mills to take advantage of economic opportunity and the possibility of upward mobility. Although many of the women were young and considered their work temporary, the mills also provided older women with a chance to develop an independent life. Robinson's description of her experience at Lowell relied on more than a half-century of memories. Read in conjunction with the contemporaneous Lowell accounts that follow, do you find her memories accurate or blurred? From a late nineteenth-century perspective, Robinson presents an overview of rights that women gained. What rights did late nineteenth-century women possess that those of Lowell lacked? What role did the lack of women's rights play in the Lowell protest and its outcome? What specific role did Robinson play in the 1836 "turn out"?[*]

In 1831 Lowell was little more than a factory village. Several corporations were started, and the cotton mills belonging to them were building. Help was in great demand; and stories were told all over the country of the new factory town, and the high wages that were offered to all classes of workpeople—stories that reached the ears of mechanics' and farmers' sons, and gave new life to lonely and dependent women in distant towns and farmhouses. Into this Yankee El Dorado, these needy people began to pour by the various modes of travel known to those slow old days. The stagecoach and the canal boat came every day, always filled with new recruits for this army of useful people. The mechanic and machinist came, each with his homemade chest of tools, and oftentimes his wife and little ones. The widow came with her little flock and her scanty housekeeping goods to open a boarding-house or variety store, and so provided a home for her fatherless children. Many farmers' daughters came to earn money to complete their wedding outfit, or buy the bride's share of housekeeping articles. . . .

The laws relating to women were such, that a husband could claim his wife wherever he found her, and also the children she was trying to shield from his influence; and I have seen more than one poor woman skulk behind her loom or her frame when visitors were approaching the end of the aisle where she worked. Some of

---

[*] From Harriet Hanson Robinson, *Loom and Spindle* or *Life Among the Early Mill Girls* (New York: T.Y. Crowell, 1898), 16–22, 37–43, 51–53.

these were known under assumed names, to prevent their husbands from trusteeing their wages. It was a very common thing for a male person of a certain kind to do this, thus depriving his wife of *all* her wages, perhaps, month after month. The wages of minor children could be trusteed, unless the children (being fourteen years of age) were given their time. Women's wages were also trusteed for the debts of their husbands, and children's for the debts of their parents. . . .

It must be remembered that at this date woman had no property rights. A widow could be left without her share of her husband's (or the family) property, a legal "encumbrance" to his estate. A father could make his will without a reference to his daughter's share of the inheritance. He usually left her a home on the farm as long as she remained single. A woman was not supposed to be capable of spending her own or of using other people's money. In Massachusetts, before 1840, a woman could not legally be treasurer of her own sewing society, unless some man were responsible for her.

The law took no cognizance of woman as a money spender. She was a ward, an appendage, a relict. Thus it happened, that if a woman did not choose to marry, or, when left a widow, to re-marry, she had no choice but to enter one of the few employments open to her, or to become a burden on the charity of some relative.

In almost every New England home could be found one or more of these women, sometimes welcome, more often unwelcome, and leading joyless, and in many instances unsatisfactory, lives. The cotton factory was a great opening to these lonely and dependent women. From a condition approaching pauperism they were at once placed above want; they could earn money and spend it as they please; and could gratify their tastes and desires without restraint, and without rendering an account to anybody. . . .

Among the older women who sought this new employment were very many lonely and dependent women, such as used to be mentioned in old wills as "encumbrances" and "relicts," and to whom a chance of earning money was indeed a new revelation. How well I remembered some of these solitary ones! As a child of eleven years, I often made fun of them—for children do not see the pathetic side of human life—and imitated them for their limp carriage and inelastic gait. I can see them now, even after sixty years, just as they looked—depressed, modest, mincing, hardly daring to look one in the face, so shy and sylvan had been their lives. But after the first pay-day came, and they felt the jungle of silver in their pockets, and had begun to feel its mercurial influence, their bowed heads were lifted, their necks seemed braced with steel, they looked you in the face, and moved blithely among their looms or frames, and walked with elastic step to and from their work. And when Sunday came, homespun was no longer their only wear; and how sedately gay in their new attire they walked to church, and how proudly they dropped their silver fourpences into the contribution-box! It seemed as if a great hope impelled them—the harbinger of the new era that was about to dawn for them and for all woman-kind.

One of the first strikes of cotton-factory operatives that ever took place in this country was that in Lowell, in October, 1836. When it was announced that the wages were to be cut down, great indignation was felt, and it was decided to strike, *en masse*. This was done. The mills were shut down, and the girls went in procession from their several corporations to the "grove" on Chapel Hill, and listened to "incendiary" speeches from early labor reformers.

One of the girls stood on a pump, and gave vent to the feelings of her companions in a neat speech, declaring that it was their duty to resist all attempts at cutting down the wages. This was the first time a woman had spoken in public in Lowell, and the event caused surprise and consternation among her audience.

Cutting down the wages was not their only grievance, nor the only cause of this strike. Hitherto the corporations had paid twenty-five cents a week towards the board of each operative, and now it was their purpose to have the girls pay the sum; and this, in addition to the cut in wages, would make a difference of at least one dollar a week. It was estimated that as many as twelve or fifteen hundred girls turned out, and walked in procession through the streets. They had neither flags nor music, but sang songs, a favorite (but rather inappropriate) one being a parody on "I won't be a nun."

> "Oh! isn't it a pity, such a pretty girl as I—
> Should be sent to the factory to pine away and die?
> Oh! I cannot be a slave,
> I will not be a slave
> For I'm so fond of liberty
> That I cannot be a slave."

My own recollection of this first strike (or "turn out" as it was called) is very vivid. I worked in a lower room, where I had heard the proposed strike fully, if not vehemently, discussed; I had been an ardent listener to what was said against this attempt at "oppression" on the part of the corporation, and naturally I took sides with the strikers. When the day came on which the girls were to turn out, those in the upper rooms started first, and so many of them left that our mill was at once shut down. Then, when the girls in my room stood irresolute, uncertain what to do, asking each other, "Would you?" or "Shall we turn out?" and not one of them having the courage to lead off, I, who began to think they would not go out, after all their talk, became impatient, and started on ahead, saying, with childish bravado, "I don't care what you do, *I* am going to turn out, whether anyone else does or not;" and I marched out, and was followed by the others.

Letters to the *Voice of Industry* (1846)

The following letters written to the *Voice of Industry*, a publication for factory workers, express growing dissatisfaction over Lowell's worsening conditions. Women argued that capitalist greed had undermined their well-being through management's insistence that they produce more yet receive a lower wage. What evidence do the women provide about worsening conditions? Why do they refer to themselves as part of the "toiling classes"? How do they justify their protest? What does the term "sister operatives" imply?*

March 13, 1846

The Female Department

NOTICE

The Female Labor Reform Association will meet every Tuesday evening, at 8 o'clock, at their Reading Room, 76 Central Street, to transact all business pertaining to the Association, and to devise means by which to promote the common interests of all the Laboring Classes. Also to discuss all subjects which shall come before the meeting. Every *Female* who realizes the great necessity of a *Reform* and improvement in the condition of the worthy, toiling classes, and who would wish to place woman in that elevated status intellectually and morally, which a bountiful Creator designed her to occupy in the scale of being, is most *cordially* invited to attend and give her influence on the side of *virtue* and *suffering humanity.*

Huldah J. Stone, Sec'y

April 24, 1846

To the Female Labor Reform Association In Manchester

SISTER OPERATIVES

As I am now in the "City of Spindles," out of employment, I have taken the liberty to occupy a few of your leisure moments in addressing the members of your Association, and pardon me for giving you a few brief hints of my own experiences as a factory Operative, before proceeding to make some remarks upon the glorious cause in which you are so arduously engaged. It would be useless to attempt to portray the hardships and privations which are daily endured, for all that have toiled within the factory walls, must be well acquainted with the present system of labor, which can be properly termed slavery.

I am a peasant's daughter, and my lot has been cast in the society of the humble laborer. I was drawn from the home of my childhood at an early age, and necessity obliged me to seek employment in the Factory . . . I have heard with the deepest interest, of your flourishing Association of which you are members, and it rejoices my heart to see so many of you contending for your rights, and making efforts to elevate the condition of your fellow brethren, and raising them from their oppressed and

---

* From the *Voice of Industry* (Lowell, Mass.), March 13, April 24, May 15, and September 11, 1846.

degraded condition, and seeing rights restored which god and Nature designed them to enjoy. Do you possess the principles of Christianity? Then do not remain silent; but seek to ameliorate the condition of every fellow being. Engage laboriously and earnestly in the work, until you see your desires accomplished. Let the proud aristocrat who has tyrannized over your rights with oppressive severity, see that there is ambition and enterprise among the "spindles," and show a determination to have your plans fully executed. Use prudence and discretion in all your ways; act independently and no longer be a slave to petty tyrants, who, if they have an opportunity, will encroach upon your privileges.

Some say that "Capital will take good care of labor," but don't believe it; don't trust them. Is it not plain, that they are trying to deceive the public, by telling them that your task is easy and plead that there is no need of reform? Too many are destitute of feeling and sympathy, and it is a great pity that they are not obliged to toil one year, and then they would be glad to see the "Ten Hour Petition" brought before the Legislature. This is plain, but true language. . . .

Ellen Monroe, Letter to the *Boston Bee* (1846)

Ellen Monroe's letter to the *Boston Bee* predates the Seneca Falls women's rights convention by two years, but expresses the same feminist spirit of protest. Monroe argued that women not only endured oppressive factory conditions, but also were deprived of the right to self-assertion and autonomy. In the letter, Monroe lists her specific grievances about gender inequality. Why does she believe that the assumption that men "protect" women is false? How was the term "She Devils" used?[*]

Sir —

I have observed that it is a common practice, among Editors, to fill their papers with advice to women, and not infrequently, with ill concealed taunts of woman's weakness. . . .

It may be, that most women are so dwarfed and weakened, that they believe that dressing, cooking, and loving . . . make up the whole of life; but Nature still asserts her rights, and there will always be those too strong to be satisfied, with a dress, a pudding, or a beau, though they may take each in turn, as a portion of life. I speak not now of the distinguished of either sex; they form a bright relief in the otherwise dark picture. Neither do I suppose that there are no exceptions, perhaps many, to the

---

[*] From Ellen Monroe, "Letter to the *Boston Bee*," in the *Voice of Industry* (Lowell, Mass.), March 13, 1846.

general rule. But to the generality of men, let the question be put. Are you not, thousands of you, as effeminate as the veriest woman of them all? You talk of your manliness; where is it? "Alas, echo answers where." You boast of the protection you offer to women. Protection! from what? From the rude and disorderly of your own sex—reform them, and women will no longer need the protection you make such a parade of giving. Protect them, do you? Let me point you to the thousands of women, doomed to lives of miserable drudgery, and receiving a "compensation which if quadrupled, would be rejected by the man-laborer, with scorn"; are they less worthy of protection because they are trying to help themselves? Because they have little inclination and less time to lisp nonsense? . . . If you would have the manliness you talk of, seek to raise those poor women from their oppressed, and too often degraded, condition; if you will not do it, go on in your old course, but prate no more of your manliness.

Bad is the condition of so many women, it would be much worse if they had nothing but your boasted protection to rely upon; but they have at last learnt the lesson, which a bitter experience teaches, that not to those who type themselves their "natural" protectors," are they to look for needful help, but to the strong and resolute of their own sex. May all good fortune attend those resolute ones, and the noble cause in which they are engaged. "*She Devils*" as some of them have been elegantly termed by certain persons, calling themselves men; let them not fear such epithets, nor shrink from the path they have chosen. . . . They are breaking the way; they shall make it smoother for those that come after them, and generations yet unborn shall live to bless them for their courage and perseverance. If we choose to sit down in our indolence, and persuade ourselves that we can do nothing, let us not censure those who are wiser and stronger than we are. It has been said that men and women are "natural enemies," which I do not believe; but if a running fight must be kept up between the two, let women have half the battlefield and fair play. The time may come when both parties will learn that they can be much better friends, when they have more equal rights. . . .

Female Labor Reform Association, *Testimony Before the Massachusetts Legislature* (1845)

The testimony of Lowell factory women who represented the Female Labor Reform Association before the Massachusetts legislature, was an early appeal for state intervention. Although they failed to achieve a ten-hour work day, their activism led to a state investigation of factory conditions. Not until the Progressive era would female factory workers secure protective legislation. What specific factory conditions do the women cite as detrimental to their well-being? Sarah Bagley played a key role in the organization. What evidence does she give about the women's health?[*]

The first petitioner who testified was Eliza R. Hemmingway. She had worked 2 years and 9 months in the Lowell Factories; 2 years in the Middlesex, and 9 months in the Hamilton Corporations. Her employment is weaving—works by the piece. The Hamilton Mill manufactures cotton fabrics. The Middlesex, woolen fabrics. She is now at work in the Middlesex Mills, and attends one loom. Her wages average from $16 to $23 a month exclusive of board. She complained of the hours for labor being too many, and the time for meals too limited. In the summer season, the work is commenced at 5 o'clock, a.m., and continued till 7 o'clock, p.m., with half an hour for breakfast and three-quarters of an hour for dinner. During eight months of the year, but half an hour is allowed for dinner. The air in the room she considered not to be wholesome. There were 293 small lamps and 61 large lamps lighted in the room in which she worked, when evening work is required. These lamps are also lighted sometimes in the morning. About 130 females, 11 men, and 12 children (between the ages of 11 and 14) work in the room with her. She thought the children enjoyed about as good health as children generally do. The children work but 9 months about of 12. The other 3 months they must attend school. Thinks that there is no day when there are less than six of the females out of the mill from sickness. Has known as many as thirty. She, herself, is out quite often, on account of sickness. There was more sickness in the Summer than in Winter months; though in the Summer, lamps are not lighted. She thought there was a general desire among the females to work but ten hours, regardless of pay. Most of the girls are from the country, who work in the Lowell Mills. The average time there is about three years. She knew one girl who had worked there 14 years. Her health was poor when she left. Miss Hemmingway said her health was better where she now worked, than it was when she worked on the Hamilton Corporation.

She knew of one girl who last winter went into the mill at half past 4 o'clock, a.m., and worked til half past 7 o'clock p.m. She did so to make more money. She earned from $25 to $30 per month. There is always a large number of girls at the gate wishing to get in before the bell rings. On the Middlesex Corporation one-fourth part of the females go into the mills before they are obliged to. They do this to make more wages. A large number come to Lowell and work in the mills to assist their husbands to pay for their farms. The moral character of the operatives is good. There was only one American female in the room with her who could not write her name.

Miss Sarah G. Bagley said she had worked in the Lowell Mills eight years and a half—six years and a half on the Hamilton Corporation, and two years on the Middlesex. She is a weaver, and works by the piece. She worked in the mills three years before her health began to fail. She is a native of New Hampshire, and went home six weeks during the summer. Last year she was out of the mill a third of the

---

[*] From "Report of the Special Committee on Hours of Labor," House Report No. 50, Massachusetts General Court Legislative Document 1845, House 1–65, 2–4.

time. She thinks the health of the operatives is not so good as the health of females who do housework or millinery business. The chief evil, so far as health is concerned, is the shortness of time allowed for meals. The next evil is the length of time employed—not giving them time to cultivate their minds. She spoke of the high moral and intellectual character of the girls. That many were engaged as teachers in the Sunday schools. That many attended the lectures of the Lowell Institute; and she thought, if more time was allowed, that more lectures would be given and more girls attend. She thought that the girls generally were favorable to the ten hour system. She had presented a petition, same as the one before the Committee, to 132 girls, most of whom said that they would prefer to work but ten hours. In a pecuniary point of view, it would be better, as their health would be improved. They would have more time for sewing. Their intellectual, moral, and religious habits would also be benefited by the change.

Miss Bagley said, in addition to her labor in the mills, she had kept evening school during the winter months, for four years, and thought that this extra labor must have injured her health.

Caroline Dall, *Women's Right to Labor* (1860)

Caroline Dall (1822–1912) was a pioneer analyst of women's work, and an early critic of their limited employment options and inequitable pay. She argued that women's right to economic independence was fundamental. What pay differentials existed between Lynn's male and female shoemakers? What were women's major employment opportunities?[*]

In 1845, there were employed in the textile manufactures of the United States, 55,828 men and 75,710 women. This proportion, or a still greater preponderance of female labor—that is, from one-third to one-half—appears in all factory returns. As an *employed* class, women seem to be more in number than men: as *employers*, they are very few.

In a New Haven clock factory, seven women are employed among seventy men, on half-wages; and the manufacturer takes great credit to himself for his liberality. At Waltham, also, a watch factory has been lately started, in which many women are employed. In the census of the city of Boston for 1845, the various employments of women are thus given:

---

[*] From Caroline H. Dall, *Women's Right to Labor, or Low Wages and Hard Work* (Boston: Walker, Wise & Co., 1860), 97–103.

Artificial-flower makers,	Comb makers,
Boardinghouse-keepers,	Confectioners,
Bookbinders,	Corset-makers,
Printers,	Corset-dealers,
Blank-book makers,	Card-makers,
Bonnet-dealers,	Professed cooks,
Bonnet-makers,	Cork-cutters,
Workers in straw,	Domestics,
Shoe and boot makers,	Dress-makers,
Band & fancy box makers,	Match-makers,
Brush-makers,	Fringe and tassel makers,
Cap-makers,	Fur-sewers,
Clothiers,	Hair-cloth weavers, and
Collar-makers,	Map-colorers.

I think you cannot fail to see, from this list, how very imperfect the enumeration is: not a single washerwoman not charwoman, for one thing, upon it. Yet here you have the occupations of 4,970 women. Of these, 4,046 are servants—a number which has, at least, doubled since then; and which leaves only 924 women for all other vocations.

It is probably known to you all how largely the rural post office duties are performed by women; petty politicians obtaining the appointment, and leaving wives and daughters to do the work. There are several Registers of the Deeds; but I only know of one—Olive Rose, of Thomaston, Me. She was elected in 1953, by 469 votes against 205; was officially notified, and required to give bonds. Her emolument depends upon fees, and ranges between three and four hundred dollars per annum . . .

I am sorry to conclude these attempts at statistics with one reliable estimate, which holds, like a nutshell, the kernel of this question of female labor.

In 1850, there were engaged in shoemaking, in the town of Lynn, 3,729 males and 6,412 females—nearly twice as many women as men; yet, in the monthly payment of wages, only half as much money was paid to women as to men. The three thousand men received seventy-five thousand dollars a month; and the six thousand women, thirty-seven thousand dollars: that is, the women's wages were, on the average, only one-quarter as much as those of men.

Helen Sumner, *Homework: Boot and Shoe Making* (1910)

This report by Helen Sumner (1876-1933) describes the role women played in the production of boots and shoes. Sumner was a labor reformer and an economist. At what point did the author believe that although women still produced shoes at home they had "definitely entered the industrial field?" How does the tone of this report differ from that of Dall?*

It was division of labor which first brought women into the boot and shoemaking industry. The introduction of machinery, indeed, later drove large numbers of them out of the business for a time. Types of machinery were soon evolved, however, which made again profitable a division of labor which could utilize the labor of women, and their restoration to the industry followed.

About 1705 or earlier, side by side with the development of the wholesale trade in boots and shoes, shoemakers or cordwainers, as they were called, began to hire their fellows and to gather them into shops where a rough division of labor was practiced. Soon afterwards they began to send the uppers out to women to be stitched and bound. From the time until the introduction of the sewing machine, the binding of shoes manufactured for the wholesale market was practically a woman's industry, carried on at home. Localities differed largely, however, in the extent of the employment of women. In Massachusetts the shoe binders appear to have been exclusively women as early as 1810, but in Philadelphia, which was also a large shoe-manufacturing center, the trade remained in the hands of men until much later. A writer in the Philadelphia Mechanics' Free Press in 1829 spoke of the employment of women in shoemaking as "derogatory to their sex."

In general, however, by 1830, and in many localities earlier, the manufacture of shoes was divided into two parts—the work of the men in small shops and the work of women in their homes. By 1837 the shoe binders of Lynn not only bound the edging but did all the inside and lighter kinds of sewing.

There were, however, two more or less roughly marked stages in women's work at shoe binding. In the first stage the family was the industrial unit, the man shoemaker being assisted by his wife and daughters in the part of the work which they could easily perform—the sewing. Even when the shoemaker worked for a "boss," he brought home his materials and turned over the work of binding to the women of the family. Gradually, however, as the business developed, it became customary for the "boss" himself to give out the shoes to be bound directly to the women. The division of labor remained the same, but it was no longer controlled by the shoemaker, but by the "boss." The women, too, instead of having their work and pay lumped with that of the head of the family—instead of being merely helpers without economic standing—now dealt directly with the employer and definitely entered the industrial field . . .

The introduction of the sewing machine, however, between 1855 and 1865, caused an almost complete transformation in the boot and shoemaking industry. Small "stitching shops" equipped with the new machines were opened. In Lynn these shops

---

* From Helen Sumner, in *Vol. IX, History of Women in Industry in the United States, Report on the Condition of Woman and Child Wage-Earners in the United States.* 61st Congress, 2d Session, Senate Document 645, 1910.

were sometimes small buildings standing by themselves, but more frequently the manufacturers fitted up rooms in the buildings where the men worked . . .

The women did not, however, after the introduction of the factory system, succeed in retaining their work as completely as they had done in textile industries. The machines were heavy and difficult to operate, especially the waxed thread sewing machine which was introduced about 1857, and, as a result, largely operated by men.

4

Moral Activism and the Contest over Woman's "Place"

Women reformers of the Jacksonian era grew to maturity at a time of democratic growth and economic expansion in which white men gained the major benefits. As more white men gained the vote, political participation crossed class lines and became a white male preserve. Not only could women not vote, the male claim to politics made it problematic whether women even could address political issues. As the Grimké sisters found, that included speaking out against slavery. In fact, the more women joined the ferment of reform that characterized the Jacksonian era, the more they encountered a chorus of outrage. They were out of their "place" or "sphere," behaving in ways that were "unnatural," "unsexed," and "unwomanly." The contest over woman's proper "place" molded the public discourse. Yet, even women like Catherine Beecher, who advocated women's private, family-oriented role, expanded the definition of appropriate gender roles to include elementary school teaching.

Within the middle-class, widening commercial opportunities for men accentuated the separation between the private sphere of female domesticity and the public sphere of male activity. Increasing numbers of middle-class husbands sought paid employment away from the home and became the sole "breadwinners." The cultural expectation that husbands be the sole providers crossed class lines, and obscured the actual life experience of the thousands of married women who took in boarders and worked at home; stitching gloves, binding shoes, or performing other types of labor that added to the family income. As manufactured goods became more widely available, more affluent women became consumers rather than producers of household goods. In towns and cities the middle-class household began to decline as a unit of economic production. Women assumed the status of housewife and performed the unpaid, although vitally necessary, functions of home and family care. As women's work, domestic labor was seen as less significant than the "real" work performed by men. The middle-class home assumed new importance as a refuge and a haven for men returning from the "real" work of business activity.

A belief system gained currency that held that the personalities, characters, and behavior of the two sexes were so sharply differentiated that each needed a separate sphere to fulfill their masculine or feminine destinies. Separate-sphere ideology emphasized the home as women's habitat and took as given a host of assumptions. Women were viewed as weak and dependent and in need of male protection. Unlike rational, purposeful men, they were considered sentimental and emotional, but also endowed with a superior degree of piety and benevolence. Cultural ssumptions created a dual standard of sexual conduct. Perceived as passionless, women were expected to be chaste, and a single pre-marital sexual encounter could destroy their reputations. Men were forgiven for similar behavior. In short, beliefs about female natures reinforced the norm of moral motherhood, and made women appear unfit for the rigor and crassness of public roles and commercial enterprise.

Domestic ideals of delicacy and weakness had little relevance to women like Elizabeth Greer, who struggled to survive on the overland trail and in the raw frontier. Poor, working-class women and enslaved black women lived beyond the parameters of male protection. The widespread appearance of prostitution involving impoverished women reflected the class-based nature of sexual parity standards. The sexual exploitation of enslaved women provides further evidence of the illusory nature of male protection. Moreover, the lives of abolitionist women and former slaves like Harriet Tubman and Sojourner Truth, reveal the race and class-based limitations of the image of women as dependent weaklings.

Middle-class women participated directly in the reform efforts that characterized the Jacksonian era. Cultural values that attributed to women moral superiority facilitated their involvement in moral purity crusades, humanitarian reforms, and elementary school teaching. Whereas Dorothea Dix embarked on a national crusade to reform conditions for the mentally ill, many other women sought to cleanse society of its sins and outlaw prostitution and drinking. They sought to have men conform to the superior standard of female morality. Women became the moral guardians of the community. Without directly challenging male domination of social and political institutions, reforming women both expanded and enriched the concept of domesticity and widened women's role in the public sphere.

Almost a century before women received the right to vote, both white and African-American women directly engaged in anti-slavery activity, and played a central role in the nation's most divise moral and political controversy. Novelist and abolotionist Harriet Beecher Stowe's *Uncle Tom's Cabin* (1852) set a new publication record. Less well-known women organized petition drives for abolition, campaigned for anti-slavery candidates, embarked on lecture tours and formed their own abolitionist societies. African-American women founded the nation's first women's anti-slavery society in Salem, Massachusetts. Former slave Harriet Tubman placed her life at risk helping others escape to freedom. Ex-slave Sojourner Truth joined white women abolitionists in their effort to achieve the dual emancipation of slaves and women.

Female abolitionist societies enabled women to strengthen their organizational and public speaking skills. In entering the public debate over the issue of slavery, outspoken women directly challenged the constraints of the domestic sphere. The Grimké sisters, Lucretia Mott, Lucy Stone, and other women who engaged in public speaking, violated a deeply entrenched social custom and provoked widespread outrage. Pelted with rocks and eggs, criticized and ridiculed, women would not be silenced. In fact, among some women, attempts at suppression produced a contradictory result: the demand for female empowerment. From a historical perspective it is clear that anti-slavery activism heightened women's awareness of their own political, social, cultural and legal subordination. Female abolitionists helped ignite and provide the leadership for America's first organized woman's movement.

Dorothea Dix, *On Behalf of the Insane* (1843)

Dorothea Dix (1802–1887) led a crusade to reform conditions for the mentally ill. Dix traveled extensively throughout Massachusetts, researching the inhumane treatment of the mentally ill who were placed in prisons. Dix submitted her testimony on prison conditions in writing to the Massachusetts legislature, because respectable women did not speak in public. Her commitment to securing reform provided the impetus for state regulation of the treatment of the mentally ill. In describing the conditions of the insane, Dix remarked that her "woman's nature shrinks with peculiar sensitiveness." How does this comment relate to pre-Civil War gender distinctions? How would the concept of "woman's nature" promote women's interest in humanitarian reform? Cite evidence of the moral outrage that permeates Dix's argument for reform.*

About two years since leisure afforded opportunity, and duty prompted me to visit several prisons and almshouses in the vicinity of this metropolis, I found, near Boston, in the jails and asylums for the poor, a numerous class brought into unsuitable connection with criminals and the general mass of paupers. I refer to idiots and insane persons, dwelling in circumstances not only adverse to their own physical and moral improvement, but productive of extreme disadvantages to all other persons brought into association with them. I applied myself diligently to trace the causes of these evils, and sought to supply remedies. As one obstacle was surmounted, fresh difficulties appeared. Every new investigation has given depth to the conviction that it is only by decried, prompt, and vigorous legislation that the evils to which I refer, and which I shall prove more fully to illustrate, can be remedied. I shall be obliged to speak with great plainness, and to reveal many things revolting to the taste, and from

---

* From "Old South Leaflets 6," (Boston, 1904), 490–95; 518–19.

which my woman's nature shrinks with peculiar sensitiveness. But truth is the highest consideration. *I tell what I have seen*—painful and shocking as the details often are—that from them you may feel more deeply the imperative obligation which lies upon you to prevent the possibility of a repetition or continuance of such outrages upon humanity. If I inflict pain upon you, and move you to horror, it is to acquaint you with sufferings which you have the power to alleviate, and make you hasten to the relief of the victims of legalized barbarity.

I come to present the strong claims of suffering humanity. I come to place before the Legislature of Massachusetts the condition of the miserable, the desolate, the outcast. I come as the advocate of helpless, forgotten, insane, and idiotic men and women; of being sunk to a condition from which the most unconcerned would start with real horror; of beings wretched in our prisons, and more wretched in our almshouses. And I cannot suppose it needful to employ earnest persuasion, or stubborn argument, in order to arrest and fix attention upon a subject only the more strongly pressing in its claims because it is revolting and disgusting in its details.

I must confine myself to few examples, but am ready to furnish other and more complete details, if required. If my pictures are displeasing, coarse, and severe, my subjects, it must be recollected, offer no tranquil, refined, or composing features. . . .

I proceed, gentlemen, briefly to call your attention to the *present* state of insane persons confined within this Commonwealth, in *cages, closets, cellars, stalls, pens*! *Chained, naked, beaten with rods,* and *lashed* into obedience. . . .

Prisons are not constructed in view of being converted into county hospitals, and almshouses are not founded as receptacles for the insane. And yet, in the face of justice and common sense, wardens are by law compelled to receive, and the masters of almshouses not to refuse, insane and idiotic subjects in all stages of mental disease and privation. . . .

I repeat it, it is defective legislation which perpetuates and multiplies these abuses. In illustration of my subject, I offer the following extracts from my Note-book and Journal: —

Springfield. In the jail, one lunatic woman, furiously mad, a State pauper, improperly situated, both in regard to the prisoners, the keepers, and herself. It is a case of extreme self-forgetfulness and oblivion to all the decencies of life, to describe which would be to repeat only the grossest scenes. She is much worse since leaving Worcester. In the almshouse of the same town is a woman apparently only needing judicious care, and some well-chosen employment, to make it unnecessary to confine her in solitude, in a dreary unfurnished room. Her appeals for employment and companionship are most touching, but the mistress replied "she had no time to attend to her."

Lincoln. A woman in a cage. *Medford*. One idiotic subject chained, and one in a close stall for seventeen years. *Pepperell*. One often doubly chained, hand and foot; another violent; several peaceable now. *Brookfield*. One man caged, comfortable. *Granville*. One often closely confined; now losing the use of his limbs from want of exercise. *Charlemont*. One man caged. *Savoy*. One man caged. *Lenox*. Two in the jail, against whose unfit condition there the jailer protests.

Dedham. The insane disadvantageously placed in the jail. In the almshouse, two females in stalls, situated in the main building; lie in wooden bunks filled with straw; always shut up. One of these subjects is supposed curable. The overseers of the poor have declined giving her a trial at the hospital, as I was informed, on account of expense.

Besides the above, I have seen many who, part of the year are chained or caged. The use of cages is all but universal. Hardly a town but can refer to some not distant period of using them; chains are less common; negligence frequent; willful abuse less frequent than suffering proceeding from ignorance, or want of consideration. I encountered during the last three months many poor creatures wandering reckless and unprotected through the country. Innumerable accounts have been sent me of persons who had roved away unwatched and unsearched after; and I have heard that responsible persons, controlling the almshouses, have not thought themselves culpable in sending away from their shelter, to cast upon the chances of remote relief, insane men and women. These, left on the highways, unfriended and incompetent to control or direct their own movements, sometimes have found refuge in the hospital, and others have not been traced. . . .

Gentlemen, I commit to you this sacred cause. Your action upon this subject will affect the present and future condition of hundreds and of thousands.

In this legislation, as in all things, may you exercise that "wisdom which is the breath of the power of God."

Catherine Beecher, *The Evils Suffered by American Women and American Children* (1846)

This document is part of Catherine Beecher's campaign for the feminization of elementary school teaching. Although Beecher (1800–1878) believed that women needed "healthful and productive labor," she did not advocate woman's rights. She limited her reform efforts to elevating women as mothers and teachers. Firmly faithful to the traditional separation between male and female spheres, she subsequently argued that voting rights for women were an unnecessary and harmful intrusion into the male sphere. What arguments does Beecher present that women rather than men should provide the nation with its elementary school teachers?*

* From Catherine Beecher, *The Evils Suffered by American Women and American Children: The Causes and the Remedy* (New York: Harper & Brothers, 1846), 3; 5–12.

The immediate object which has called us together, is an enterprise now in progress, the design of which is *to educate destitute American children, by the agency of American women.* It is an effort which has engaged the exertions of a large number of ladies of various sects, and of all sections in our country, and one which, though commencing in a humble way and on a small scale, we believe is eventually to exert a most extensive and saving influence through the nation. . . .

Few are aware of the deplorable destitution of our country in regard to the education of the rising generation, or of the long train of wrongs and sufferings endured by multitudes of young children from this neglect.

The last twelve years I have resided chiefly in the West, and my attention has been directed to the various interests of education. In five of the largest western states I have spent from several weeks to several months—I have traveled extensively and have corresponded or conversed with well-informed gentlemen and ladies on this subject in most of the western states. And I now have materials for presenting the real situation of vast multitudes of American children, which would "cause the ear that heareth it to tingle." But I dare not do it. It would be so revolting—so disgraceful—so heartrending—so incredible—that in the first place, I should not be believed; and in the next place such an outcry of odium and indignation would be aroused, as would impede efforts to remedy the evil. The only thing I can safely do is to present some statistics, which cannot be disputed, because they are obtained from *official documents*, submitted by civil officers to our national or state legislatures. Look then at the census, and by its data we shall find that *now* there are nearly *a million* adults who cannot read and write, and more than *two million* children utterly illiterate, and entirely without schools. Look at individual states, and we shall find Ohio and Kentucky, the two best supplied of our western states, demanding *five thousand* teachers each, to supply them in the same ratio as Massachusetts is supplied. *Ten thousand* teachers are now needed in Ohio and Kentucky alone, to furnish schools for more than two hundred thousand children, who otherwise must grow up in utter ignorance. . . .

Let us now turn to another class of our countrywomen—the *female operatives* in our shops and mills. Unfortunately, this subject cannot be freely discussed without danger of collision with the vast pecuniary and party interests connected with it. I therefore shall simply *state facts*, without expressing the impressions of my own mind.

Last year, I spent several days in Lowell, for the sole purpose of investigating this subject. I conversed with agents, overseers, clergymen, physicians, editors, ladies resident in the place, and a large number of the operatives themselves. All seem disposed to present the most favorable side of the picture; and nothing unfavorable was said except as drawn forth by my questions. . . .

Let me now present the facts I learned by observation or inquiry on the spot. I was there in mid-winter, and every morning I was wakened at *five*, by the bells calling to labor. The time allowed for dressing and breakfast was so short, as many told me, that both were performed hurriedly, and then work at the mills was begun by lamplight, and proceeded without remission till twelve, and chiefly in the standing position. Then half an hour only allowed for dinner, from which the time for going and returning was deducted. Then back to the mills, to work till seven o'clock, the last part of the time by lamplight. Then returning, washing, dressing, and supper occupied another hour. Thus ten hours only remained for recreation and sleep. Now eight hours' sleep is required for laborers, and none in our country are employed in labor more hours than the female operatives in mills. Deduct eight hours for sleep and only *two hours* remain for shopping, mending, making, recreation, social intercourse, and *breathing the pure air*. For it must be remembered that all the hours of labor are spent in rooms where lamps, together with from forty to eighty persons, are exhausting the healthful principle of the air, where the temperature, both summer and winter, on account of the work, must be kept at 70¼ and in some rooms at 80¼, and where the air is loaded with particles of cotton thrown from thousands of cards, spindles, and looms. . . .

In regard to *intellectual advantages*, such as night schools, lectures, reading and composition, all time devoted to these must be taken from the hours required for recreation or needful repose. . . .

I asked one of the young operatives if they could not take turns reading aloud while sewing. She replied that they were all either too tired, or they wished a little time to talk, so they never succeeded when they attempted it. As to the periodical, the *Lowell Offering*, I found that of six thousand women, many of them schoolteachers, but about *twenty* were contributors to its pages, while the best pieces were written by the two lady editors, neither of whom are operatives, though both had been so at former periods. All writing by actual operatives is probably done in hours which should have been given to sleep. . . .

Now, without expressing any opinion as to the influence, on health and morals, of taking women away from domestic habits and pursuits, to labor with men in shops and mills, I simply ask if it would not be *better* to put the thousands of men who are keeping school for young children into the mills, and employ the women to train the children?

Wherever education is most prosperous, there woman is employed more than man. In Massachusetts, where education is highest, five out of seven of the teachers are women; while in Kentucky, where education is so much lower, five out of six of the teachers are men.

Another cause of depression to our sex is found in the fact that there is no profession for women of education and high position which, like law, medicine, and theology, opens the way to competence, influence and honor, and presents motives for exertion. Woman ought never to be led to married life except under the promptings of pure affection. To marry for an establishment, a position, or for something to do, is a deplorable wrong. But how many women, for want of a high and honorable profession to engage their time, are led to this melancholy course. This is not so because Providence has not provided an ample place for such a profession for woman, but because custom or prejudice, or a low estimate of its honorable character, prevents her from entering it. The educating of children, that is the true and noble profession of a woman—that is what is worthy of the noblest powers and affections of the noblest minds.

A Temperance Activist (1853)

Women who advocated temperance were confined to auxillary status in male-dominated temperance societies. Women's activism on behalf of temperance awakened male concern that women were stepping beyond their domestic roles. While most temperance women protested peacefully, this newspaper article describes a "novel case"—the actual destruction of property of a saloon owner. What personal factors motivated the woman's destructive behavior? What bearing on the case would her status as a "pious mother" have?[*]

A Heroic Woman—Mrs. Margaret Freeland, of Syracuse, was recently arrested upon a warrant issued on complaint of Emanuel Rosendale, a rum-seller, charging her with forcing an entrance to his house, and with stones and clubs smashing his doors and windows, breaking his tumblers and bottles, and turning over his whiskey barrels and spilling their contents. Great excitement was produced by this novel case. It seems that the husband of Mrs. Freeland was a drunkard—that he was in the habit of abusing his wife, turning her out of doors, etc., and this was carried so far that the police frequently found it necessary to interfere to put a stop to his ill-treatment of his family. Rosendale, the complainant, furnished Freeland with the liquor which turned him into a demon. Mrs. Freeland had frequently told him of her sufferings and besought him to refrain from giving her husband the poison. But alas! she appealed to a heart of stone. He disregarded her entreaties and spurned her from his door. Driven to desperation she armed herself, broke into the house, drove out the base-hearted landlord and proceeded upon the work of destruction.

She was brought before the court and demanded a trial. The citizens employed Charles B. Sedgwick, Esq., as her counsel, and prepared to justify her assault upon legal grounds. Rosendale, being at once arrested on complaint of Thomas L. Carson for selling liquor unlawfully, and feeling the force of the storm that was gathering over his head, appeared before the Justice, withdrew his complaint against Mrs. Freeland, paid the costs, and gave bail on the complaint of Mr. Carson, to appear at the General Sessions and answer to an indictment should there be one found.

Mrs. Freeland is said to be "the pious mother of a fine family of children, and a highly respectable member of the Episcopal Church."

---

[*] From *The Lily*, June 1853, in Elizabeth Cady Stanton, Susan B. Anthony, and Matilda J. Gage, *History of Woman Suffrage*, ed. (New York: Fowler and Wells, 1881), I: 475.

Elizabeth Emery and Mary P. Abbott, Letter to *The Liberator* (1836)

Women wrote letters to William Lloyd Garrison's abolitionist newspaper, *The Liberator*, that reflected their abolitionist commitment. The following letter by Elizabeth Emery and Mary P. Abbot, of Andover, Massachusetts, expressed the intensity of their moral outcry against slavery. What justification did they provide for women's abolitionist activism? What is the significance of the phrase "Her oppressed sister cries aloud for help"? In what ways does the letter express bi-racial sisterhood?*

Andover, Massachusetts, August 22, 1836

Mr. Editor:

In these days of women's doings, it may not be amiss to report the proceedings of some ladies in Andover. The story is now and then told of a new thing done here, as the opening of a railroad, or the building of a factory, but we have news better than all—it is the formation of a "Female Antislavery Society."

The call of our female friends across the waters—the energetic appeal of those untiring sisters in the work of emancipation in Boston—above all, the sighs, the groans, the deathlike struggles of scourged sisters in the South—these have moved our hearts, our hands. We feel that woman has a place in this Godlike work, for women's woes, and women's wrongs, are borne to us on every breeze that flows from the South; woman has a place, for she forms a part in God's created intelligent instrumentality to reform the world. God never made her to be inactive nor in all cases to follow in the wake of man. When man proves recreant to his duty and faithless to his Maker, woman, with her feeling heart, should rouse him—should start his sympathies—should cry in his ear, and raise such a storm of generous sentiment, as shall never let him sleep again. We believe God gave woman a heart to feel—an eye to weep—a hand to work—a tongue to speak. Now let her use that tongue to speak on slavery. Is it not a curse—a heaven-daring abomination? Let her employ that hand, to labor for the slave. Does not her sister in bonds, labor night and day without reward? Let her heart grieve, and her eye fill with tears, in view of a female's body dishonored—a female's mind debased—a female's soul forever ruined! Woman nothing to do with slavery! Abhorred the thought!! We will pray to abhor it more and more. Is not woman abused—women trampled upon—woman spoiled of her virtue, her probity, her influence, her joy! And this, not in India—not in China—not in

---

* From Elizabeth Emery and Mary P. Abbott, "Letter to *The Liberator*," *The Liberator"* 6, August 27, 1836, 138.

Turkey—not in Africa but in America—in the United States of America, in the birthplace of Washington, the father of freedom, the protector of woman, the friend of equality and human rights!

Woman out of her place, in feeling, playing, and acting for the slave! Impious idea! Her oppressed sister cries aloud for help. She tries to lift her manacled hand—to turn her bruised face—to raise her tearful eye, and by all these, to plead a remembrance in our prayers—an interest in our labors. . . . Woman then may not be dumb. Christian sisters of Boston! We gladly respond to your call. We will "leave no energy unemployed—no righteous means untried. We will grudge no expense—yield to no opposition—forget fatigue, till by the strength of prayer and sacrifice, the spirit of love shall have overcome sectional jealousy—political rivalry—prejudice against color—cowardly concession of principle—wicked compromise with sin—devotion to gain, and spiritual despotism, which now bear with a mountain's weight upon the slave." As Christian women, we will do a Christian woman's duty.

The Constitution of our Society is so similar to that of other Antislavery Societies, it may not be necessary to give a copy of it. Our preamble gives our creed:

"We believe American Slavery is a sin against God—at war with the dictates of humanity, and subversive of the principles of freedom, because it regards rational beings as goods and chattel; robs them of compensation for their toil—denies to them the protection of law—disregards the relation of husband and wife, brother and sister, parent and child; shuts out from the intellect the light of knowledge; overwhelms hope in despair and ruins the soul—thus sinking to the level of brutes, more than one million of American females, who are created in God's image, a little lower than the angels', and consigns them over to degradation, physical, social, intellectual and moral: consequently, every slaveholder is bound instantly to cease from all participation in such a system. We believe that we should have no fellowship with these works of darkness, but rather reprove them—and that the truth spoken in love, is mighty to the removal of slavery, as of all other sins."

On such a creed, we base the constitution, which binds us together, and which we omit. . . .

[M]ay fearful foreboding lead the slave holder to timely repentance.

Elizabeth Emery, President
Mary P. Abbott, Rec. Secretary

Pastoral Letter to New England Churches (1837)

The Congregational clergy denounced outspoken women abolitionists in this Pastoral Letter. The Grimké sisters were the particular target of their wrath. The letter spelled out in detail why the "obtrusive and ostentatious" behavior of the women was "unnatural" and defied Christian precepts. The clergy urged women to remain strictly within their God-ordained female sphere. Ministers reminded women that their essential character was like a vine that needed to cling to men for protection and support. What other arguments did the clergy provide to support female subordination and passivity? What positive role did they assign to women?[*]

We invite your attention to the dangers which at present seem to threaten the female character with widespread and permanent injury.

The appropriate duties and influence of woman are clearly stated in the New Testament. Those duties and that influence are unobtrusive and private, but the source of mighty power. When the mild, dependent, softening influence of woman upon the sternness of man's opinions is fully exercised, society feels the effects of it in a thousand forms. The power of woman is in her dependence, flowing from the consciousness of that weakness which God has given her for her protection, and which keeps her in those departments of life that form the character of individuals and of the nation. There are social influences which females use in promoting piety, and the great objects of Christian benevolence which we cannot too highly commend. We appreciate the unostentatious prayers and efforts of woman in advancing the cause of religion at home and abroad; in Sabbath-schools; in leading religious inquirers to the pastors for instruction; and in all such associated effort as becomes the modesty of her sex; and earnestly hope that she may abound more and more in these labors of piety and love.

But when she assumes the place and tone of man as a public reformer, our care and protection of her seem unnecessary; we put ourselves in self-defense against her; she yields the power which God has given her for protection, and her character becomes unnatural. If the vine, whose strength and beauty is to lean upon the trellis-work and half conceal its clusters, thinks to assume the independence and the overshadowing nature of the elm, it will not only cease to bear fruit, but fall in shame and dishonor into the dust. We cannot, therefore, but regret the mistaken conduct of those who encourage females to bear an obtrusive and ostentatious part in measures of

---

[*] From "Pastoral Letter of the General Association of Massachusetts to the Congretional Churches Under Their Care," reprinted in *The Liberator*, August 11, 1837.

reform, and countenance any of that sex who so far forget themself as to incinerate in the character of public lecturers and teachers.

Sarah Grimké, *Reply to Pastoral Letter* (1837)

Antislavery women such as the Grimké sisters dramatically departed from what many men and women considered appropriate female behavior. The daughters of a southern slave owner, both Sarah and Angelina Grimké became Quakers and joined the abolitionist crusade. The Grimké sisters lectured on behalf of William Lloyd Garrison's American Anti-Slavery Society. In her reply to the *Pastoral Letter*, Sarah Grimké (1792–1873) directly addressed the question of women speaking in public. Lashing out against the "self-styled lords of creation," she demanded equality and moral accountability for women. Grimké's reply was a pioneer feminist's argument for women's power. What evidence did she offer to support her defense for women's equality with men? Why did she equate women's submission with hypocrisy?[*]

[The Pastoral Letter] says, "We invite your attention to the dangers which at present seem to threaten the FEMALE CHARACTER with widespread and permanent injury." I rejoice that they have called the attention of my sex to this subject, because I believe if woman investigates it, she will soon discover that danger is impending, though from a totally different source from that which the Association apprehends—danger from those who, having long held the reins of *usurped* authority, are unwilling to permit us to fill that sphere which God created us to move in, and who have entered into league to crush the immortal mind of woman. I rejoice, because I am persuaded that the rights of woman, like the rights of slaves, need only be examined, to be understood and asserted, even by some of those who are now endeavoring to smother the irrepressible desire for mental and spiritual freedom which glows in the breast of many who hardly dare to speak their sentiments.

"The appropriate duties and influence of woman are clearly stated in the New Testament. Those duties are unobtrusive and private, but the sources of *mighty power*. When the mild, *dependent*, softening influence of woman upon the sternness of man's opinions, is fully exercised, society feels the effects of it in a thousand ways." No one can desire more earnestly than I do, that woman may move exactly in the sphere which her Creator has assigned her; and I believe her having been displaced from that

---

[*] From Sarah Grimké, "Province of Women: The Pastoral Letter," *The Liberator*, October 6, 1837.

sphere, has introduced confusion into the world. It is therefore of vast importance to herself, and to all the rational creation, that she should ascertain what are her duties and privileges as a responsible and immortal being. The New Testament has been referred to, and I am willing to abide by its decision, and must enter my protest against the false translations of some passages by the MEN who did that work, and against the perverted interpretations by the MEN who undertook to write commentaries thereon. I am inclined to think, when we are admitted to the honor of studying Greek and Hebrew, we shall produce some various readings of the Bible, a little different from those we now have.

I find the Lord Jesus defining the duties of his followers in his sermon on the Mount, laying down grant principles by which they should be governed, without any preference to sect or condition:—"Ye are the light of the world. A city that is set on a hill cannot be hid. Neither do men light a candle and put it under a bushel, but on a candlestick, and it giveth light unto all that are in the house. Let your light so shine before men, that they may see your good works, and glorify your Father which is in heaven." I follow him through all his precepts, and find him giving the same directions to women as to men, never even referring to the distinction now so strenuously insisted upon between masculine and feminine virtues: this is one of the anti-Christian "traditions of men" which are taught instead of the "commandments of God." Men and women were CREATED EQUAL; they are both moral and accountable beings, and whatever is right for man to do, is right for woman to do.

But the influence of woman, says the Association, is to be private and unobtrusive; her light is not to shine before man like that of her brethren; but she is passively to let the lords of the creation, as they call themselves, put the bushel over it, lest peradventure it might appear that the world has been benefited by the rays of her candle. Then her quenched light is of more use than if it were set on the candlestick:—"Her influence is the source of mighty power." This has ever been the language of man since he laid aside the whip as a means to keep woman in subjection. He spares her body, but the war he has waged against her mind, her heart, and her soul, has been no less destructive to her as a moral being. How monstrous is the doctrine that the woman is to be dependent on man! Where in all the sacred scriptures is this taught? But, alas, she has too well learned the lesson which he has labored to teach her. She has surrendered her dearest RIGHTS, and has been satisfied with the privileges which man has assumed to grant her, whilst he has amused her with the show of power, and absorbed all the reality into himself. He has adorned the creature, whom God gave him as companion, with baubles and gewgaws, turned her attention to personal attractions, offered incense to her vanity, and made her the instrument of his selfish gratification, a plaything to please his eye, and amuse his hours of leisure.—"Rule by obedience, and by submission sway," or in other words, study to be a hypocrite, pretend to submit, but gain your point, has been the code of household morality which woman has been taught. The poet has sung in sickly strains the loveliness of woman's dependence upon man, and now we find it re-echoed by those who profess to teach the religion of the Bible. God says, "Cease ye from man whose breath is in his nostrils, for wherein is he to be accounted of?" Man says, depend upon me. God says, "He will teach us of his ways." May says, believe it or not; I am to be your teacher. This doctrine of dependence upon man is utterly at variance with the doctrine of the Bible. In that book I find nothing like the softness of woman, nor the sternness of man; but both are equally commanded to bring forth the fruits of the Spirit—Love, meekness, gentleness.

But we are told, "the power of woman is in her dependence, flowing from a consciousness of that weakness which God has given her for her protection." If physical weakness is alluded to, I cheerfully concede the superiority; if brute force is what my brethren are claiming, I am willing to let them have all the honor they desire; but if they mean to intimate that mental or moral weakness belongs to woman more than to man, I utterly disclaim the charge; our powers of mind have been crushed, as far as man could do it; our sense of morality has been impaired by his interpretation of our duties, but nowhere does God say that he has made any distinction between us as moral and intelligent beings. . . .

Angelina Grimké, *An Appeal to the Woman of the Nominally Free States* (1838)

Angelina Grimké (1805–1879) countered efforts to silence abolitionist women, with the insistence that all moral beings—whether men or women—shared the same moral rights and duties. Her arguments directly challenged the effort to limit women to the domestic sphere. She also claimed that sisterhood crossed racial barriers. In her outcry against racial injustice in the North, Grimké noted how racism damaged the lives of free black women. What examples of northern racism does she cite? Why did she believe that the "degradation of slavery" fostered the oppression of free blacks?[*]

[In] a country where women are degraded and brutalized, and where their exposed persons bleed under the lash—where they are sold in the shambles of "negro brokers"—robbed of their hard earnings—torn from their husbands, and forcibly plundered of their virtue and their offspring; surely in *such* a country, it is very natural that *women* should wish to know "the reason *why*"—especially when these outrages of blood and nameless horror are practiced in violation of the principles of our national Bill of Rights and the Preamble of our Constitution. We do not, then, and cannot concede the position, that because this is a *political subject* woman ought to

---

[*] From Angelina Grimké, *An Appeal to the Woman of the Nominally Free States*, Issued by an Anti-Slavery Convention of American Women, 2nd ed. (Boston: Isaac Knapp, 1838), 13–16, 19–23, 49–53, 60–61.

fold their hands in idleness, and close their eyes and ears to the "horrible things" that are practiced in our land. The denial of our duty to act, is a bold denial of our right to act; and if we have no right to act, then may *we* well be termed "the white slaves of the North"—for, like our brethren in bonds, we must seal our lips in silence and despair. . . .

Slavery exerts a most deadly influence over the morals of our country, not only over that portion of it where it actually exists as a "domestic institution," but like the miasma of some pestilential pool, it spreads its desolating influence far beyond its own boundaries. Who does not know that licentiousness is a crying sin at the North as well as at the South? and who does not admit that the manners of the South in this respect have had a wide and destructive influence on Northern character? Can crime be fashionable and common in one part of the Union and unrebuked by the other, without corrupting the very heart's blood of the nation, and lowering the standard of morality everywhere? Can Northern men go down to the well-watered plains of the South to make their fortune, without bowing themselves in the house of Rimmon and drinking the waters of that river of pollution which rolls over the plain of Sodom and Gomorrah? Do they return uncontaminated to their homes, or does not many a Northerner dig the grave of his virtue in the Admahs and Zeboims of our Southern States. And can our theological and academic institutions be opened to the sons of the planter without endangering the purity of the morals of our own sons, by associations with men who regard the robbery of the poor as no crime, and oppression as no wrong? Impossible! . . .

But this is not all; our people have erected a false standard by which to judge men's character. Because in the slaveholding States colored men are plundered and kept in abject ignorance, are treated with disdain and scorn, so here, too, in profound deference to the South, we refuse to eat, or drive, or walk, or associate, or open our institutions of learning, or even our zoological institutions to people of color, unless they visit them in the capacity of *servants*, of menials in humble attendance upon the Anglo-American. Who ever heard of a more wicked absurdity in a Republican country?

Have Northern women, then, nothing to do with slavery, when its demoralizing influence is polluting their domestic circles and blasting the fair character of *their* sons and brothers? Nothing to do with slavery when *their* domestics are often dragged by the merciless kidnapper from the hearth of their nurseries and the arms of their little ones? Nothing to do with slavery when Northern women are chained and driven like criminals, and incarcerated in the great prison-house of the South? Nothing to do with slavery? . . .

We have hitherto addressed you more as moral and responsible beings, than in the distinctive character of women; we have appealed to you on the broad ground of *human rights* and human responsibilities, rather than on that of your peculiar duties as women. We have pursued this course of argument designedly, because, in order to prove that you have any duties to perform, it is necessary first to establish the principle of moral being for all our rights, and all our duties grow out of this principle. *All moral beings have essentially the same rights and the same duties,* whether they be male or female. . . .

The Colored Women of the North Are Oppressed

[Another] reason we would urge for the interference of northern women with the system of slavery is, that in consequence of the odium which the degradation of slavery has attached to *color* even in the free States, our *colored sisters* are dreadfully oppressed here. Our seminaries of learning are closed to them, they are almost entirely banished from our lecture rooms, and even in the house of God they are separated from their white brethren and sisters as though we were afraid to come in contact with a colored skin. . . .

Here, then, are some of the bitter fruits of that inveterate prejudice which the vast proportion of northern women are cherishing towards their colored sisters; and let us remember that every one of us who denies the influence of this prejudice, . . . is awfully guilty in the sight of Him who is no respecter of persons. . . .

But our colored sisters are oppressed in other ways. As they walk the streets of our cities, they are continually liable to be insulted with the vulgar epithet of "nigger"; no matter how respectable or wealthy, they cannot visit the Zoological Institute of New York except in the capacity of nurses or servants—no matter how worthy, they cannot gain admittance into or receive assistance from any of the charities of this city. In Philadelphia, they are cast out of the Widow's Asylum, and their children are refused admittance to the House of Refuge, the Orphan's House and the Infant School connected with the Almshouse, though into these are gathered the very offscouring of our population. These are only specimens of that soul-crushing influence from which the colored women of the north are daily suffering. Then, again, some of them have been robbed of their husbands and children by the heartless kidnapper, and others have themselves been dragged into slavery. If they attempt to travel, they are exposed to great indignities and great inconveniences. Instances have been known of their actually dying in consequence of the exposure to which they were subjected on board of our steamboats. No money could purchase the use of a berth for a delicate female because she had a colored skin. Prejudice, then, degrades and fetters the minds, persecutes and murders the bodies of our free colored sisters. Shall *we* be silent at such a time as this? . . .

Much may be done, too, by sympathizing with our oppressed colored sisters, who are suffering in our very midst. Extend to them the right hand of fellowship on the broad principles of humanity and Christianity, treat them as *equals*, visit them as *equals*, invite them to cooperate with you in the Anti-Slavery and Temperance and Moral Reform Societies—in Maternal Associations and Prayer Meetings and Reading Companies. . . .

Multitudes of instances will continually occur in which you will have the opportunity of *identifying yourselves with this injured class* of our fellow-beings: embrace these opportunities at all times and in all places, in the true nobility of our great Exemplar, who was ever found among the *poor and the despised*, elevating and blessing them with his counsels and presence. In this way, and this alone, will you be enabled to subdue that deep-rooted prejudice which is doing the work of oppression in the free States to a most dreadful extent.

When this demon has been cast out of your hearts, when *you* can recognize the colored woman as a WOMAN—*then* will you be prepared to send out an appeal to our Southern sisters, entreating them to "go and do likewise."

Benjamin Drew, *Narratives of Escaped Slaves* (1855)

Enslaved women encountered both sexual exploitation and physical abuse. Long hours in cotton fields ran counter to domestic ideals, as did women's various forms of resistance, including escape. Benjamin Drew, an abolitionist, recorded the stories of fugitive slaves who had escaped to Canada. Because of the difficulty of fleeing slavery with small children, fewer enslaved women than men made the dangerous journey to freedom. What abuses convinced women to risk their lives and escape?[*]

Mrs. James Steward

The slaves want to get away bad enough. They are not contented with their situation.

I am from the eastern shore of Maryland. I never belonged but to one master; he was very bad indeed. I was never sent to school, nor allowed to go to church. They were afraid we would have more sense than they. I have a father there, three sisters, and a brother. My father is quite an old man, and he is used very badly. Many a time he has been kept at work a whole long summer day without sufficient food. A sister of mine has been punished by his taking away her clothes and locking them up, because she used to run when master whipped her. He kept her at work with only what she could pick up to tie on her for decency. He took away her child which had just begun to walk, and gave it to another woman—but she went and got it afterward. He had a large farm eight miles from home. Four servants were kept at the house. My master could not manage to whip my sister when she was strong. He waited until she was confined, and the second week after her confinement he said, "Now I can handle you, now you are weak." She ran from him, however, and had to go through water, and was sick in consequence.

I was beaten at one time over the head by my master, until the blood ran from my mouth and nose: then he tied me up in the garret, with my hands over my head—then he brought me down and put me in a little cupboard, where I had to sit cramped up,

---

[*] From *A Northside View of Slavery: The Refuge*, or *The Narratives of Fugitive Slaves in Canada, Related by Themselves*, Benjamin Drew, ed. (Boston: John P. Jowett, 1856), 41–3, 50–1, 138, 140–1, 224–27.

part of the evening, all night, and until between four and five o'clock, next day, without any food. The cupboard was near a fire, and I thought I should suffocate.

My brother was whipped on one occasion until his back was as raw as a piece of beef, and before it got well, master whipped him again. His back was an awful sight.

We were all afraid of master: when I saw him coming, my heart would jump up into my mouth, as if I had seen a serpent.

I have been wanting to come away for eight years back. I waited for Jim Seward to get ready. Jim had promised to take me away and marry me. Our master would allow no marriages on the farm. When Jim had got ready, he let me know—he brought to me two suits of clothes—men's clothes—which he had bought on purpose for me. I put on both suits to keep me warm. We eluded pursuit and reached Canada in safety.

Mrs. Nancy Howard

I was born in Anne Arundel county, Maryland—was brought up in Baltimore. After my escape, I lived in Lynn, Mass., seven years, but I left there through fear of being carried back, owing to the fugitive slave law. I have lived in St. Catherine's less than a year.

The way I got away was—my mistress was sick, and went into the country for her health. I went to stay with her cousin. After a month, my mistress was sent back to the city to her cousin's, and I waited on her. My daughter had been off three years. A friend said to me—"Now is your chance to get off." At last I concluded to go—the friend supplying me with money. I was asked no questions on the way north.

My idea of slavery is, that it is one of the blackest, the wickedest things everywhere in the world. When you tell them the truth, they whip you to make you lie. I have taken more lashes for this, than for any other thing, because I would not lie.

One day I set the table, and forgot to put on the carving-fork—the knife was there. I went to the table to put it on a plate. My master said,—"Where is the fork?" I told him "I forgot it." He says,—"You d—d black b—, I'll forget you!"—at the same time hitting me on the head with the carving knife. The blood spurted out—you can see. (Here the woman removed her turban and showed a circular cicatrices denuded of hair, about an inch in diameter, on the top of her head.) My mistress took me into the kitchen and put on camphor, but she could not stop the bleeding. A doctor was sent for. He came but asked no questions. I was frequently punished with raw hides—was hit with tongs and poker and anything. I used when I went out, to look up at the sky, and say, "Blessed Lord, oh, do take me out of this!" It seemed to me I could not bear another lick. I can't forget it. I sometimes dream that I am pursued, and when I wake, I am scared almost to death.

Harriet Tubman, Excerpts from *A Biography by Her Contemporaries* (c. 1880)

Based on a series of interviews by abolitionists, Harriet Tubman's biography described her escape from slavery, as well as her vital role in the underground railroad. Known as "Moses, the deliverer of her people," Tubman (1820–1913) personally risked death and repeatedly returned to the South to lead as many as three hundred slaves to freedom. In what ways did Tubman's life contradict beliefs about woman's behavior?[*]

One of the teachers lately commissioned by the New England Freedmen's Aid Society is probably the most remarkable woman of this age. That is to say, she has performed more wonderful deeds by the native power of her own spirit against adverse circumstances than any other. She is well known to many by the various names which her eventful life has given her; Harriet Garrison, Gen. Tubman, &c; but among the slaves she is universally known by her well-earned title of *Moses*—Moses the deliverer. She is a rare instance, in the midst of high civilization and intellectual culture, of a being of great native powers, working powerfully, and to beneficent ends, entirely unaided by schools or books.

Her maiden name was Araminta Ross. She is the granddaughter of a native African, and has not a drop of white blood in her veins. She was born in 1820 or 1821, on the Eastern Shore of Maryland. Her parents were slaves, but married and faithful to each other, and the family affection is very strong. She claims that she was legally freed by a will of her first master, but his wishes were not carried into effect.

She seldom lived with her owner, but was usually "hired out" to different persons. She once "hired her time," and employed it in rudest farming labors, ploughing, carting, driving the oxen, &c., to so good advantage that she was able in one year to buy a pair of steers worth forty dollars.

When quite young she lived with a very pious mistress; but the slaveholder's religion did not prevent her from whipping the young girl for every slight or fancied fault. Araminta found that this was usually a morning exercise; so she prepared for it by putting on all the thick clothes she could procure to protect her skin. She made sufficient outcry, however, to convince her mistress that her blows had full effect; and in the afternoon she would take off her wrappings, and dress as well as she could. When invited into family prayers, she preferred to stay on the landing, and pray for herself; "and I prayed to God," she says "to make me strong and able to fight, and

[*] From *Slave Testimony: Two Centuries of Letters, Speeches, Interviews, and Autobiographies*, ed. John W. Blassingame (Baton Rouge: Lousiana State University Press, 1977), 457–465. Reprinted by permission of Louisina State University Press. Copyright © 1977 by Louisiana State University Press.

that's what I've allers prayed for since." It is in vain to persuade her that her prayer was a wrong one. She always maintains it to be sincere and right, and it has certainly been fully answered.

In her youth she received a severe blow on her head from a heavy weight thrown by her master at another slave, but which accidentally hit her. The blow produced a disease of the brain which was severe for a long time, and still makes her very lethargic. She cannot remain quiet for fifteen minutes without appearing to fall asleep. It is not a refreshing slumber; but a heavy, weary condition which exhausts her. She therefore loves great physical activity, and direct heat of the sun, which keeps her blood actively circulating. She was married about 1844 to a free colored man named John Tubman, but never had any children. Owing to changes in her owner's family, it was determined to sell her and some other slaves; but her health was so much injured, that a purchaser was not easily found. At length she became convinced that she would soon be carried away, and she decided to escape. . . .

She remained two years in Philadelphia, working hard and carefully hoarding her money. Then she hired a room, furnished it as well as she could, bought a nice suit of men's clothes, and went back to Maryland for her husband. But the faithless man had taken to himself another wife. Harriet did not dare venture into her presence, but sent word to her husband where she was. He declined joining her. At first her grief and anger were excessive. She said, "she did not care what massa did to her, she thought she would go right in and make all the trouble she could, she was determined to see her old man once more" but finally she thought "how foolish it was just for temper to make mischief" and that, "if he could do without her, she could without him," and so "he dropped out of her heart," and she determined to tie her life to brave deeds. Thus all personal aims died out of her heart; and with her simple brave motto "I can't die but once," she began the work which has made her Moses—the deliverer of her people. Seven or eight times she has returned to the neighborhood of her former home, always at the risk of death in the most terrible forms, and each time has brought away a company of fugitive slaves, and led them safely to the free States, or to Canada. Every time she went, the dangers increased. In 1857 she brought away her old parents, and, as they were too feeble to walk, she was obliged to hire a wagon, which added greatly to the perils of the journey. In 1860 she went for the last time, and among her troop was an infant whom they were obliged to keep stupefied with laudanum to prevent its outcries. This was a period of great excitement and Moses was not safe even in the New York states; but her anxious friends insisted upon her taking refuge in Canada.

Elizabeth Dixon Smith Greer, Journal (1847–1850)

With her husband and family, Elizabeth Dixon Smith Greer made the journey from Indiana to Oregon. Westward migration was often an unwelcome disruption in the lives of many women. Responsible for the care of seven children and an infant, Greer recorded her incredible physical hardships during the rigorous journey. She survived and witnessed the death of her husband, who may have been a victim of cholera. In what ways did the circumstances of the journey West contradict the image of women as frail and in need of male protection?[*]

Dear Friends—By your request I have endeavored to keep a record of our journey from "the States" to Oregon, though it is poorly done, owing to my having a young babe and besides a large family to do for; and, worst of all, my education is very limited.

April 21, 1847—Commenced our journey from La Porte, Indiana, to Oregon; made fourteen miles. . . .

November 18—My husband is sick. It rains and snows. We start this morning around the falls with our wagons. We have 5 miles to go. I carry my babe and lead, or rather carry, another through snow, mud and water, almost to my knees. It is the worst road that a team could possibly travel. I went ahead with my children, and I was afraid to look behind me for fear of seeing the wagons turn over into the mud and water with everything in them. My children gave out with cold and fatigue and could not travel, and the boys had to unhitch the oxen and bring them and carry the children on to camp. I was so cold and numb that I could not tell by the feeling that I had any feet at all. We started this morning at sunrise and did not get to camp until after dark, and there was not one dry thread on one of us—not even my babe. I had carried my babe and I was so fatigued that I could scarcely speak or step. When I got here I found my husband lying in Welch's wagon, very sick. He had brought Mrs. Polk down the day before and was taken sick here. We had to stay up all night, for our wagons are left halfway back. I have not told half we suffered. I am not adequate to the task. Here were some hundreds camped, waiting for boats to come and take them down the Columbia to Vancouver or Portland or Oregon City.

November 19—My husband is sick and can have but little care. Rain all day.

---

[*] From *35th Transactions of the Oregon Pioneer Association*, (1907), 153, 171–178.

November 20—Rain all day. It is almost an impossibility to cook, and quite so to keep warm or dry. I froze or chilled my feet so that I cannot wear a shoe, so I have to go around in the cold water barefooted.

November 21—Rain all day. The whole care of everything falls upon my shoulders. I cannot write any more at present.

November 30—Raining. This morning I ran about trying to get a house to get into with my sick husband. At last I found a small, leaky concern, with two families already in it. Mrs. Polk had got down before us. She and another widow was in this house. My family and Welch's went in with them, and you could have stirred us with a stick. Welch and my oldest boy was driving the cattle around. My children and I carried up a bed. The distance was nearly a quarter of a mile. Made it down on the floor in the mud. I got some men to carry my husband up through the rain and lay him on it, and he never was out of that shed until he was carried out in his coffin. Here lay five of us bedfast at one time . . . and we had no money, and what few things we had left that would bring money, I had to sell. I had to give 10 cents a pound for fresh pork, 75 cents per bushel for potatoes, 4 cents a pound for fish. There are so many of us sick that I cannot write any more at present. I have not time to write much, but I thought it would be interesting to know what kind of weather we have in the winter.

1848—January 14—Rain this morning. Warm weather. We suppose it has rained half of the time that I have neglected writing.

January 15—My husband is still alive, but very sick. There is no medicine here except at Fort Vancouver, and the people there will not sell one bit—not even a bottle of wine.

February 1—Rain all day. This day my dear husband, my last remaining friend, died.

February 2—Today we buried my earthly companion. Now I know what none but widows know; that is, how comfortless is a widow's life, especially when left in a strange land, without money or friends, and the care of seven children. Cloudy. . . .

5

Woman's Rights: Pioneer Feminists Champion Gender Equity

The women who played key roles in America's first women's rights movement lived in an era when separate-sphere beliefs were widely asserted by both men and women. Articles and books proclaimed women's unique domestic gifts and their responsibility—as Caroline Gilman noted—to create marital harmony through self-sacrifice and denial. Still, countercurrents prevailed. The pre-Civil War period was filled with reform activism and evangelical religious enthusiasm. Women flocked to religious revivals and, filled with moral purpose, joined abolitionist and temperance crusades that took them beyond the confines of their homes.

As the Grimké sisters had before them, women found their reformist efforts blocked by men who sought to end their public speaking, and terminate their encroachment in what men defined as their own political sphere. After Lucretia Mott and Elizabeth Cady Stanton were forced to sit in the gallery behind a screen at an anti-slavery conference in London, they organized the first woman's rights conference at Seneca Falls in 1848. Lucy Stone's commitment to women's rights intensified as a result of men's efforts—including drenching her with cold water—to end her public speaking on behalf of abolition.

Mott, Stanton, and Stone, along with Susan B. Anthony, Ernestine Rose, Amelia Bloomer, and Caroline Dall were pioneer advocates of women's rights. They sought to limit men's exclusive power and to free women from the constraints of the domestic sphere. They initiated a struggle to end male domination of religious, political, legal, educational, and professional institutions. Women's rights received male support, including that of Frederick Douglass, the nation's leading African-American abolitionist, who was present at Seneca Falls, and witnessed the Declaration of Sentiments' lengthy indictment against men's usurpation of power.

Women's rights advocates argued from the fundamental American belief that the exercise of political power must rest on the consent of the governed. With this in mind, they demanded that women be given the right to vote. Voting directly would give women access to the public sphere and political power. Voting was a direct challenge to male power, and met with extreme resistance, not only from men but also from women intent on preserving women's separate domestic identity.

Pioneer feminists championed the right of all women to determine their own identity because much of what they found intolerable—denial of educational and professional opportunities—depended on tying women at birth to exclusive domesticity. They combated gender inequities that sustained male power and privilege and at the same time created female dependency. They lashed out against all assumptions that limited women's achievement and undermined self-confidence. Critical of the sexual double standard, they wanted men as well as women to be held to a single standard of sexual responsibility.

Women's rights advocates also challenged men's power within marriage. Of major concern was the legal tradition of *femme covert,* that resulted in the loss of the wife's legal identity and the husband's right to her property, wages, and guardianship of children. The tradition of losing one's maiden name when one married was symbolic of women's loss of identity in marriage. To combat this, Elizabeth Cady Stanton added her married name (Stanton) to her maiden name, and Lucy Stone kept her maiden name after her marriage to Henry Blackwell. Stanton, Ernestine Rose, and Susan B. Anthony played central roles in the reform of married women's legal status in New York state. Their demand for women's autonomy and married women's legal rights was built on American ideals of inalienable rights, individual conscience, and personal liberty. As women they claimed all the rights traditionally reserved for men. They also acknowledged gender difference in terms of women's familial roles and perceived moral and spiritual superiority. However, they believed that most of the differences between men and women were not innate, but due to divergent cultural expectations and social roles.

Their rebellion against prescribed gender roles also extended to dress reform. Stanton, Anthony, Amelia Bloomer and others advocated that women exchange their layers of petticoats and voluminous skirts for a short dress worn over pants, that would provide greater comfort. Known as the "bloomer" outfit, the appearance of women in pants provoked outrage. In San Francisco, a woman wearing bloomers was arrested and found guilty of disturbing the peace. Anxious to promote more significant reforms, women's rights advocates abandoned their dress-reform effort and returned to restrictive clothing that made physical exercise impossible and freedom of movement difficult.

Elizabeth Cady Stanton, *Declaration of Sentiments* (1848)

Elizabeth Cady Stanton (1815–1902) played a major role in drafting the Declaration that was presented at the convention at Seneca Falls, New York, in 1848. The Declaration is possibly the most significant document in the history of U.S. women. It summarized the way in which feminists believed men usurped power and tyrannized women. The document paralleled the Declaration of Independence—the abusive power of men was substituted for that of England. The inclusion of the demand for women's suffrage proved to be the most controversial aspect of the argument for woman's rights. What is meant by the Declaration's allegation that men have assigned to women "a sphere of action?" Did the Declaration deny or uphold the view of women's moral superiority? In what ways did the Declaration speak for all women? In what ways did it reflect the particular experience of white middle-class women?[*]

When, in the course of human events, it becomes necessary for one portion of the family of man to assume among the people of the earth a position different from that which they have hitherto occupied, but one to which the laws of nature and of nature's God entitle them, a decent respect to the opinions of mankind requires that they should declare the causes that impel them to such a course.

We hold these truths to be self-evident: that all men and women are created equal; that they are endowed by their Creator with certain inalienable rights; that among these are life, liberty and the pursuit of happiness; that to secure these rights governments are instituted, deriving their just powers from the consent of the governed. Whenever any form of government becomes destructive of these ends, it is the right of those who suffer from it to refuse allegiance to it, and to insist upon the institution of a new government, laying its foundation on such principles, and organizing its powers in such form, as to them shall seem most likely to effect their safety and happiness. Prudence, indeed, will dictate that governments long established should not be changed for light and transient causes; and accordingly all experience has shown that mankind are more disposed to suffer, while evils are sufferable, than to right themselves by abolishing the forms to which they are accustomed. But when a long train of abuses and usurpations, pursuing invariably the same object, evinces a design to reduce them under absolute despotism, it is their duty to throw off such

---

[*] From "Declaration of Sentiments," ed. Elizabeth Cady Stanton, Susan B. Anthony, and Matilda J. Gage, in *History of Woman Suffrage* (Rochester: Charles Mann, 1881), I: 67–94.

government, and to provide new guards for their future security. Such has been the patient sufferance of the women under this government, and such is now the necessity which constrains them to demand the equal station to which they are entitled.

The history of mankind is a history of repeated injuries and usurpations on the part of man toward woman, having in direct object the establishment of an absolute tyranny over her. To prove this, let facts be submitted to a candid word.

He has never permitted her to exercise her inalienable right to the elective franchise.

He has compelled her to submit to laws, in the formation of which she had no voice.

He has withheld from her rights which are given to the most ignorant and degraded men—both natives and foreigners.

Having deprived her of this first right of a citizen, the elective franchise, thereby leaving her without representation in the halls of legislation, he has oppressed her on all sides.

He has made her, if married, in the eye of the law, civilly dead.

He has taken from her all right in property, even to the wages she earns.

He has made her, morally, an irresponsible being, as she can commit many crimes with impunity, provided they be done in the presence of her husband. In the covenant of marriage, she is compelled to promise obedience to her husband, he becoming, to all intents and purposes, her master, the law giving him power to deprive her of her liberty, and to administer chastisement.

He has so framed the laws of divorce, as to what shall be the proper causes, and in case of separation, to whom the guardianship of the children shall be given, as to be wholly regardless of the happiness of women—the law, in all cases, going upon a false supposition of the supremacy of man, and giving all power into his hands.

After depriving her of all rights as a married woman, if single, and the owner of property, he has taxed her to support a government which recognizes her only when her property can be made profitable to it.

He has monopolized nearly all the profitable employments, and from those she is permitted to follow, she receives but a scanty remuneration. He closes against her all the avenues to wealth and distinction which he considers most honorable to himself. As a teacher of theology, medicine, or law, she is not known.

He has denied her the facilities for obtaining a thorough education, all colleges being closed against her.

He allows her in Church, as well as in State, but a subordinate position, claiming Apostolic authority for her exclusion from the ministry, and, with some exceptions, from any public participation in the affairs of the Church.

He has created a false public sentiment by giving to the world a different code of morals for men and women, by which the moral delinquencies which exclude women from society are not only tolerated, but deemed of little account in man.

He has usurped the prerogative of Jehovah himself, claiming it as his right to assign for her a sphere of action, when that belongs to her conscience and to her God.

He has endeavored, in every way he could, to destroy her confidence in her own powers, to lessen her self-respect, and to make her willing to lead a dependent and abject life.

Now, in the view of this entire disfranchisement of one-half of the people of this country, their social and religious degradation, in view of the unjust laws above mentioned, and because women do feel themselves aggrieved, oppressed, and fraudulently deprived of their most sacred rights, we insist that they have immediate admission to all the rights and privileges which belong to them as citizens of the United States.

In entering upon the great work before us, we anticipate no small amount of misconception, misrepresentation, and ridicule; but we shall use every instrumentality within our power to effect our object. We shall employ agents, circulate tracts, petition the State and National legislatures, and endeavor to enlist the pulpit and the press on our behalf. We hope this Convention will be followed by a series of Conventions embracing every part of the country.

Women of Philadelphia (1848)

This letter to a Philadelphia newspaper was written by a man outraged by women's demand for equal rights. The writer emphasized that "a woman is nobody, a wife is everything." His argument reflected the widely held belief that women acquired identity and importance only when married. Moreover, women didn't need rights because as mothers, next to God, they were all-powerful. What evidence is given that women already influence human affairs "without being politicians?" Was this an accurate assessment? What social purpose would assertions about maternal and wifely influence serve? *

Our Philadelphia ladies not only possess beauty, but they are celebrated for discretion, modesty, and unfeigned diffidence, as well as wit, vivacity, and good nature. Whoever heard of a Philadelphia lady setting up for a reformer, or standing out for woman's rights, or insisting to *man* the election grounds, raise a regiment, command a legion, or address a jury? Our ladies glow with a higher ambition. They soar to rule the hearts of their worshippers, and secure obedience by the scepter of affection. The tenure of

---

* From *The Public Ledger and Daily Transcript* (Philadelphia), in ed. Elizabeth Cady Stanton, Susan B. Anthony, and Matilda J. Gage, *History of Woman Suffrage* (Rochester: Charles Mann, 1881), I, 804–5.

their power is a law of nature, not a law of man, and hence they fear no insurrection, and never experience the shock of a revolution in their dominions. But all women are not as reasonable as our of Philadelphia. The Boston ladies contend for the rights of women. The New York girls aspire to mount the rostrum, to do all the voting, and, we suppose all the fighting too. . . .

Our Philadelphia girls object to fighting and holding office. They prefer the baby-jumper to the study of Coke and Lyttleton, and the ballroom to the Palo Alto battle. The object to having a George Sand for President of the United States; a Corinna for Governor; a Fanny Wright for Mayor; or a Mrs. Partington for Postmaster . . .Women have enough influence over human affairs without being politicians. Is not everything managed by female influence? Mothers, grandmothers, aunts and sweethearts manage everything. Men have nothing to do but to listen and obey the "of course, my dear, you will, and of course, my dear, you won't." Their rule is absolute; their power unbounded. Under such a system men have no claim to rights, especially "equal rights."

A woman is nobody. A wife is everything. A pretty girl is equal to ten thousand men, and a mother is, next to God, all-powerful . . .The ladies of Philadelphia, therefore, under the influence of the most serious "sober second thoughts" are resolved to maintain their rights as Wives, Belles, Virgins, and Mothers, and not as Women.

Caroline Gilman, *Recollections of a Southern Matron* (1838)

Male authority flourished on southern plantations. The following excerpt is from a novel written by a northern woman who moved with her husband to Charleston, South Carolina. Caroline Gilman (1794–1888) intended the book to be a guide for the creation of marital harmony. She recommended a sacrifice of independent thought and action. Note how the wife denies her own wishes in order to please her husband. Why do you suppose that the author considered it so vital for women to remain submissive to their husbands? Would her advice have equal or less relevance for women in the North? What does she mean by the remark that a good wife must "study self-control almost to hypocrisy"? [*]

---

[*] From Caroline Howard Gilman, *Recollections of a Southern Matron* (New York: Harper & Brothers, 1838), 250–57.

The planter's bride, who leaves a numerous and cheerful family in her paternal home, little imagines the change which awaits her in her own retired residence. She dreams of an independent sway over her household, devoted love and unbroken intercourse with her husband, and indeed longs to be released from the eyes of others, that she may dwell only beneath the sunbeam of his. And so it was with me. After our bustling wedding and protracted journey, I looked forward to the retirement at Bellevue as a quiet port in which I should rest with Arthur, after drifting so long on general society. The romance of our love was still in its glow, as might be inferred by the infallible sign of his springing to pick up my pocket-handkerchief whenever it fell. . . .

For several weeks all kinds of droll associations were conjured up, and we laughed at anything and nothing. What cared we for fashion and pretension? There we were together, asking for nothing but each other's presence and love. At length it was necessary for him to tear himself away to superintend his interests. I remember when his horse was brought to the door for his first absence of two hours; an observer would have thought that he was going on a far journey, had he witnessed that parting; and so it continued for some days, and his return at each time was like the sun shooting through a three days' cloud.

But the period of absence was gradually protracted; then a friend sometimes came home with him, and their talk was of crops and politics, draining the fields and draining the revenue, until I (country ladies will believe me) fell off into a state as nearly approaching sleep as a straight-backed chair would allow. . . .

Arthur was a member of a social club—but he had allowed several citations to pass unnoticed, until it occurred to him that he was slighting his friends; I thought so too, and said so, without permitting the sigh to escape that lay at the bottom of my heart, at the idea of his passing an evening away from me.

"They shall not keep me long from you, my love," he said, as we parted; "I have little joy without you." . . .

This club engagement, however, brought on others. I was not selfish, and even encouraged Arthur to go to hunt and to dinner parties, although hoping that he would resist my urging. He went frequently, and a growing discomfort began to work upon my mind. I had undefined forebodings; I mused about past days; my views of life became slowly disorganized; my physical powers enfeebled; a nervous excitement followed; I nursed a moody discontent, and ceased a while to reasons clearly. Woe to me had I yielded to this irritable temperament! I began immediately, on principle, to busy myself about my household. The location of Bellevue was picturesque—the dwelling airy and commodious; I had, therefore, only to exercise taste in external and internal arrangements to make it beautiful throughout. I was careful to consult my husband in those points which interested him, without annoying him with mere trifles. If the reign of romance was really waning, I resolved not to chill his noble confidence, but to make a steadier light rise on his affections. If he was absorbed in reading, I sat quietly waiting the pause when I should be rewarded by the communication of ripe ideas; if I saw that he prized a tree which interfered with my flowers, I sacrificed my preference to a more sacred feeling; if any habit of his annoyed me, I spoke of it once or twice calmly, and then bore it quietly if unreformed; I welcomed his friends with cordiality, entered into their family interests, and stopped my yawns, which, to say the truth, was sometimes an almost desperate effort, before they reached eye or ear.

This task of self-government was not easy. To repress a harsh answer, to confess a fault, and to stop (right or wrong) in the midst of self-defense, in gently submission, sometimes requires a struggle like life and death; but these *three* efforts are the golden threads with which domestic happiness is woven; once being the fabric with this woof, and trials shall not break nor sorrow tarnish it.

Men are not often unreasonable; their difficulties lie in not understanding the moral and physical structure of our sex. They often wound through ignorance, and are surprised at having offended. How clear it is, then, that woman loses by petulance and recrimination! Her first study must be self-control, almost to hypocrisy. A good wife must smile amid a thousand perplexities, and clear her voice to tones of cheerfulness when her frame is drooping with disease, or else languish alone. Man, on the contrary, when trials beset him, expects to find her ear and heart a ready receptacle; and, when sickness assails him, her soft hand must nurse and sustain him. . . .

Wakes from love's romantic dream,

His eyes may open on a sweet esteem.

Let him know nothing of the struggle which follows the first chill of the affectations; let no scenes of tears and apologies be acted to agitate him, until he becomes accustomed to agitation; thus shall the star of domestic peace arise in fixedness and beauty above them, and shine down in gentle light on their lives, as it has on ours.

Lucretia Mott, *Discourse on Women* (1849)

One of the best-known advocates of abolition and woman's rights, Lucretia Mott (1793–1880) lectured extensively. Her background and experience as a Quaker prepared her for public speaking. As was the case with other pioneer feminists, Mott encountered women's refusal to support equal rights. To what did she attribute women's resistance to their own independence? What does the remark "she hugs her chains" mean? Would the wife described by Gilman fit this description? *

---

* From Lucretia Mott, *Discourse on Women*, December 1849, 12-20.

The question is often asked, "What does woman want, more than she enjoys? What is she seeking to obtain? Of what rights is she deprived? What privileges are withheld from her?" I answer, she asks nothing as a favor, but as a right, she wants to be acknowledged a moral, responsible being. She is seeking not to be governed by laws, in the making of which she has no voice. She is deprived of almost every right in civil society, and is a cipher in the nation, except in the right of presenting a petition. In religious society her disabilities, as already pointed out, have greatly retarded her progress. Her exclusion from the pulpit or ministry—her duties marked out for her by her equal brother, man, subject to creeds, rules, and disciplines made for her by him—this is unworthy of her true dignity. In marriage, there is assumed superiority, on the part of the husband, and admitted inferiority, with a promise of obedience, on the part of the wife. This subject calls loudly for examination, in order that the wrong may be redressed. Customs suited to darker ages in Eastern countries are not binding upon enlightened society. The solemn covenant of marriage may be entered into without these lordly assumptions, and humiliating concessions and promises. . . .

So with woman. She has so long been subject to the disabilities and restrictions, with which her progress has been embarrassed, that she has become enervated, her mind to some extent paralyzed; and, like those still more degraded by personal bondage, she hugs her chains. Liberty is often presented in its true light, but it is liberty for man. . . .

Liberty is not less a blessing, because oppression has so long darkened the mind that it cannot appreciate it. I would therefore urge, that woman be placed in such a situation in society, by the yielding of her rights, and have such opportunities for growth and development, as shall raise her from this low, enervated and paralyzed condition, to a full appreciation of the blessing of entire freedom of mind. . . .

"The law of husband and wife, as you gather it from the books, is a disgrace to any civilized nation. The theory of the law degrades the wife almost to the level of slaves. When a woman marries, we call her condition coverture, and speak of her as a *femme covert*. The old writers call the husband baron, and sometimes, in plain English, lord. . . .The merging of her name in that of her husband is emblematic of the fate of all her legal rights. The torch of Hymen serves but to light the pile on which these rights are offered up. The legal theory is, that marriage makes the husband and wife one person, and that person is the *husband*. On this subject, reform is loudly called for. There is no foundation in reason or expediency, for the absolute and slavish subjection of the wife to the husband, which forms the foundation of the present legal relations. Were woman, in point of fact, the abject thing which the law, in theory, considers her to be when married, she would not be worthy of the companionship of man."

Emily Collins, *Reminiscences of the Suffrage Trail* (c. 1881)

Emily Collins' recollections were included in Elizabeth Cady Stanton, Susan B. Anthony, and Matilda Joselyn Gage's *History of Women Suffrage*. Countless women connected the anti-slavery struggle to the need for women's rights. The parallel between the wrongs of the slave and the wrongs of women is shown by Collins' descriptions of wife beating. Men's power over women provided the basis for physical abuse. Does this issue continue to have relevance today? In what ways are these recollections similar to those of Harriet Robinson? [*]

I was born and lived almost forty years in South Bristol, Ontario County—one of the most secluded spots in Western New York; but from the earliest dawn of reason I pined for that freedom of thought and action that was then denied to all womankind. I revolted in spirit against the customs of society and the laws of the State that crushed my aspirations, and debarred me from the pursuit of almost any object worthy of an intelligent, rational mind. But not until that meeting at Seneca Falls in 1848, of the pioneers in the cause, which gave this feeling of unrest form and voice, did I take action. Then I summoned a few women in our neighborhood together, and formed an Equal Suffrage Society, and sent petitions to our Legislature; but our efforts were little known beyond our circle, as we were in communication with no person or newspaper. Yet there was enough of wrong in our narrow horizon to rouse some thought in the minds of all.

In those early days a husband's supremacy was often enforced in the rural districts by corporeal chastisement, and it was considered by most people as quite right and proper—as much so as the correction of refractory children in like manner. I remember in my own neighborhood a man who was a Methodist class leader and exhorted, and one who was esteemed a worthy citizen, who, every few weeks, gave his wife a beating with a horsewhip. He said it was necessary, in order to keep her in subjection, and because she scolded so much. Now this wife, surrounded by six or seven little children, whom she must wash, dress, feed, and attend to day and night, was obliged to spin and weave cloth for all the garments of the family. She had to milk the cows, make butter and cheese, do all the cooking, washing, making, and mending for the family, and, with the pains of maternity forced upon her every eighteen months, was whipped by her pious husband, "because she scolded." And pray, why should he not have chastised her? The laws made it his privilege—and the

[*] From Emily Collins, *Reminiscences of the Suffrage Trail*, in ed. Elizabeth Cady Stanton, Susan B. Anthony, and Matilda J. Gage, *History of Woman Suffrage* (Rochester: Charles Mann, 1881), I: 67–94.

Bible, as interpreted, made it his duty. It is true, women repined at their hard lot; but it was thought to be fixed by a divine decree, for "The man shall rule over these," and "Wives, be subject to your husbands," and "Wives, submit yourselves unto your husbands as unto the Lord," caused them to consider their fate inevitable, and to feel that it would be contravening God's law to resist it. It is ever thus; where Theology enchains the soul, the Tyrant enslaves the body. But can anyone, who has any knowledge of the laws that govern our being of heredity and pre-natal influences—be astonished that our jails and prisons are filled with criminals, and our hospitals with sickly specimens of humanity? As long as the mothers of the race are subject to such unhappy conditions, it can never be materially improved. Men exhibit some common sense in breeding all animals except those of their own species.

All through the Anti-Slavery struggle, every word of denunciation of the wrongs of the Southern slave, was, I felt, equally applicable to the wrongs of my own sex. Every argument for the emancipation of the colored man, was equally one for that of woman, and I was surprised that all abolitionists did not see the similarity in the condition of the two classes. I read, with intense interest, everything that indicated an awakening of public or private thought to the idea that woman did not occupy her rightful position in the organization of society; and, when I read the lectures of Ernestine L. Rose and the writings of Margaret Fuller, and found that other women entertained the same thoughts that had been seething in my own brain, and realized that I stood not alone, how my heart bounded with joy! The arguments of that distinguished jurist, Judge Hurlburt, encouraged me to hope that men would ultimately see the justice of our cause, and concede to women their natural rights.

I hailed with gladness any aspiration of women toward an enlargement of their sphere of action. . . .

But, it was the proceedings of the Convention, in 1848, at Seneca Falls, that first gave a direction to the efforts of the many women, who began to feel the degradation of their subject condition, and its baneful effects upon the human race. They then saw the necessity for associated action, in order to obtain the elective franchise, the only key that would unlock the doors of their prison. . . .

Would to heaven that women could be persuaded to use the funds they acquire by their sewing-circles and fairs, in trying to raise their own condition above that of "infants, idiots, and lunatics," with whom our statutes class them, instead of spending the money in decorating their churches, or sustaining a clergy, most of whom are striving to rivet the chains still closer that bind, not only our own sex, but the oppressed of every class and color.

The elective franchise is now the one object for which we must labor; that once attained, all the rest will be easily acquired. Moral Reform and Temperance Societies may be multiplied *ad infinitum*, but they have about the same effect upon the evils they seek to cure, as clipping the top of a hedge would have toward extirpating it. Please forward me a copy of the petition for suffrage. We will engage to do all we can, not only in our own town, but in the adjoining ones of Richmond, East Bloomfield, Canandaigua, and Naples. I have promises of aid from people of influence in obtaining signatures. In the meantime we wish to disseminate some able work upon the enfranchisement of women. We wished to represent our Assemblyman elect, whoever he may be, with some work of this kind, and solicit his candid attention to the subject. People are more willing to be convinced by the calm perusal of an argument, than in a personal discussion. . . .

The Unwelcome Child (1845)

Very few documents provide evidence about the private lives of married couples, and sexual issues were not discussed in public. The wife's statements concern marital duties that include her sexual submission. The wife's claim to the "justice of her personal rights in regard to maternity" has remained basic to the argument for reproductive freedom. When this letter was written, women had limited options to controlling pregnancy. Women's rights advocates supported voluntary motherhood—the wife's right to abstain from sexual relations. The prevalence of abortion may have been a factor in the decline of the birthrate that occurred during the nineteenth century. According to the evidence, how did the husband enforce his claim to his wife's body? Do you think the husband's behavior expressed societal norms?[*]

Before we married, I informed him (the husband) of my dread of having children. I told him I was not yet prepared to meet the sufferings and responsibilities of maternity. He entered into an arrangement to prevent it for a specified time. This agreement was disregarded. After the legal form was over and he felt that he could now indulge his passion without loss of reputation, and under legal and religious sanctions, he insisted on the surrender of my person to his will. He violated his promise at the beginning of our united life. That fatal bridal night! . . .I can never forget it. It sealed the doom of our union, as it does of thousands.

He was in feeble health; so was I; and both of us mentally depressed. But the sickly germ was implanted, and conception took place. We were poor. . . .In September, 1838, we came to ——, and settled in a new country. In the March following my child . . .was born. After three months' struggle, I became reconciled to my, at first, unwelcome child. . . .

---

[*] From Henry C. Wright, *The Unwelcome Child* (Boston: B. Marsh, 1858) as cited in John Cowan, M.D. and W.R.C. Latson, *What All Married People Should Know* (Chicago: G.W. Ogilvie & Co., 1903), 214-218.

In one year I found I was again to be a mother. I was in a state of frightful despair. My first born was sickly and troublesome, needing constant care and nursing. My husband chopped wood for our support. . . .I felt that death would be preferable to maternity under such circumstances. A desire and determination to get rid of my child entered into my heart. I consulted a lady friend, and by her persuasion and assistance, killed it. Within less than a year, maternity was again imposed upon me, with no better prospect of doing justice to my child. It was a most painful conviction to me; I felt that I could not have another child at the time . . .

I consulted a physician, and told him of my unhappy state of mind. . . . He told me how to destroy it. After experimenting on myself three months, I was successful. I killed my child about five months after conception. . . .

Soon after the birth of my [second] child, my husband insisted on his accustomed injustice. Without any wish of my own, maternity was again forced upon me. I dared no attempt to get rid of the child, abortion seemed so cruel, so inhuman, unnatural and repulsive. I resolved again, for my child's sake, to do the best I could for it. Though I could not joyfully welcome, I resolved quietly to endure its existence.

After the birth of this child, I felt that I could have no more to share our poverty, and to suffer the wrongs and trials of an unwelcome existence. I felt that I had rather die at once, and thus end my life and my power to be a mother together. My husband cast the entire care of the family on me. . . .

In this state, known as it was to my husband, he thrust maternity on me twice. I employed a doctor to kill my child, and in the destruction of it, which should have been the vigor of my life, ended my power to be a mother. . . . I suffered, as woman alone can suffer, not only in body, but in bitter remorse and anguish of soul. . . .

Such has been my false religious and social education, that, in submitting my person to his passion, I did it with the honest conviction that in marriage my body became the property of my husband. He said so; all women to whom I applied for counsel said it was my duty to submit; that husbands expected it, had a right to it, and must have this indulgence whenever they were excited, or suffer; and that in this way alone could wives retain the love of their husbands. I had no alternative but silent, suffering submission to his passion, and then procure abortion or leave him, and thus resign my children to the tender mercies of one with whom I could not live myself. Abortion was most repulsive to every feeling of my nature. It seemed degrading, and a times rendered me an object of loathing to myself.

When my firstborn was three months old, I had a desperate struggle for my personal liberty. My husband insisted on his right to subject my person to his passion, before my babe was two months old. I saw his conduct then in all its degrading and loathsome injustice. I pleaded, with tears and anguish, for my own and my child's sake, to be spared; and had it not been for my helpless child I should then have ended the struggle by bolting my legal bonds. For its sake I submitted to that outrage, and to my own conscious degradation. For its sake, I concluded to take my chances in the world with other wives and mothers, who, as they assured me, and as I then knew, were, all around me subjected to like outrages and driven to the degrading practice of abortion.

But, even then, I saw and argued the justice of my personal rights in regard to maternity. . .I insisted on my right to say when and under what circumstances I would accept of him the office of maternity, and become the mother of his child. I insisted that it was for me to say when and how often I should subject myself to the liability of becoming a mother. But he became angry with me; claimed ownership over me; insisted that I, as a wife, was to submit to my husband "*in all things*"; threatened to leave me and my children, and declared I was not fit to be a wife. Fearing some fatal consequences to my child or to myself—being alone, destitute, and far from helpful friends, in the far West, and fearing that my little one would be left to want—I stifled all expression of my honest convictions, and ever after kept my aversion and painful struggles in my own bosom. . . .

Sojourner Truth, *A'n't I a Woman?* (1851)

Frances Gage, a suffrage advocate, recorded this speech by Sojourner Truth (c. 1797–1883) at the women's rights convention in Akron, Ohio (1851). Although Gage added rhetorical flourishes, the speech expressed Truth's sentiments. An ex-slave with an equal commitment to abolitionism and woman's rights, Truth galvanized audiences. In her speech Truth responded to clergymen's anti-suffrage arguments that God had given men "superior intellect" and limited women to motherhood and domesticity. Using her own experiences as a former slave who had survived physical and emotional oppression, Truth challenged the assumption that women are weak. In establishing an image of women's strength, what particular qualities did Truth emphasize? [*]

Sojourner Truth, Mrs. Stowe's "Lybian Sibyl," was present at this Convention. Some of our younger readers may not know that Sojourner Truth was once a slave in the State of New York, and carries today as many marks of the diabolism of slavery, as ever scarred the back of a victim in Mississippi. Though she can neither read nor write, she is a woman of rare intelligence and commonsense on all subjects. She is still living, at Battle Creek, Michigan, though now 110 years old. Although the

[*] From Sojourner Truth, "Ain't I a Woman?" in *History of Woman Suffrage,* ed. Elizabeth Cady Stanton, Susan B. Anthony, and Matilda J. Gage, (Rochester: Charles Mann, 1881), I: 403–04.

exalted character and personal appearance of this noble woman have been often portrayed, and her brave deeds and words many times rehearsed, yet we give the following graphic picture of Sojourner's appearance in one of the most stormy sessions of the Convention, from reminiscences by Frances D. Gage.

Sojourner Truth. The leaders of the movement trembled on seeing a tall, gaunt black woman in a gray dress and white turban, surmounted with an uncouth sunbonnet, march deliberately into the church, walk with the air of a queen up the aisle, and take her seat upon the pulpit steps. A buzz of disapprobation was heard all over the house, and there fell on the listening ear, "An abolition affair!" "Woman's rights and niggers!" "I told you so!" "Go to it, darkey!"

I chanced on that occasion to wear my first laurels in public life as president of the meeting. At my request order was restored, and the business of the Convention went on. Through all these sessions old Sojourner, quiet and reticent as the "Lybian Statue," sat crouched against the wall on the corner of the pulpit stairs, her sun-bonnet shading her eyes, her elbows on her knees, her chin resting upon her broad, hard palms. At intermission she was busy selling the "Life of Sojourner Truth," a narrative of her own strange and adventurous life. Again and again, timorous and trembling ones came to me and said, with earnestness, "Don't let her speak, Mrs. Gage, it will ruin us. Every newspaper in the land will have our cause mixed up with abolition and niggers, and we shall be utterly denounced." My only answer was, "We shall see when the time comes."

The second day the work waxed warm. Methodist, Baptist, Episcopal, Presbyterian and Universalist ministers came in to hear and discuss the resolutions presented. One claimed superior rights and privileges for man, on the ground of "superior intellect"; another, because of the "manhood of Christ; if God had desired the equality of woman, He would have given some token of His will through the birth, life and death of the Saviour." Another gave us a theological view of the "sin of our first mother."

There were very few women in those days who dared to "speak in meeting"; and the august teachers of the people were seemingly getting the better of us, while the boys in the galleries, and the sneers among the pews, were hugely enjoying the discomfiture, as they supposed, of the "strong-minded." Some of the tender-skinned friends were on the point of losing dignity, and the atmosphere betokened a storm. When, slowly from her seat in the corner rose Sojourner Truth, who, till now, had scarcely lifted her head. "Don't let her speak!" gasped half a dozen in my ear. She moved slowly and solemnly to the front, laid her old bonnet at her feet, and turned her great speaking eyes to me. There was a hissing sound of disapprobation above and below. I rose and announced "Sojourner Truth," and begged the audience to keep silence for a few moments.

The tumult subsided at once, and every eye was fixed on this almost Amazon form, which stood nearly six feet high, head erect, and eyes piercing the upper air like one in a dream. At her first word there was a profound hush. She spoke in deep tones, which, though not loud, reached every ear in the house, and away through the throng at the doors and windows.

"Wall, chilren, whar dar is so much racket dar must be somethin' out o' kilter. I tink dat 'twixt de niggers of de Sof and de womin at de Noft, all talkin' 'bout rights, de white men will be in a fix pretty soon. But what's all dis here talkin' 'bout?

"Dat man ober dar say dat womin needs to be helped into carriages, and lifted ober ditches, and to hab de best place everywhar. Nobody eber helps me into carriages, or ober mud-puddles, or gibs me any best place!" And raising herself to her full height, and her voice to a pitch like rolling thunder, she asked, "And a'n't I a woman? Look at me! Look at my arm! (and she bared her right arm to the shoulder, showing her tremendous muscular power). I have ploughed, and planted, and gathered into barns, and no man could head me! And a'n't I a woman? I could work as much and eat as much as a man—when I could get it—and bear de lash as well! And a'n't I a woman? I have borne thirteen chilren, and seen 'em mos' all sold off to slavery, and when I cried out with my mother's grief, none but Jesus heard me! And a'n't I a woman?

"Den dey talks 'bout dis ting in de head; what dis dey call it?" ("Intellect," whispered some one near.) "Dat's it, honey. What's dat got to do wid womin's rights or nigger's rights? If my cup won't hold but a pint, and yours holds a quart, wouldn't ye be mean not to let me half my little half-measure full?" And she pointed her significant finger, and sent a keen glance at the minister who had made the argument. The cheering was long and loud.

"Den dat little man in black dar, he say women can't have as much rights as men 'cause Christ wan't a woman! Whar did your Christ come from?" Rolling thunder couldn't have stilled that crowd, as did those deep, wonderful tones, as she stood there with outstretched arms and eyes of fire. Raising her voice still louder, she repeated, "Whar did your Christ come from? From God and a woman! Man had nothin' to do wid Him." Oh, what a rebuke that was to that little man.

Turning again to another objector, she took up the defense of Mother Eve. I cannot follow her through it all. It was pointed, and witty, and solemn; eliciting at almost every sentence deafening applause, and she ended by asserting: "If de fust woman God ever made was strong enough to turn the world upside down all alone, dese women togedder (and she glanced her eyes over the platform) ought to be able to turn it back, and get it right side up again! And now dey is asking to do it, de men better let 'em." Long-continued cheering greeted this. "'Bleeged to ye for hearin' on me, and now ole Sojourner han't got nothin' more to say."

Amid roars of applause, she returned to her corner, leaving more than one of us with streaming eyes, and hearts beating with gratitude. She had taken us up in her strong arms and carried us safely over the slough of difficulty by turning the whole tide in our favor. I have never in my life seen anything like the magical influence that subdued the mobbish spirit of the day, and turned the sneers and jeers of an excited crowd into notes of respect and admiration. Hundreds rushed up to shake hands with her, and congratulate the glorious old mother, and bid her Godspeed on her mission of "testifyin' again concerning the wickedness of this 'ere people."

Ernestine Rose, *This Is the Law but Where Is the Justice of It?* (1852)

Ernestine Rose was a pioneer in the struggle to give married women legal rights. She played a key role in agitating for legal reform that led to New York State's Married Women's Property Act. A Polish Jewish immigrant, Rose (1810–1892) joined the mainly native-born Protestant women's rights crusade and frequently gave public lectures. In this speech to a woman's rights convention, she presented a vehement argument against a husband's ownership of his wife, and the denial of freedom and equality that ran counter to the promise of republican life. Rose also claimed that the duties of married women were as "indispensable" and more "arduous" than those of husbands. Would this be an accurate description of married women's roles?[*]

Here, in this far-famed land of freedom, under a Republic that has inscribed on its banner the great truth that "all men are created free and equal, and endowed with inalienable rights to life, liberty, and the pursuit of happiness" . . . even here, in the very face of this eternal truth, woman, the mockingly so-called "better half" of man, has yet to plead for her rights, nay, for her life. For what is life without liberty, and what is liberty without equality of rights? And so for the pursuit of happiness, she is not allowed to choose any line of action that might promote it; she has only thankfully to accept what man in his magnanimity decides is best for her to do, and this is what he does not choose to do himself.

Is she then not included in that declaration? Answer, ye wise men of the nation, and answer truly; add not hypocrisy to oppression! Say that she is not created free and equal, and therefore (for the sequence follows on the premise) that she is not entitled to life, liberty, and the pursuit of happiness. But with all the audacity arising from an assumed superiority, you dare not so libel and insult humanity as to say, that she is not included in that declaration; and if she is, then what right has man, except that of might, to deprive woman of the rights and privileges he claims for himself? And why,

[*] From Ernestine Rose, "This is the Law but Where is the Justice of it All?", in *History of Woman Suffrage*, ed. Elizabeth Cady Stanton, Susan B. Anthony, and Matilda J. Gage, (Rochester: Charles Mann, 1881), I: 237–41.

in the name of reason and justice, why should she not have the same rights? Because she is woman? Humanity recognizes no sex; virtue recognizes no sex; mind recognizes no sex; life and death, pleasure and pain, happiness and misery, recognize no sex. . . . Like him she enjoys or suffers with her country. Yet she is not recognized as his equal!

In the laws of the land she has no rights; in government she has no voice. And in spite of another principle, recognized in this Republic, namely, that "taxation without representation is tyranny," she is taxed to defray the expenses of that unholy, unrightous custom called war, yet she has no power to give her vote against it. From the cradle to the grave she is subject to the power and control of man. Father, guardian, or husband—one conveys her like some piece of merchandise over to the other.

At marriage she loses her entire identity, and her being is said to have become merged in her husband. Has nature thus merged it? Has she ceased to exist and feel pleasure and pain? . . .And when at his nightly orgies, in the grog-shop and the oyster-cellar, or at the gamingtable, he squanders the means she helped, by her co-operation and economy, to accumulate, and she awakens to penury and destitution; will it supply the wants of her children to tell them that, owing to the superiority of man she had no redress by law, and that as her being was merged in his, so also ought theirs to be? What an inconsistency, that from the moment she enters that compact, in which she assumes the high responsibility of wife and mother, she ceases legally to exist, and become a purely submissive being. Blind submission in woman is considered a virtue, while submission is itself wrong, and resistance to wrong is virtue, alike in woman as in man.

But it will be said that the husband provides for the wife, or in other words, he feeds, clothes, and shelters her! I wish I had the power to make everyone before me fully realize the degradation contained in that idea. Yes! He *keeps* her, and so he does a favorite horse: by law they are both considered his property. Both may, when the cruelty of the owner compels them to run away, be brought back by the strong arm of the law. . . .

Carry out the republican principle of universal suffrage, or strike it from your banners and substitute "Freedom and Power to one half of society, and Submission and Slavery to the other." Give woman the elective franchise. Let married women have the same right to property that their husbands have; for whatever the difference in their respective occupations, the duties of the wife are as indispensable and far more arduous than the husband's. Why then should the wife, at the death of her husband, not be his heir to the same extent that he is heir to her? In this inequality there is involved another wrong. When the wife dies, the husband is left in the undisturbed possession of all there is, and the children are left with him; no change is made, no stranger intrudes on his home and his affliction. But when the husband dies, the widow, at best receives but a mere pittance, while strangers assume authority denied to the wife. The sanctuary of affection must be desecrated by executors; everything must be ransacked and assessed, lest she should steal something out of her own house; and to cap the climax, the children must be placed under guardians. When the husband dies poor, to be sure, no guardian is required, and the children are left for the mother to care and toil for, as best she may. But when anything is left for their maintenance, then it must be placed in the hands of strangers for safekeeping!

According to a late act, the wife has a right to the property she brings at marriage, or receives in any way after marriage. Here is some provision for the favored few; but for the laboring many, there is none. The mass of the people commence life with no other capital than the union of heads, hearts, and hands. To the benefit of this best of capital, the wife has no right. If they are unsuccessful in married life, who suffers more the bitter consequences of poverty than the wife? But if successful, she cannot call a dollar her own. The husband may will away every dollar of the personal property, and leave her destitute and penniless, and she has no redress. . . This is law, but where is the justice of it?

Lucy Stone and Henry B. Blackwell, *Marriage Contract* (1855)

Like many feminists, Lucy Stone (1818–1893) initially was committed to abolition. In 1855 she married Henry Blackwell, a leading abolitionist and women's rights advocate. Stone's marriage contract went beyond that of Elizabeth Cady Stanton, who merely omitted the word "obey" from her 1840 marriage contract. Not only did Lucy Stone keep her maiden name, but her contract also addressed property and guardianship rights. Why was the issue of property rights so important for pre-Civil War feminists? Would poorer women be equally concerned?[*]

While acknowledging our mutual affection by publicly assuming the relationship of husband and wife, yet in justice to ourselves and a great principle, we deem it a duty to declare that this act on our part implies no sanction of, nor promise of voluntary obedience to such of the present laws of marriage, as refuse to recognize the wife as an independent, rational being, while they confer upon the husband an injurious and unnatural superiority, investing him with legal powers which no honorable man would exercise, and which no man should possess. We protest especially against the laws which give to the husband:

---

[*] From Lucy Stone and Henry B. Blackwell, "Marriage Contract," in *History of Woman Suffrage*, ed. Elizabeth Cady Stanton, Susan B. Anthony, and Matilda J. Gage, (Rochester: Charles Mann, 1881), I: 260–61.

1. The custody of the wife's person.

2. The exclusive control and guardianship of their children.

3. The sole ownership of her personal, and use of her real estate, unless previously settled upon her, or placed in the hands of trustees, as in the case of minors, lunatics, and idiots.

4. The absolute right to the product of her industry.

5. Also against laws which give to the widower so much larger and more permanent an interest in the property of his deceased wife, than they give to the widow in that of the deceased husband.

6. Finally, against the whole system by which "the legal existence of the wife is suspended during marriage," so that in most States, she neither has a legal part in the choice of her residence, nor can she make a will, nor sue or be sued in her own name, nor inherit property.

We believe that personal independence and equal human rights can never be forfeited, except for crime; that marriage should be an equal and permanent partnership and so recognized by law; that until it is so recognized, married partners should provide against the radical injustice of present laws, by every means in their power.

We believe that where domestic difficulties arise, no appeal should be made to legal tribunals under existing laws, but that all difficulties should be submitted to the equitable adjustment of arbitrators mutually chosen.

Thus reverencing law, we enter our protest against rules and customs which are unworthy of the name, since they violate justice, the essence of law.

Henry B. Blackwell
Lucy Stone

State of New York, *Married Women's Property Act* (1860)

This legislation was the result of years of effort on the part of women reformers, including Elizabeth Cady Stanton, Susan B. Anthony and Ernestine Rose to end married women's loss of legal identity. A victory for equal rights, the legislation ended the common-law tradition of *femme covert*. Unlike an earlier 1848 New York act, the 1860 reform also gave women the right to keep their wages. What provisions of this act would most benefit working wives?[*]

The People of the State of New York, represented in Senate and Assembly, do enact as follows:

Section I. The property, both real and personal, which any married woman now owns, as her sole and separate property; that which comes to her by descent, devise, bequest, gift or grant; that which she acquires by her trade, business, labor, or services, carried on or performed on her sole or separate account; that which a woman married in this State owns at the time of her marriage, and the rents, issues, and proceeds of all such property, shall notwithstanding her marriage, be and remain her sole and separate property, and may be used, collected and invested by her in her own name, and shall not be subject to the interference or control of her husband, or liable for his debts, except such debts as may have been contracted for the support of herself or her children, by her as his agent.

2. A married woman may bargain, sell, assign, and transfer her separate personal property, and carry on any trade or business, and perform any labor or services on her sole and separate account, and the earnings of any married woman from her trade, business, labor, or services shall be her sole and separate property, and may be used or invested by her in her own name.

3. Any married woman possessed of real estate as her separate property may bargain, sell and convey such property, and enter into any contract in reference to the same; but no such conveyance or contract shall be valid without the assent, in writing, of her husband, except as hereinafter provided. . . .

4. Any married woman may, while married, sue and be sued in all matters having relation to her property, which may be her sole and separate property, or which may hereafter come to her by descent, devise, bequest, or the gift of any person except her husband, in the same manner as if she were sole. And any married woman may bring and maintain an action in her own name, for damages against any person or body corporate, for any injury to her person or character, the same as if she were sole; and the money received upon the settlement of any such action, or recovered upon a judgment, shall be her sole and separate property.

8. No bargain or contract made by any married woman, in respect to her sole and separate property. . . shall be binding upon her husband, or render him and his property in any way liable therefor.

---

[*] From "Married Women's Property Act," New York, 1860, in *History of Woman Suffrage,* ed. Elizabeth Cady Stanton, Susan B. Anthony, and Matilda J. Gage, (Rochester: Charles Mann), I: 1881.

9. Every married woman is hereby constituted and declared to be the joint guardian of her children, with her husband, with equal powers, rights, and duties in regard to them, with the husband.

10.   At the decease of husband or wife, leaving no minor child or children, the survivor shall hold, possess, and enjoy life estate in one-third of all the real estate of which the husband or wife died seized.

11.   At the decease of the husband or wife intestate, leaving minor child or children, the survivor shall hold, possess, and enjoy all the real estate of which the husband or wife died seized, and all the rents, issues, and profits thereof during the minority of the youngest child, and one-third thereof during his or her natural life.

6

The Civil War, Reconstruction and Gender Politics

Hardship and the labor scarcity of wartime cast women in untraditional roles. Throughout the divided nation they assumed the management of running farms and plantations. Many performed the male-designated task of ploughing. The Civil War also propelled thousands of women into service as hospital nurses and distributors of medical supplies. Women in both the North and the South responded to the military crisis and organized soldiers' aid societies. In the absence of adequate government provisions and nursing care, women's participation was lifesaving. In the North they played a central role in the work of the United States Sanitary Commission. Nursing the wounded was an outgrowth of women's traditional role; caring for sick family members. Women who entered the hospitals confronted the hostility of male doctors, who found them annoying and intrusive; however, like Phoebe Yates Pember, they persevered. Nursing subsequently gained recognition as an appropriate occupation. Yet until the Civil War, it was considered "unladylike" for women to nurse wounded men.

Although nursing became permissible for women, male doctors continued to exclude women from the medical profession. Furthermore, the Supreme Court upheld women's exclusion from the legal profession on the grounds that the practice of law and womanhood were incompatible. However, wartime scarcity opened the field of clerical work to women, and growing numbers of women were employed as clerks after peace was restored. The expanding field of teaching continued to offer women occupational opportunities, and during Reconstruction large numbers of African-American and white women left their homes in order to meet the educational needs of newly freed blacks.

During the Civil War, women suffragists, many who were also abolitionists, set aside women's rights to devote their full attention to the campaign for the emancipation of slaves. With emancipation achieved, women's rights leaders resumed their struggle for the ballot. Their suffragist crusade was far removed from the experiences of newly freed black women who joined their husbands in the impoverished life of sharecroppers. Many took in laundry or worked as domestics to supplement their husbands' marginal wages. For the vast majority of married African-American women, the normative single male breadwinner was a myth. Work—combined with family care—remained the focus of their lives.

Although Reconstruction brought the promise of political rights and citizenship for African-American men, the promise was not extended to women. The passage of the Fourteenth and Fifteenth Amendments guaranteed all men the right to vote. To Elizabeth Cady Stanton and Susan B. Anthony, the exclusion of women from the amendments was an inexcusable betrayal on the part of abolitionist men who had foremely had linked women's rights to emancipation. Abolitionist men now urged women to be patient as it was the "negro's" hour. Dismissing patience, Stanton and Anthony severed ties with their former comrades and remained unreconciled to the Fifteenth Amendment. Embittered and defiant, they organized the National Woman's Suffrage Association (NWSA), a comprehensive equal rights association.

Through their radical publication, *The Revolution*, they promoted a wide range of economic and social reforms for women, as well as the right to vote. Always ahead of her time, Stanton advocated liberalized divorce laws. She initially defended the rebel Victoria Woodhull, who advocated free love and broke the rules for respectable female sexual behavior. As leader of the Equal Rights Party, Woodhull also became the first woman in the United States to run for president in 1872. Distancing themselves from Woodhull's increasingly notorious behavior, Stanton and Anthony conducted massive petition drives and repeatedly and unsuccessfully sought congressional approval for woman's suffrage. In 1872 Anthony tested the right of women as citizens to vote—she was tried and fined for attempting to vote. In *Minor v. Happrestell*, the Supreme Court rejected the argument that women, as citizens, had a constitutional right to vote.

Less radical women followed Lucy Stone and joined the American Woman's Suffrage Association (AWSA). The AWSA included abolitionist men and recognized the Fifteenth Amendment. Focusing their efforts completely on the right to vote, the AWSA campaigned for suffrage on the state level. For more than twenty years, the rival associations pursued their separate objectives and strategies. However, deeply rooted assumptions, similar to those of Amelia Barr, about women's unique biological and emotional nature and the domestic sphere, made it difficult for women's rights leaders to secure a constituency for the vote. Both groups proved ineffectual in building a mass base of support. Reunited in 1890 as the National American Woman's Suffrage Association (NAWSA), the suffrage cause continued to lack significant public support until the 1900s. Only in the West, in Wyoming, Idaho, Utah, and Colorado, had women gained the right to vote. The pro-suffrage position of Western states reflected the relatively higher status of women. In the west, women provided vital labor and were not as tightly bound by convention as their eastern counterparts.

Mary Boykin Chesnut, *A Confederate Lady's Diary* (1861)

The daughter and wife of wealthy southern senators, Mary Boykin
Chesnut (1823–1886) lived a plantation mistress's life of class and
race privilege. Her diary provides evidence of male slave owner's
sexual exploitation of enslaved women. Chesnut's primary
concern was the impact of this sexual misconduct on wives. What
evidence does Chesnut offer to support her allegation about
interracial sexual relations between owners and enslaved
women?*

I wonder if it be a sin to think slavery a curse to any land. Sumner said not one word
of this hated institution which is not true. Men & women are punished when their
masters & mistresses are brutes & not when they do wrong—& then we live
surrounded by prostitutes. An abandoned woman is sent out of any decent house
elsewhere. Who thinks any worse of a Negro or Mulatto woman for being a thing we
can't name. God forgive *us*, but ours is a *monstrous* system & wrong & iniquity.
Perhaps the rest of the world is as bad. This is *only* what I see: like the patriarchs of
old, our men live all in one house with their wives & their concubines, & the Mulattos
one sees in every family exactly resemble the white children—& every lady tells you
who is the father of all the Mulatto children in everybody's household, but those in
her own, she seems to think drop from the clouds or pretends so to think—. Good
women we have, *but* they talk of *nastiness tho* they never do wrong; they talk day &
night of —. My disgust sometimes is boiling over—but they are, I believe, in conduct
the purest women God ever made. Thank God for my countrywomen—alas for the
men! No worse than men everywhere, but the lower their mistresses, the more
degraded they must be.

My mother-in-law told me when I was first married not to send my female
servants in the street on errands. They were there tempted, led astray—& then she
said placidly, "So they told *me* when I came here—& I was very particular, *but you
see with what* result." Mr. Harris said it was so patriarchal. So it is—flocks & herds &
slaves—& wife Leah does not suffice. Rachel must be *added*, if not *married* & all the
time they seem to think themselves patterns—models of husbands & fathers.

Mrs. Davis told me "everybody described my husband's father as an odd
character, a Millionaire who did nothing for his son whatever, left him to struggle
with poverty," &c. I replied, "Mr. Chesnut Senior thinks himself the best of fathers—

---

* From Mary Boykin Chesnut, "A Confederate Lady's Diary," (1861) as published in C. Van Woodward and
Elizabeth Muhlenfeld, *The Private Mary Chestnut : The Unpublished Civil War Diaries*, (New York: Oxford
University Press, 1984), 41–43. Reprinted by permission of Harold Ober Associates.

& his son thinks likewise. I have nothing to say—but it is true, he has no money but what he makes as a lawyer," &c. Again I say, my countrywomen are as pure as angels—tho surrounded by another race who are—the social evil!

Clara Barton, *Nursing on the Firing Line* (c. 1870)

> In this document, Clara Barton (1821–1912) described the ordeals she faced as a battlefield nurse. Although she won national acclaim for her nursing, her contribution to the Civil War also involved fundraising and collecting and distributing medical supplies. Like other Civil War women nurses, Barton had to overcome enormous resistance. How did Barton deal with the argument that nursing wounded soldiers was inappropriate and "unseemly for a woman"? *

I was strong and thought I might go to the rescue of the men who fell. The first regiment of troops, the old 6th Mass. that fought its way through Baltimore, brought my playmates and neighbors, the partakers of my childhood; the brigades of New Jersey brought scores of my brave boys, the same solid phalanx; and the strongest legions from old Herkimer brought the associates of my seminary days. They formed and crowded around me. What could I do but go with them, or work for them and my country? The patriot blood of my father was warm in my veins. The country which he had fought for, I might at least work for, and I had offered my service to the government in the capacity of a double clerkship at twice $1400 a year, upon discharge of two disloyal clerks from its employ—the salary never to be given to me, but to be turned back into the U.S. Treasury then poor to beggary, with no currency, no credit. But there was no law for this, and it could not be done, and I would not draw salary from our government in such peril, so I resigned and went into direct service of the sick and wounded troops wherever found.

But I struggled long and hard with my sense of propriety—with the appalling fact that I was only a woman whispering in one ear, and thundering in the other the groans of suffering men dying like dogs—unfed and unsheltered, for the life of every institution which had protected and educated me!

I said that I struggled with my sense of propriety and I say it with humiliation and shame. I am ashamed that I thought of such a thing.

---

* From Perry Epler, *Life of Clara Barton* (New York: Macmillan, 1915), 31–32, 35–43, 45, 59, 96–98.

When our armies fought on Cedar Mountain, I broke the shackles and went to the field. . . .

Five days and nights with three hours sleep—a narrow escape from capture—and some days of getting the wounded into hospitals at Washington, brought Saturday, August 30. And if you chance to feel, that the positions I occupied were rough and unseemly for a *woman*—I can only reply that they were rough and unseemly for *men*. But under all, lay the life of the nation. I had inherited the rich blessing of health and strength of constitution—such as are seldom given to woman—and I felt that some return was due from me and that I ought to be there. . . .

You generous thoughtful mothers and wives have not forgotten the tons of preserves and fruits with which you filled our hands. Huge boxes of these stood beside that railway track. Every can, jar, bucket, bowl, cup or tumbler, when emptied, that instant became a vehicle of mercy to convey some preparation of mingled bread and wine, or soup or coffee to some helpless famishing sufferer who partook of it with the tears rolling down his bronzed cheeks, and divide his blessings between the hands that fed him and his God. I never realized until that day how little a human being could be grateful for, and that day's experience also taught me the utter worthlessness of that which could not be made to contribute directly to our necessities. The bit of bread which would rest on the surface of a gold eagle was worth more than the coin itself.

But the most fearful scene was reserved for the night. I have said that the ground was littered with dry hay and that we had only two lanterns, but there were plenty of candles. The wounded were laid so close that it was impossible to move about in the dark. The slightest misstep brought a torrent of groans from some poor mangled fellow in your path.

Consequently here were seen persons of all grades, from the careful man of God who walked with a prayer upon his lips, to the careless driver hunting for his lost whip—each wandering about among this hay with an open flaming candle in his hands.

The slightest accident, the mere dropping of a light could have enveloped in flames this whole mass of helpless men.

How we watched and pleaded and cautioned as we worked and wept that night! How we put socks and slippers upon the cold, damp feet, wrapped your blankets and quilts about them, and when we had no longer these to give, how we covered them in the hay and left them to their rest!. . . .

Phoebe Yates Pember, Excerpts from *A Southern Woman's Story (1879)*

Phoebe Yates Pember was a member of the plantation aristocracy. In 1862 she was appointed to the position of matron at the Chimborazo Hospital in Richmond, Virginia. In the following excerpt, Yates recounts the activism of southern women on behalf of the Confederacy. Her story serves as a reminder that men governed hospital nursing. The presence of women in hospitals was bitterly resented although desperately needed. What information does Pember's account supply about male resentment?[*]

The women of the South had been openly and violently rebellious from the moment they thought their states' rights touched. They incited the men to struggle in support of their views, and whether right or wrong, sustained them nobly to the end. They were the first to rebel—the last to succumb. Taking an active part in all that came within their sphere, and often compelled to go beyond this when the field demanded as many soldiers as could be raised; feeling a passion of interest in every man in the gray uniform of the Confederate service; they were doubly anxious to give comfort and assistance to the sick and wounded. In the course of a long and harassing war, with port blockaded and harvests burnt, rail tracks constantly torn up, so that supplies of food were cut off, and sold always at exorbitant prices, no appeal was ever made to the women of the South, individually or collectively, that did not meet with a ready response. There was no parade of generosity; no published lists of donations, inspected by public eyes. What was contributed was given unostentatiously, whether a barrel of coffee or the only half bottle of wine in the giver's possession.

About this time one of these large hospitals was to be opened, and the wife of George W. Randolph, Secretary of War, offered me the superindendence—rather a startling proposition to a woman used to all the comforts of luxurious life. Foremost among the Virginia women, she had given her resources of mind and means to the sick, and her graphic and earnest representations of the benefit a good and determined woman's rule could effect in such a position, settled the result in my mind. The natural idea that such a life would be injurious to the delicacy and refinement of a lady—that her nature would become deteriorated and her sensibilities blunted, was rather appalling. But the first step only costs, and that was soon taken.

---

[*] From Phoebe Yates Pember, *A Southern Woman's Story: Life in Confederate Richmond* edited by Bell Irwin Wiley (Jackson, TN: McCowat-Mercer, 1959). Reprinted by permission of Broadfoot Publishing.

A preliminary interview with the surgeon-in-chief gave necessary confidence. He was energetic—capable—skillful. A man with ready oil to pour upon troubled waters. Difficulties melted away beneath the warmth of his ready interest, and mountains sank into mole-hills when his quick comprehension had surmounted and leveled them. However troublesome daily increasing annoyances became, if they could not be removed, his few and ready words sent applicants and grumblers home satisfied to do the best they could. Wisely he decided to have an educated and efficient woman at the head of his hospital, and having succeeded, never allowed himself to forget that fact.

The day after my decision was made found me at "headquarters," the only two-story building on hospital ground, then occupied by the chief surgeon and his clerks. He had not yet made his appearance that morning, and while awaiting him, many of his corps, who had expected in horror the advent of female supervision, walked in and out, evidently inspecting me. There was at the time a general ignorance on all sides, except among the hospital officials, of the decided objection on the part of the latter to the carrying out of a law which they prognosticated would entail "petticoat government"; but there was no mistaking the stage-whisper which reached my ears from the open door of the office that morning, as the little contract surgeon passed out and informed a friend he met, in a tone of ill-concealed disgust, that *"one of them had come."*

Susie King Taylor, *Reminiscences of an Army Laundress* (1902)

Susie King Taylor (1848–1912) was one of the five thousand slaves who escaped to the Union army. She accompanied the 33rd U.S. Colored Troops in which her husband served. This excerpt from her reminiscences described the variety of services female army followers such as Taylor performed. In what ways did Taylor's duties affirm conventional gender roles?[*]

I was enrolled as company laundress, but I did very little of it, because I was always busy doing other things through camp, and was employed all the time doing something for the officers and comrades. . . .

The first colored troops did not receive any pay for eighteen months, and the men had to depend wholly on what they received from the commissary, established by Gen.

[*] From Susie King Taylor, *Reminiscences of My Life in Camp with the 33rd United States Colored Troops* (Boston: Author, 1902), 15–16, 26– 28, 32–35.

Saxton. A great many of these men had large families, and as they had no money to give them, their wives were obliged to support themselves and children by washing for the officers of the gunboats and the soldiers, and making cakes and pies, which they sold to the boys in camp. Finally, in 1863, the government decided to give them half pay, but the men would not accept this. They wanted "full pay or nothing." They preferred rather to give their services to the state, which they did until 1864, when the government granted them full pay with all the back pay due. . .

I learned to handle a musket very well while in the regiment and could shoot straight and often hit the target. I assisted in cleaning the guns and used to fire them off, to see if the cartridges were dry, before cleaning and re-loading, each day. I thought this was great fun. I was also able to take a gun all apart and put it together again. . . .

We had fresh beef once in a while, and we would have soup, and the vegetables they put in the soup were dried and pressed; they looked like hops. Salt beef was our standby. Sometimes the men would have what we called slap-jacks. This was flour made into bread and spread thin on the bottom of the mess-pan to cook; each man had one of them with a pint of tea for his supper, or a pint of tea and five or six hardtack. I often got my own meals and would fix some dishes for the noncommissioned officers also.

About the first of June, 1864, the regiment was ordered to Folly Island, staying there until the latter part of the month, when it was ordered to Morris Island. We landed on Morris Island between June and July, 1864. This island was a narrow strip of sandy soil, nothing growing on it but a few bushes and shrubs. The camp was one mile from the boat landing, called Pawnell Landing, and the landing one mile from Fort Wagner. . . .

The regiment under Colonel Trowbridge did garrison duty, but they had troublesome times from Fort Gregg, on James Island, for the rebels would throw a shell over our island every now and then. Finally orders were received for the boys to prepare to take Fort Gregg, each man to take 150 rounds of cartridges, canteens of water, hardtack and salt beef. This order was sent three days prior to starting, to allow them to be in readiness. I helped as many as I could to pack haversacks and cartridge boxes.

About four o'clock, July 2, the charge was made. The firing could be plainly heard in camp. I hastened down to the landing and remained there until eight o'clock that morning. When the wounded arrived, or rather began to arrive, the first one brought in was Samuel Anderson of our company. He was badly wounded. Then others of our boys, some with their legs off, arm gone, foot off, and wounds of all kinds imaginable. They had to wade through creeks and marshes, as they were discovered by the enemy and shelled very badly. A number of the men were lost, some got fastened in the mud and had to cut off the legs of their pants, to free themselves. The 103rd New York suffered the most, as their men were very badly wounded.

My work now began. I gave my assistance to try to alleviate their sufferings. I asked the doctor at the hospital what I could get for them to eat. They wanted soup, but that I could not get; but I had a few cans of condensed milk and some turtle eggs, so I thought I would try to make some custard. I had doubts as to my success, for cooking with turtle eggs was something new to me, but the adage has it, "Nothing ventured, nothing done," so I made a venture and the result was a very delicious custard. This I carried to the men, who enjoyed it very much. My services were given at all times for the comfort of these men. I was on hand to assist whenever needed.

Charlotte Forten, *Letter to William Lloyd Garrison* (1862)

A member of one of the nation's most prominent free African-American families, Charlotte Forten (1837–1914) joined other women who served as teachers to contraband slaves under the protection of the Union army. In what ways did Forten find her teaching experience "great happiness" yet "more fatiguing than at the North"?

St. Helena's Island, South Carolina

November 20, 1862

My Dear Friend:

St. Helena's Island, on which I am, is about six miles from the mainland of Beaufort. I must tell you that we were rowed hither from Beaufort by a crew of negro boatmen, and that they sang for us several of their own beautiful songs. There is a peculiar wildness and solemnity about them which cannot be described, and the people accompany the singing with a singular swaying motion of the body which seems to make it more effective.

As far as I have been able to observe, the negroes here rejoice in their new-found freedom. It does me good to see how *jubilant* they are over the downfall of their "secesh" masters. I do not believe that there is a man, woman, or even a child that would submit to be made a slave again. They are a truly religious people. They speak to God with a loving familiarity. Another trait that I have noticed is their natural courtesy of manner. There is nothing cringing about it, but it seems inborn, and one

* From Charlotte Forten, "Letter to William Lloyd Garrison," in Dorothy Sterling, *We are Your Sisters: Black Women in the Nineteeth Century*, (New York: Norton, 1984), 280 -81.

might almost say elegant. It marks their behavior toward each other as well as to the white people.

My school is about a mile from here, in the little Baptist church, which is in a grove of white oaks. These trees are beautiful—evergreen—and every branch heavily draped with long, bearded moss, which gives them a strange, mournful look. There are two ladies in the school besides myself—Miss T and Miss M—both of whom are most enthusiastic teachers. At present, our school is small—many of the children being ill with whooping cough—but in general it averages eighty or ninety. It is a great happiness to teach them. I wish some of those persons at the North who say the race is hopelessly and naturally inferior could see the readiness with which these children, so long oppressed and deprived of every privilege, learn and understand.

I have some grown pupils—people on our own plantation—who take lessons in the evenings. It will amuse you to know that one of them,—our man-of-all-work—is name *Cupid*. (Venuses and Cupids are very common here.) He told me he was "feared" he was almost too old to learn, but I assured him that that was not the case, and now he is working diligently at the alphabet. One of my people—Harry—is a scholar to be proud of. He makes most wonderful improvement. I never saw anyone so determined to learn. . . .

These people have really a great deal of musical talent. It is impossible to give you any idea of their songs and hymns. They are so wild, so strange, and yet so invariably harmonious and sweet. There is one of their hymns—"Roll Jordan Roll"—that I never listen to without seeming to hear, almost to feel, the rolling of waters. There is a great rolling wave of sound through it all. . . .

After the lessons, we talk freely to the children, often giving them slight sketches of some of the great and good men. Before teaching them the "John Brown" song, which they learned to sing with great spirit, Miss T. told them the story of the brave old man who had died for them. I told them about Toussaint, thinking it well they should know what one of their own color had done. They listened attentively and seemed to understand. We found it rather hard to keep their attention in school. It is not strange, as they have been so entirely unused to intellectual concentration. It is necessary to interest them every moment, in order to keep their thoughts from wandering. Teaching here is consequently far more fatiguing than at the North.

Elizabeth Cady Stanton, *On Marriage and Divorce* (c. 1850)

Elizabeth Cady Stanton and Susan B. Anthony established a journal called *The Revolution* as a forum for women's rights. In the following article, Stanton (1815–1902) discussed the need for more liberal divorce laws. Her radical stand on personal issues such as marriage and divorce alienated more cautious women reformers. How did Stanton link the power of men to the abuse of women? On what grounds did she advocate divorce? [*]

All this talk about the indissoluble tie and the sacredness of marriage, irrespective of the character and habits of the husband, is for its effect on woman. She never could have been held the pliant tool she is today but for the subjugation of her religious nature to the idea that in whatever condition she found herself as man's subject, that condition was ordained of Heaven; whether burning on the funeral pile of her husband in India, or suffering the slower torture of bearing children every year in America to drunkards, diseased, licentious men, at the expense of her own life and health, and the enfeebling of both the mind and body of her progeny. Women would not live as they now do in this enlightened age in violation of every law of their being, giving the very heyday of their existence to the exercise of one animal function, if subordination to man had not been made through the ages the cardinal point of their religious faith and daily life. It requires but little thought to see that. . .the indissoluble tie was found to be necessary in order to establish man's authority over woman. The argument runs thus:

Men all admit that if two cannot be agreed they must part. This may apply to partners in business, pastor and people, physician and patient, master and servant, and many other relations in life; but in the case of parent and child, husband and wife, as their relations cannot be dissolved, there must be some alternate authority to decide all matters on which they cannot agree, hence man's headship. These cases should be distinguished, however; the child is free to act on his own opinions, by law, at a certain age, and the tie is practically dissolved between him and the parent so soon as he earns his own bread. The child is under the parent's control only during its minority; but the wife's condition is perpetual minority, lifelong subjection to authority, with no appeal, no hope on the indissoluble tie theory. The practical effect of this is to make tyrants of men and fools of women. There never was a human being yet on this footstool godlike enough to be trusted with the absolute control of any living thing. Men abuse each other. Look in your prisons, jails, asylums, battle-fields and camps, they abuse their horses, dogs, cats. . . . They abuse their own children, and of course they will abuse their wives, taught by law and gospel that they own them as property, especially as a wife can vex and thwart a man, as no other living thing can.

It is sheer folly at this age of the world to waste ink or words on marriage as an indissoluble tie and on the husband's divinely ordained authority, for woman's growing self-respect and keep perception of the drift of these dogmas enable her at last to see that the long and weary bondage her sex has endured through the centuries was based in the beginning on these twin heresies. . . .

---

[*] From Elizabeth Cady Stanton, "On Marriage and Divorce," reprinted in Paulina Wright Davis, *History of the National Woman's Rights Movement for Twenty Years... From 1850 to 1870* (New York: Journeymen Printers' Cooperative Association, 1871), 62-83.

Bradwell v. Illinois (1869)

Law was even more of a male preserve than medicine. In Bradwell v. Illinois, the Supreme Court upheld traditional gender roles. Like other restrictive arguments made in the post-Civil War period, women's feminine natures and reproductive function were used to deny them the right to practice law. The last lines of the document refer to the fact that the plaintiff was married. Apparently, the court found married women pursuing careers "repugnant." In what ways did the concept of gender influence the court's decision?[*]

In regard to that amendment, counsel for plaintiff in this court truly says that there are certain privileges and immunities which belong to a citizen of the United States as such; otherwise it would be nonsense for the XIV Amendment to prohibit a State from abridging them, and he proceeds to argue that admission to the bar of a State of a person who possesses the requisite learning and character is one of those which a State may not deny.

In this latter proposition we are not able to concur with counsel. We agree with him that there are privileges and immunities belonging to citizens of the United States, in that relation and character, and that it is these, and these alone, which a State is forbidden to abridge. But the right to admission to practice in the courts of a State is not one of them. The right in no sense depends on citizenship of the United States. . . .

[From a Concurring Opinion]

The claim that, under the XIV Amendment of the Constitution, which declares that no State shall make or enforce any law which shall abridge the privileges and immunities of citizens of the United States, the statute law of Illinois, or the common law prevailing in that State, can no longer be set up as a barrier against the right of female to pursue any lawful employment for a livelihood (the practice of law included) assumes that it is one of the privileges and immunities of women as citizens to engage in any and every profession, occupation, or employment in civil life.

It certainly can not be affirmed, as a historical fact, that this has ever been established as one of the fundamental privileges and immunities of the sex. On the contrary, the civil law, as well as nature herself, has always recognized a wide difference in the respective spheres and destinies of man and woman. Man is, or should be, woman's protector and defender. The natural and proper timidity and

---

[*] From *Bradwell v. Illinois*, Supreme Court of the United States, 1873, 83 U.S. (16 Wallace) 130, 141.

delicacy which belongs to the female sex evidently unfits it for many of the occupations of civil life. The constitution of the family organization, which is founded in the divine ordinance, as well as in the nature of things, indicates the domestic sphere as that which properly belongs to the domain and functions of womanhood. The harmony, not to say identity, of interests and views which belong, or should belong, to the family institution is repugnant to the idea of a woman adopting a distinct and independent career from that of her husband.

Amelia Barr, *Discontented Women* (1896)

Amelia Barr (1831–1919) was a novelist who wrote romantic stories about love and married life. Her argument against suffrage provides an excellent example of how anti-suffragists used gendered arguments to deny women the ballot. Note how Barr contrasts "virile virtues" with "feminine softness." Men possess reason but women cannot go beyond their feminine natures, which "substitute sentiment for reason." Anti-suffragists viewed women's desire to vote as unnatural discontent. Barr linked women's discontent to Eve and believed it was natural for women but could be controlled. Her stress on woman's "original sin" contradicted the conventional nineteenth-century emphasis on womanly virtue. However, her argument generally reflects separate-sphere beliefs. Would any part of Barr's argument have relevance today?[*]

Discontent is a vice six thousand years old, and it will be eternal; because it is in the race. Every human being has a complaining side, but discontent is bound up in the heart of woman; it is her original sin. For if the first woman had been satisfied with her conditions, if she had not aspired to be "as gods," and hankered after unlawful knowledge, Satan would hardly have thought it worth his while to discuss her rights and wrongs with her. That unhappy controversy has never ceased; and, without reason, woman has been perpetually subject to discontent with her conditions and, according to her nature, has been moved by its influence. Some, it has made peevish, some plaintive, some ambitious, some reckless, while a noble majority have found in its very control that serene composure and cheerfulness which is granted to those who conquer, rather than to those who inherit.

---

[*] From Amelia Barr, "Discontented Women," in *North American Review* 162 (February 1896), 201, 205–207, 209.

Finally, women cannot get behind or beyond their nature, and their nature is to substitute sentiment for reason—a sweet and not unlovely characteristic in womanly ways and places; yet reason, on the whole, is considered a desirable necessity in politics. . . . Women may cease to be women, but they can never learn to be men and feminine softness and grace can never do the work of the virile virtues of men. Very fortunately this class of discontented women have not yet been able to endanger existing conditions by combinations analogous to trades unions; nor is it likely they ever will; because it is doubtful if women, under any circumstances, could combine at all. Certain qualities are necessary for combination, and these qualities are represented in women by their opposites. . . .

The one unanswerable excuse for woman's entrance into active public life of any kind, is *need* and alas! need is growing daily, as marriage becomes continually rare, and more women are left adrift in the world without helpers and protectors. But this is a subject too large to enter on here, though in the beginning it sprung from discontented women, preferring the work and duties of men to their own work and duties. Have they found the battle of life any more ennobling in masculine professions, than in their old feminine household ways? Is work done in the world for strangers, any less tiresome and monotonous, than work done in the house for father and mother, husband and children? If they answer truly, they will reply "the home duties were the easiest, the safest and the happiest."

Of course all discontented women will be indignant at any criticism of their conduct. The expect every one to consider their feelings without examining their motives. Paddling in the turbid maelstrom of life, and dabbling in politics and the most unsavory social questions, they still think men, at least, ought to regard them as the Sacred Sex. But women are not sacred by grace of sex, if they voluntarily abdicate its limitations and its modesties, and make a public display of unsexed sensibilities, an unabashed familiarity with subjects they have nothing to do with. If men criticize such women with asperity it is not to be wondered at; they have so long idealized women, that they find it hard to speak moderately. They excuse them too much, or else they are too indignant at their follies, and unjust and angry in their denunciation. Women must be criticized by women; then they will hear the bare uncompromising truth, and be the better for it.

7

Building Sisterhood: Gender, Race, Ethnicity, and the Limits of Inclusion

The last decades of the nineteenth century were characterized by the founding of women's institutions and organizations. These separate institutions both reflected and intensified the assumptions that women had an identity so different from men, that they needed a separate sphere to fulfill their womanly roles. Separate institutions may have resulted from woman's secondary status, but they also enabled women to forge positive identities, strengthen the bonds of sisterhood, and create supportive networks. The continued refusal of men to grant women an opportunity for higher education provided the impetus for the establishment of separate female colleges, which had rigorous academic standards comparable to those of male institutions. In pursuit of a college education, M. Carey Thomas and other women of her generation had to surmount the pervasive assumption that women were intelluctually inferior as well as the dismal medical warnings of "experts" like Edward H. Clarke, that intellectual activity strained the weak female brain and nervous system leading to the eventual collapse of the reproductive organs.

The proliferation of women's clubs also expressed women's response to exclusion from male organizations, as well as the need to create an environment where they could gather socially and participate in cultural and intellectual activity. Club objectives quickly widened and became community oriented. Club women promoted projects such as kindergartens, libraries, playgrounds, and civic beautification. They lobbied for uncontaminated food and milk, clean streets, and better "municipal housekeeping." In 1890, thousands of local clubs formed the General Federation of Women's Clubs (GFWC). The GFWC played a major role in securing the passage of the Pure Food and Drug Act and promoted protective legislation for women and children. Club women's activism indicated how permeable the boundaries were between public and private spheres. As housewives, women responded to a wide range of public issues that affected the security of their homes and neighborhoods and the well-being of their families.

Activism grew out of traditional community service and the women's associations that had flourished since the 1800s. Club membership reached two million by 1915. Women's clubs expressed no concern for gender inequities, and the GFWC did not support the suffrage movement until 1914. Yet, critics like ex-President Grover Cleveland, who took the ideology of separate spheres literally, viewed club involvement as the abandonment of motherhood and predicted national calamity if women continued their "club habit".

One of the most popular female organizations of the era, the Women's Christian Temperance Union (WCTU) was determined to rid the nation of alcohol. Unlike the pre-Civil War temperance activists who were auxiliaries in a male-directed movement, women led and managed the WCTU. Prohibition was an infinitely more popular cause than women's rights. WCTU chapters sprang up throughout the United States. The WCTU attempted to control male behavior and especially sought to end drunken husbands' abuse of their wives. Under Frances Willard's leadership the WCTU linked women's suffrage to the protection of the nation's homes and families.

Sisterhood institutions were exclusive rather than inclusive; colleges, clubs, and organizations rarely crossed race, class, or ethnic lines. Denied access to white-only clubs, African-American middle-class women launched their own club movement. In their commitment to community service and female sociability, African-American clubs paralleled those of white women. However, black club women also sought to eradicate the racist stereotyping of black females as sexually promiscuous— a race and gender view that justified white male sexual exploitation. Recognizing the intersection of race, class, and gender—the multiple burdens African American women confronted—club women took the motto "lifting as we climb." They emphasized that improved conditions for black women could be gained only in the context of greater racial equality and opportunities for all African-Americans. In organizing the National Association of Colored Women (NACW) in 1896, African-American women created the first nationally organized civil rights association.

The late nineteenth century was characterized by heightened racism, nativism, and increasing class conflict. Jim Crow laws and segregated social patterns prevailed throughout the South, and were validated by the Supreme Court in the 1896 *Plessy* v. *Ferguson* decision. Not only in the South, but throughout the nation, white supremacist values molded social behavior. Defying racial hostility, outspoken African American women followed the example of Ida B. Wells and Mary Church Terrell and opposed both the injustice and daily indignities of segregation as well as the deadly practice of lynching.

As was the case during previous westward expansion, opportunity for white Americans to start "new" lives on the Great Plains and in the far west brought devastation to native peoples. Susette La Flesche, of Omaha ancestry, describes how the combined efforts of the U.S. government, army, and settlers caused the displacement of Native Americans from their ancestral lands. Subsequent governmental efforts to privatize tribal holdings and assimilate indigenous people demonstrated little concern or respect for Native American culture and ethnic identity.

Zitkala-Sa's recollections of her school days relate the trauma of coerced Americanization.

Edward H. Clarke, *Sex in Education* (1874)

A Harvard Medical School trustee, Dr. Edward H. Clarke argued against higher education for women at a time when increasing numbers of young women were applying to medical schools. At Harvard, Clarke voted against opening admission to women. In Clarke's medical opinion, intellectual effort ruined the mental and reproductive health of college women. Arising out of a combination of medical ignorance and a lengthy tradition that argued for women's limited intellectual capacity, Clarke's views also expressed the increasing cultural emphasis on the need to safeguard female reproductive function. What evidence did Clarke provide that a college education puts women's "complicated reproductive mechanisms" at risk? [*]

This case needs very little comment: its teachings are obvious. Miss D—went to college in good physical condition. During the four years of her college life, her parents and the college faculty required her to get what is popularly called an education. Nature required her, during the same period, to build and put in working order a large and complicated reproductive mechanism, a matter that is popularly ignored—shoved out of sight like a disgrace. She naturally obeyed the requirements of the faculty, which she could see, rather than the requirements of the mechanism within her, that she could not see. Subjected to the college regimen, she worked four years in getting a liberal education. Her way of work was sustained and continuous, and out of harmony with the rhymical periodicy of the female organization. The stream of vital and constructive force evolved within her was turned steadily to the brain, and away from the ovaries and their accessories. The result of this sort of education was, that these last-mentioned organs, deprived of sufficient opportunity and nutriment, first began to perform their functions with pain, a warning of error that was unheeded; then, to cease to grow; next, to set up once a month a grumbling torture that made life miserable; and, lastly, the brain and the whole nervous system, disturbed, in obedience to the law, that, if one member suffers, all the members suffer,

---

[*] From Edward H. Clark, M.D., *Sex in Education*, or *A Fair Chance for the Girls* (Boston: James R. Osgood and Co., 1873), 78-87.

became neuralgic and hysterical. And so Miss D—spent the next few years succeeding her graduation in conflict with dysmenorrehea, headache, neuralgia, and hysteria. Her parents marveled at her ill health; and she furnished another text for the often-repeated sermon on the delicacy of American girls.

It may not be unprofitable to give the history of one more case of this sort. Miss E—had an hereditary right to a good brain and to the best cultivation of it. Her father was one of our ripest and broadest American scholars, and her mother one of our most accomplished American women. They both enjoyed excellent health. Their daughter had a literary training—an intellectual, moral, and aesthetic half of education, such as their supervision would be likely to give, and one that few young men of her age receive. Her health did not seem to suffer at first. She studied, recited, walked, worked, stood, and the like, in the steady and sustained way that is normal to the male organization. She *seemed* to evolve force enough to acquire a number of languages, to become familiar with the natural sciences, to take hold of philosophy and mathematics, and to keep in good physical case while doing all this. At the age of twenty-one she might have been presented to the public, on Commencement Day, by the president of Vassar College or of Antioch College or of Michigan University, as the wished-for result of American liberal female culture. Just at this time, however, the catamenical function began to show signs of failure of power. No severe or even moderate illness overtook her. She was subjected to no unusual strain. She was only following the regimen of continued and sustained work, regardless of Nature's periodical demands for a portion of her time and force, when, without any apparent cause, the failure of power was manifested by moderate dysmenorrehoea and diminished excretion. Soon after this the function ceased altogether, and up to this present writing, a period of six or eight years, it has shown no more signs of activity than an amputated arm. In the course of a year or so after the cessation of the function, her head began to trouble her. First there was headache, then a frequent congested condition, which she described as a "rush of blood" to her head; and, by and by, vagaries and foreboding and despondent feelings began to crop out. Coincident with this mental state, her skin became rough and coarse, and an inveterate acne covered her face. She retained her appetite, ability to exercise, and sleep. A careful local examination of the pelvic organs, by an expert, disclosed no lesion or displacement there, no ovarian or other inflammation. Appropriate treatment faithfully persevered in was unsuccessful in recovering the lost function. I was finally obliged to consign her to an asylum.

M. Carey Thomas, *Present Tendencies in Women's Education* (1908)

The following document was written by M. Carey Thomas (1857–1935) more than twenty-five years after Dr. Clarke's attack on college education for women. Thomas served as the president of Bryn Mawr, one of the nation's most prestigious women's colleges, which opened in 1885. What did the author mean by the statement that when women first began to attend college, little was known about the effect higher education would have on their health? *

The passionate desire of the women of my generation for higher education was accompanied throughout its course by the awful doubt, felt by women themselves as well as by men, as to whether women as a sex were physically and mentally fit for it. I think I can best make this clear to you if I refer briefly to my own experience. I cannot remember the time when I was not sure that studying and going to college were the things above all others which I wished to do. I was always wondering whereto it could be really true, as everyone thought, that boys were cleverer than girls. Indeed, I cared so much that I never dared ask any grown-up person the direct question, not even my father or mother, because I feared to hear the reply. I remember often praying about it, and begging God that if it were true that because I was a girl I could not successfully master Greek and go to college and understand things, to kill me at once, as I could not bear to live in such an unjust world. When I was a little older I read the Bible entirely through with passionate eagerness, because I had heard it said that it proved that women were inferior to men. Those were not the days of the higher criticism. I can remember weeping over the account of Adam and Eve because it seemed to me that the curse pronounced on Eve might imperil girls' going to college; and to this day I can never read many parts of the Pauline epistles without feeling again the sinking of the heart with which I used to hurry over the verses referring to women's keeping silence in the churches and asking their husbands at home. I searched not only the Bible, but all other books I could get for light on the woman question. I read Milton with rage and indignation. Even as a child I knew him for the woman-hater he was. The splendor of Shakespeare was obscured to me then by the lack of intellectual power in his greatest woman characters. Even now it seems to me that only Isabella in *Measure for Measure* thinks greatly, and weighs her actions greatly, like Hamlet or a Brutus. . . .

---

* From M. Carey Thomas, "Present Tendencies in Women's Education," *Publications of the Association of Collegiate Alumnae*, 3, February 1908.

But how vast the difference between then and now in my feeling, and in the feelings of every woman who has had to do with the education of girls! Then I was terror-struck lest I, and ever other woman with me, were doomed to live as pathological invalids in a universe merciless to woman as a sex. Now we know that it is not we, but the man who believes such things about us, who is himself pathological, blinded by neurotic mists of sex, unable to see that women for one-half of the kindly race of normal, healthy human creatures in the world; that women, like men, are quickened and inspired by the same great traditions of their race by the same love of learning, the same love of science, the same love of abstract truth; that women, like men, are immeasurably benefited, physically, mentally, and morally, and are made vastly better mothers, as men are made vastly better fathers, by subordinating the distracting instincts of sex to the simple human fellowship of similar education, and similar intellectual and social ideals.

It was not to be wondered at that we were uncertain in those old days as to the ultimate result of women's education. Before I myself went to college I had seen only one college woman. I had heard that such a woman was staying at the house of an acquaintance. I went to see her with fear. Even if she had appeared in hoofs and horns I was determined to go to college all the same. But it was a relief to find this Vassar graduate tall and handsome and dressed like other women. When, five years later, I went to Leipzig to study after I had graduated from Cornell, my mother used to write me that my name was never mentioned to her by the women of her acquaintance. I was thought by them to be as much of a disgrace to my family as if I had eloped with the coachman. Now, women who have been to college are as plentiful as blackberries on summer hedges. . . .

We did not know when we began whether woman's health could stand the strain of college education. We were haunted in those days by the clanging chains of that gloomy little specter, Dr. Edward H. Clarke's *Sex in Education*. With trepidation of spirit, I made my mother read it, and was much cheered by her remark that, as neither she, nor any of the women she knew, had ever seen girls or women of the kind described in Dr. Clarke's book, we might as well act as if they did not exist. Still we did not *know* whether colleges might not produce a crop of just such invalids. Doctors insisted that they would. We women could not be sure until we had tried the experiment. Now we have tried it, and tried it for more than a generation, and we know that college women are not only not invalids, but that they are better physically than other women in their own class of life . . .

We did not really know anything about even the ordinary everyday intellectual capacity of women when we began to educate them. We were not even sure that they inherited their intellects from their fathers as well as their mothers. We were told that their brains were too light, their foreheads too small, their reasoning powers too defective, their emotions too easily worked upon to make good students. None of these things has proved to be so. . . .

Anna Manning Comfort, *Only Heroic Women Were Doctors Then* (1916)

Even before the Civil War, a few women became doctors. Elizabeth Blackwell was the first woman in the United States to earn a medical degree in 1849. In 1857, she joined her sister and another female doctor and opened the New York Infirmary for Women and Children. Some years later they established the New York Medical College and Hospital for Women from which Comfort graduated. Comfort's testimony emphasized the vital role women's medical institutions played in providing women with an opportunity to practice medicine. Why were male doctors so resistant to women entering the medical profession?[*]

Changes in the position of women in the world of the last fifty years were emphasized by Dr. Anna Manning Comfort, graduate of the New York Medical College and Hospital for Women in its first class in 1865, at a luncheon in her honor, given by the Faculty and Trustees of the college at Delmonico's yesterday. Dr. Comfort was graduated at the age of 20, and she is only in the early seventies, alert and well preserved, though she has had a vigorous career, has been married, and is the mother of three children.

"Students of today have no idea of conditions as they were when I studied medicine," said Dr. Comfort. "It is difficult to realize the changes that have taken place. I attended the first meeting when this institution was proposed, and was graduated from the first class. We had to go to Bellevue Hospital for our practical work, and the indignities we were made to suffer are beyond belief. There were 500 young men students taking post-graduate courses, and we were jeered at and catcalled, and the 'old war horses,' the doctors, joined the younger men.

"We were considered aggressive. They said women did not have the same brains as men and were not trustworthy. All the work at the hospital was made as repulsively unpleasant for us as possible. There were originally six in the class, but all but two were unable to put up with the treatment to which we were subjected, and dropped out. I trembled whenever I went to the hospital and I said once that I could not bear it. Finally the women went to the authorities, who said that if we were not respectfully treated they would take the charter from the hospital!

"As a physician there was nothing that I could do that satisfied people. If I wore square-toed shoes and swung my arms they said I was mannish, and if I carried a

---

[*] From "Only Heroic Women Were Doctors Then," the *New York Times*, April 9, 1916.

parasol and wore a ribbon in my hair they said I was too feminine and if I smiled they said I had too much levity.

"They tore down my sign when I began to practice, the drugstores did not like to fill my prescriptions, and the other doctors would not consult with me. But that little band of women made it possible for the other women who have come later into the field to do their work. When my first patients came and saw me they said I was too young, and they asked in horrified tones if I had studied dissecting just like the men. They were shocked at that, but they were more shocked when my bills were sent in to find that I charged as much as a man.

"I believe in women entering professions," said Dr. Comfort, "but I also believe in motherhood. For the normal woman it is no more of a tax to have a profession as well as a family life, than it is for man to carry on the multitudinous duties he has outside the family. I had three sons of my own and two adopted ones, and I am as proud of my motherhood as of my medical career. I gave as much of my personality to my children in an hour than some mothers do in ten. My children honored me and have been worthwhile in the world."

There were many expressions of esteem for Dr. Comfort, and she was overcome when it was announced that money had been raised for an Anna Manning Comfort scholarship at the hospital.

Letters of regret were read from John Burroughs and Colonel Theodore Roosevelt among others.

"I believe in women in the medical profession, and in politics, and in all worthy pursuits," said John Burroughs.

"I am amazed to learn that this is the only institution in this State, and one of two in the United States, exclusively for the woman medical student," said Colonel Roosevelt. "There should be others, and women of refinement would be drawn into the profession who will not study medicine in a coeducational college, and more women doctors are needed."

Dr. Walter G. Crump, who spoke of the need for medical colleges exclusively for women, said:

"We learn from the [1910] Fexner report that there is an overproduction of doctors, but nine out of ten of the women doctors practice. There are demands continually for women physicians which cannot be filled. They are needed in many places where women and girls are to be under a physician's care."

Martha E. D. White, *Work of the Woman's Club* (1904)

> In this document Martha E. D. White described how the club movement helped shape public opinion. Even without the vote, club women successfully publicized community needs, and increasingly gained a political voice. What specific evidence does White offer about the way club activity shaped community life and influenced national policy?*

But even without the personal enlightenment that counts for so much, women's clubs have been a potent factor in determining public opinion. As organizations, they have realized that "in public opinion we are all legislators by our birthright." And in practice, they have found that they could actually legislate by means of this power. Legislative work is undertaken by all the state federations, in urging and securing the passage of laws that deal with the conditions of women and children. In Massachusetts, Connecticut, and Illinois, the state federations have promoted the passage of a bill giving joint and equal parental guardianship to minor children. The Juvenile Court Law has been secured in California, Illinois, Maryland and Nebraska. The Louisiana Federation has worked successfully for the Probationary Law, and in Texas an industrial school has been established. Laws to raise the standard of public morality, to segregate and classify defective and delinquent classes, to secure the services of women as factory inspectors, police matrons, and on boards of control, are other measures for which women's clubs have successfully worked.

But it is in the work for the extension of libraries that women's clubs have more fully demonstrated their ability to further an educational project. Many states in the Union have made no provision for the establishment of free libraries, and in others, where there is the necessary legislation, local conditions prevent their adequate establishment. Realizing keenly what a dearth of books means to a community, women's clubs have promptly initiated in many states systems of traveling libraries to satisfy the needs of the people until free libraries could be established on a permanent basis. In Oklahoma and Indian territory the federation collected one thousand volumes. These were classified and divided into fifty libraries, and each was sent on its enlightening pilgrimage. Kansas is sending to its district schools and remote communities 10,000 books divided into suitable libraries. The women of Ohio circulate 900 libraries; Kentucky is sending sixty-four to its mountaineers. In Maine the traveling library has become a prized educational opportunity. Its success has secured the appointment of a Library Commission and the enactment of suitable library legislation. This movement is extensive, and as an indication of what

---

* From Martha E. D. White, "Work of the Woman's Club,"*Atlantic Monthly*, 93, May 1904.

organized women can do, when the issue is concrete and appealing, it is significant. At a recent federation meeting in Massachusetts, no orator of the day made so eloquent an appeal as did the neat and convenient case of good books that invited our inspection before it should be sent to a remote community in the Tennessee Mountains. . . .

Six years ago the General Federation undertook to help solve certain industrial problems, notably to further organization among working-women; to secure and enforce child labor legislation where needed; to further attendance at school; and to secure humane conditions under which labor is performed. State federations have acted in accordance with the General Federation's plans to appoint standing industrial committees, procure investigations, circulate literature, and create a public sentiment in favor of these causes. In Illinois this indirect power was of much aid in securing a Child Labor Law. In other communities something has been accomplished by way of enacting new laws or enforcing existing ones, showing that organized women readily avail themselves of the chance for indirect service in promoting the intelligent efforts of the federations.

Grover Cleveland, *Woman's Mission and Woman's Clubs* (1905)

Former President Grover Cleveland's attack on women's clubs reflected an outpouring of anxiety over any activity that took women away from their domestic and maternal concerns. Cleveland considered motherhood to be part of the divine and natural order. His effort to link club membership with the destruction of family life and the nation's well-being typified conservative fears that any departure from their God-ordained roles would result in national ruin. How did Cleveland link the suffrage movement with the "club habit?" Why did he believe that club membership subverted "true womanhood?" In what ways were his views similar to those of John Abbott? What, if any, relevance, would his views have today? In view of White's summary of women's clubs' achievements, would it be more reasonable to argue that rather than being a "menace", clubs were a national benefit? *

---

* From Grover Cleveland, "Woman's Mission and Woman's Clubs," in *Ladies Home Journal* 22, May 1905.

The restlessness and discontent to which I have referred is most strongly manifested in a movement which has for a long time been on foot for securing women the right to vote and otherwise participate in public affairs. Let it here be distinctly understood that no sensible man has fears of injury to the country on account of such participation. It is its dangerous, undermining effect on the characters of the wives and mothers of our land that we fear. This particular movement is so aggressive, and so extreme in its insistence, that those whom it has fully enlisted may well be considered as incorrigible. At a very recent meeting of these radicals a high priestess of the faith declared: "No matter how bad the crime a woman commits, if she can't vote, and is classed with idiots and criminals and lunatics, she should not be punished by the same laws as those who vote obey." This was said when advocating united action on the part of the assembled body to prevent the execution of a woman proved guilty of the deliberate and aggravated murder of her husband. The speaker is reported to have further announced as apparently the keynote of her address: "If we could vote we'd be willing to be hanged." It is a thousand pities that all the wives found in such company cannot sufficiently open their minds to see the complete fitness of the homely definition which describes a good wife as "a woman who loves her husband and her country with no desire to run either;" and what a blessed thing it would be if every mother, and every woman, whether mother, wife, spinster or maid, who either violently demands or wildly desires for women a greater share in the direction of public affairs, could realize the everlasting truth that "the hand that rocks the cradle is the hand that rules the world."

There is comfort in the reflection that, even though these extremists may not be amenable to reformation, there is a fair prospect that their manifest radicalism and their blunt avowal of subverting purposes will effectively warn against a dangerously wide acceptance of their theories.

The real difficulty and delicacy of our topic becomes more apparent when we come to speak of the less virulent and differently directed club movements that have crossed the even tenor of the way of womanhood. I do not include those movements which amount to nothing more than woman's association or cooperation in charitable, benevolent and religious work, largely local in its activities, and in all its qualities and purposes entirely fitted to a woman's highest nature and best impulses. I speak more especially of the woman's clubs of an entirely different sort which have grown up in all sections of our land, and which have already become so numerous that in the interest of their consolidated management a "National Federation of Woman's Clubs" has been created. I speak also of the vast number of associations less completely organized, but no less exacting of time and attention, whose professed purposes are in many instances the intellectual improvement or entertainment of the women composing their membership. Doubtless in numerous cases the objects of these clubs and associations are shown in such a light and are made to appear so good, or at least so harmless, that a consceintious woman, unless she make a strong fight against self-delusion, may quite easily persuade herself that affiliated with them would be certainly innocent and perhaps even within her dictates of duty. The danger of self-delusion lies in her supposition that she is consulting the need of relaxation, or the duty of increased opportunity for intellectual improvement, when in point of fact, and perhaps imperceptibly to herself, she is taking counsel of her discontent with the humdrum of her home life. . . .

Woman's Danger of the Club Habit

No woman who enters upon such a retaliatory course can be sure that the man she seeks to punish will be otherwise affected than to be made the more indifferent to home, and the more determined to enlarge the area of his selfish pleasures. She can be sure, however, that cheerlessness will invade her home, and that if children are there they will be irredeemably deprived of the mysterious wholesomeness and delight of an atmosphere which can only be created by a mother's loving presence and absorbing care. She can also be certain that, growing out of the influence which her behavior and example are sure to have upon the conduct of the wives and mothers within the range of her companionship, she may be directly responsible for marred happiness in other households, and that as an aider and abettor of woman's clubs she must bear her share of liability for the injury they may inflict upon the domestic life of our land. It must be abundantly evident that, as agencies for retaliation or man's punishment, woman's clubs are horribly misplaced and miserably vicious.

To the honest-minded women who are inclined to look with favor upon such of these clubs as indicate beneficent purposes or harmless relaxation, it is not amiss to suggest that these purposes and characteristics are naturally not only of themselves expansive, but that membership in one such organization is apt to create a club habit which, if it does not lead to other smaller affiliations, induces toleration and defense of club ideas in general. It is in this way that many conscientious women, devoted to their home duties and resentful of any suspicion to the contrary, through apparently innocent club membership, subordinate their household interests, and are lost to the ranks of the defenders of home against such club influences and consequences as the unbiased judgment of true womanhood would unhesitatingly condemn. The woman is fortunate and well poised who, having yielded to whatever allurements there may be in a single club membership, can implicitly rely upon her ability to resist persuasion to additional indulgence, and can fix the exact limit of her surrender to its infatuation. It is quite evident that she ought not take the first step toward such membership before considering the matter with a breadth of view sufficient to take in all its indirect possibilities, as well as its immediate and palpable consequences.

Woman's Clubs Not Only Harmful, but a Menace

I am persuaded that without exaggeration of statement we may assume that there are woman's clubs whose objects and intents are not only harmful, but harmful in a way that directly menaces the integrity of our homes and the benign disposition and character of our wifehood and motherhood; that there are others harmless in intent, but whose tendency is toward waster of time and perversion of effort, as well as toward the formation of the club habit, and the toleration or active patronage of less innocent organizations; that there are also associations of women whose purposes of charity, religious enterprise or intellectual improvement are altogether laudable and worthy. Leaving this latter class out of account, and treating the subject on the theory that only the other organizations mentioned are under consideration, I believe that it should be boldly declared that the best and safest club for a woman to patronize is her home. American wives and American mothers, as surely as "the hand that rocks the cradle is the hand that rules the world," had, through their nurture of children and their influence over men, the destinies of our Nation in their keeping to a greater extent than any other single agency. It is surely not soft-hearted sentimentalism which insists that, in a country where the people rule, a decisive share in securing the perpetuity of its institutions falls upon the mothers who devote themselves to teaching their children who are to become rulers, lessons of morality and patriotism and disinterested citizenship. Such thoughts suggest how supremely great is the stake of our country in woman's unperverted steadfastness, and enjoin in the necessity of its protection against all risks and temptations.

The Real Path of True Womanhood

I am in favor of according to women the utmost social enjoyment; and I am profoundly thankful that this, in generous and sufficient measure, is within their reach without encountering the temptations or untoward influences so often found in the surroundings of woman's clubs.

For the sake of our country, for the sake of our homes, and for the sake of our children, I would have our wives and mothers loving and devoted, though all others may be sordid and heedless; I would have them disinterested and trusting, though all others may be selfish and cunning; I would have them happy and contented in following the Divinely appointed path of true womanhood, though all others may grope in the darkness of their own devices.

National Association of Colored Women, *Club Activities* (1906)

The following is an excerpt from an annual NACW report that documents African-American women's club activities. In an era when government provided nominal attention to the needs of poor blacks, clubs provided social services that sustained the lives of the community's most impoverished. What were some of the causes club women supported?

Women's Christian, Social and Literary Club of Peoria, Ill.

We, the Women's Christian, Social and Literary Club of Peoria, Ill. beg leave to submit the following report for 1905–1906: We have a membership of 15 active members and 7 honorary members. . . .Our motto is "For God and Humanity.". . . Last year we had a good school for the little ones, and did much good and realized $5.50 for the work. . . . We have seventeen pupils. We have donated to the Baptist Church $15 and to the A.M.E. Church $17 . . .Assisted 44 different persons. We meet every Monday afternoon. . . .

On June 28, 1906, we made arrangements to purchase 5 1/2 acres of land on which we will erect an industrial home and school for all ages of our people. This piece of land cost us $6000. It is a handsome place, and it is now laid out in 36 lots, thirty by one hundred twenty-five feet. After paying all expenses and $150 on the place, we will have left in the bank $5. Respectfully submitted, Mrs. Anna R. Fields, Founder and President.

Phillis Wheatley Home Association of Detroit

The Phillis Wheatley Home Association of Detroit, Michigan was organized in 1897, the object begin the establishment of a home for our aged colored women. In 1897 a few earnest women met . . . and they were without funds but each one contributed her mite and the Committee rented a building. Furnishings were solicited . . . applications were received and on our opening day seven old ladies were received in the Phillis Weatley Home. In 1901 the Phillis Wheatley Home Association was incorporated under the state laws, and seeing the necessity of having a permanent building, we purchased the property at 176 East Elizabeth Street at a cost of $4000, paying $1300 cash. We have at present 12 inmates. . . .We have 24 members, regular meetings are held every Tuesday evening. Cash receipts (from donations for the past two years, 1904–1906) includes $1847. Respectfully submitted, Eliza Wilson, President.

Sojourner Truth Club of Montgomery, Ala.

The Sojourner Truth Club of Montgomery, Alabama furnished a reading room, this being the only one of its kind available for colored people in our city. It has six tables, two bookcases, three sets of bookshelves, one and a half dozen chairs, stove pictures, floor coverings of linoleum, rugs, twelve to fifteen current periodicals, 300 or more books. The room is lighted by shaded incandescent lights. The librarian is hired and the hours are from 3 p.m. to 9 p.m. Back of the reading room we had recently furnished a club room with a small table, two dozen chairs, matting, rugs, curtains, stove and pictures. It makes quite a cozy appearance. A third room we hope to furnish is a kitchen. Here we hope to have cooking lessons given for the benefit of the public. All this is paid for by 25¢-per-month membership dues and fundraising affairs held by the club. They have also invited guest speakers, such as Dr. Booker T. Washington, W. E. B. DuBois and Kelly Miller. The membership is 29.

Frances Willard, *On Behalf of Home Protection* (1884)

Under Frances Willard's (1839–1898) leadership, the Women's Christian Temperance Union (WCTU) supported the effort for suffrage. Although WCTU women avoided the confrontational issues of gender equity involved in the crusade for women's rights, Willard directly linked the women's vote to the issue of home protection and temperance. Within this context, the vote became a means to extend a mother's protection of her sons to the maternal protection of the nation. Why would this argument for the vote be less threatening than those found in the earlier "Declaration of Sentiments?" *

Dear Christian women who have crusaded in the rum shops, I urge that you begin crusading in halls of legislation, in primary meetings, and the offices of excise commissioners. Roll in your repetitions, burnish your arguments, multiply your prayers. Go to the voters in your town—procure the official list and see them one by one—and get them pledged to a local ordinance requiring the votes of men and women before a license can be issued to open rum shop doors beside your homes; go to the Legislature with the same; remember this may be just as really Christian a work as praying in saloons was in those other glorious days. Let us not limit God, whose modes of operation are so infinitely varied in nature and grace. I believe in the correlation of spiritual forces, and that the heat which melted hearts to tenderness in the Crusade is soon to be the light which shall reveal our opportunity and duty as the Republic's daughters.

Longer ago than I shall tell, my father returned one night to the far–off Wisconsin home where I was reared; and, sitting by my mother's chair, with a child's attentive ear, I listened to their words. He told us of the news that day had brought about Neal Dow and the great fight for prohibition down in Maine, and then he said: "I wonder if poor, rum–cursed Wisconsin will ever get a law like that?" And mother rocked a while in silence in the dear old chair I love, and then she gently said:

"YES, JOSIAH, THERE'LL BE SUCH A LAW OVER THE LAND SOME DAY, WHEN WOMEN VOTE."

My father had never heard her say so much before. He was a great conservative; so he looked tremendously astonished, and replied, in his keen, sarcastic voice: "And pray, how will you arrange it so that women shall vote?" Mother's chair went to and fro a little faster for a minute, and then, looking not into his face, but into the

* From Frances Willard, "On Behalf of Home Protection," in *Women and Temperance* or *The Work and Workers of the Women's Christian Temperance Union,*(Hartford, Conn.: Park Publishing Co., 1884), 457–59.

flickering flames of the grate, she slowly answered: "Well, I say to you, as the apostle Paul said to his jailer, 'You have put us into prison, we being Romans, and you must come and take us out.'"

That was a seed–thought in a girl's brain and heart. Years passed on, in which nothing more was said upon this dangerous theme. My brother grew to manhood, and soon after he was twenty–one years old he went with his father to vote. Standing by the window, a girl of sixteen years, a girl of simply, homely face, not at all strong–minded, and altogether ignorant of the world, I looked out as they drove away, my father and my brother, and as I looked I felt a strange ache in my heart, and tears sprang to my eyes. Turning to my sister Mary, who stood beside me, I saw that the dear little innocent seemed wonderfully sober, too. I said: "Don't you wish we could go with them when we are old enough? Don't we love our country just as well as they do?" and her little frightened voice piped out: "Yes, of course we ought. Don't I know that? but you mustn't tell a soul—not mother, even; we should be called strong–minded."

In all the years since then I have kept these things, and many others like them, and pondered them in my heart; but two years of struggle in this temperance reform have shown me, as they have ten thousand other women, so clearly and so impressively, my duty, that I HAVE PASSED THE RUBICON OF SILENCE and am ready for any battle that shall be involved in this honest declaration of the faith that is within me . . .Ah, it is women who have given the costliest hostages to fortune. Out into the battle of life they have sent their best beloved, with fearful odds against them, with snares that men have legalized and set for them on every path. Beyond the arms that held them so long, their boys have gone forever. Oh! by the danger they have dared; by the hours of patient watching over beds where helpless children lay; by the incense of ten thousand prayers wafted from their gentle lips to Heaven, I charge you give them power to protect, along life's treacherous highway, those whom they have so loved. Let it no longer be that they must sit back among the shadows, hopelessly mourning over their strong staff broken, and their beautiful rod; but when the sons they love shall go forth into life's battle, still let their mothers walk beside them, sweet and serious, and clad in the garments of power.

Zitkala–Sa, *The School Days of an Indian Girl* (1900)

Founder and first president of the National Council of American Indians, Zitkala–Sa (1876–1938) described the pain of her disrupted identity. In the article that follows she describes how Americanization left her in a cultural void. Even though she was uprooted from her native beliefs, she failed to fully adapt to

American culture. How does this source add to our knowledge of power relationships between Native Americans and European Americans?[*]

The first turning away from the easy, natural flow of my life occurred in an early spring. It was in my eighth year; in the month of March, I afterward learned. At this ago I knew but one language, and that was my mother's native tongue. . . .

The Cutting of My Long Hair.

The first day in the land of apples was a bitter cold one; for the snow still covered the ground, and the trees were bare. A large bell rang for breakfast, its loud metallic voice crashing through the belfry overhead and into our sensitive ears. The annoying clatter of shoes on bare floors gave us no peace. The constant clash of harsh noises, with an undercurrent of many voices murmuring an unknown tongue, made a bedlam within which I was securely tied. And though my spirit tore itself in struggling for its lost freedom, all was useless.

A paleface woman, with white hair, came up after us. We were placed in a line of girls who were marching into the dining room. These were Indian girls, in stiff shoes and closely clinging dresses. The small girls wore sleeved aprons and shingled hair. As I walked noiselessly in my soft moccasins, I felt like sinking to the floor, for my blanket had been stripped from my shoulders. I looked hard at the Indian girls, who seemed not to care that they were even more immodestly dressed than I, in their tightly fitting clothes. While we marched in, the boys entered at an opposite door. I watched for the three young braves who came in our party. I spied them in the rear ranks, looking as uncomfortable as I felt.

A small bell was tapped, and each of the pupils drew a chair from under the table. Supposing this act meant they were to be seated, I pulled out mine and at once slipped into it from one side. But when I turned my head, I saw that I was the only one seated, and all the rest at our table remained standing. Just as I began to rise, looking shyly around to see how chairs were to be used, a second bell was sounded. All were seated at last, and I had to crawl back into my chair again. I heard a man's voice at one end of the hall, and I looked around to see him. But all the others hung their heads over their plates. As I glanced at the long chain of tables, I caught the eyes of a paleface woman upon me. Immediately I dropped my eyes, wondering why I was so keenly watched by the strange woman. The man ceased his mutterings, and then a third bell was tapped. Everyone picked up his knife and fork and began eating. I began crying instead, for by this time I was afraid to venture anything more.

But this eating by formula was not the hardest trial in that first day. Late in the morning, my friend Judéwin gave me a terrible warning. Judéwin knew a few words

---

[*] From Zitkala-Sa (Gertrude Simmons Bonnin), "The School Days of an Indian Girl," *Atlantic Monthly* 89, January–March 1900.

of English; and she had overheard the paleface woman talk about cutting our long, heavy hair. Our mothers had taught us that only unskilled warriors who were captured had their hair shingled by the enemy. Among our people, short hair was worn by mourners, and shingled hair by cowards!

We discussed our fate for some moments, and when Judéwin said, "We have to submit, because they are strong," I rebelled.

"No, I will not submit! I will struggle first!" I answered.

I watched my chance, and when no one noticed I disappeared. I crept up the stairs as quietly as I could in my squeaking shoes—my moccasins had been exchanged for shoes. Along the hall I passed, without knowing whither I was going. Turning aside to an open door, I found a large room with three white beds in it. The windows were covered with dark green curtains, which made the room very dim. Thankful that no one was there, I directed my steps toward the corner farthest from the door. On my hands and knees I crawled under the bed, and cuddled myself in the dark corner.

From my hiding place I peered out, shuddering with fear whenever I heard footsteps nearby. Though in the hall loud voices were calling my name, and I knew that even Judéwin was searching for me, I did not open my mouth to answer. Then the steps were quickened and the voices became excited. The sounds came nearer and nearer. Women and girls entered the room. I held my breath and watched them open closet doors and peep behind large trunks. Someone threw up the curtains, and the room was filled with sudden light. What caused them to stoop and look under the bed I do not know. I remember being dragged out, though I resisted by kicking and scratching wildly. In spite of myself, I was carried downstairs and tied fast in a chair.

I cried aloud, shaking my head all the while until I felt the cold blades of the scissors against my neck, and heard them gnaw off one of my thick braids. Then I lost my spirit. Since the day I was taken from my mother I had suffered extreme indignities. People had stared at me. I had been tossed about in the air like a wooden puppet. And now my long hair was shingled like a coward's! In my anguish I moaned for my mother, but no one came to comfort me. Not a soul reasoned quietly with me, as my own mother used to do; for now I was only one of many little animals driven by a herder.

Susette LaFlesche, *The Plight of the Ponca Indians* (1879)

An Omaha Indian, Susette LaFlesche (1854–1903) spent her childhood on a reservation. She devoted her life to documenting Native American suffering. Both in terms of cultural background and the extent of their victimization, Native American women's life experiences were vastly different from those of European-

American women. What particular "wrongs" does LaFlesche address? In what way is her account similar to that of Zitkala-Sa?[*]

I have lived all my life, with the exception of two years, which I spent at school in New Jersey, among my own tribe, the Omahas, and I have had an opportunity, such as is accorded to but few, of hearing both sides of the "Indian question." I have at times felt bitterly toward the white race, yet were it not for some who have shown all kindness, generosity and sympathy toward one who had no claims on them but that of common humanity, I shudder to think what I would now have been. As it is, my faith in justice and God has sometimes almost failed me, but, I thank God, only almost. It crushed our hearts when we saw a little handful of poor, ignorant, helpless, but peaceful people, such as the Poncas were, oppressed by a mighty nation, a nation so powerful that it could well have afforded to show justice and humanity if it only would. It was so hard to feel how powerless we were to help those we loved so dearly, when we saw our relatives forced from their homes and compelled to go to a strange country at the point of the bayonet. The whole Ponca tribe were rapidly advancing in civilization; cultivated their farms, and their schoolhouses and churches were well filled, when suddenly they were informed that the government required their removal to Indian Territory. My uncle said it came so suddenly upon them that they could not realize it at first, and they felt stunned and helpless. He also said if they had had any idea of what was coming, they might have successfully resisted; but as it was, it was carried rigidly beyond their control. Every objection they made was met by the word "soldier" and "bayonet." The Poncas had always been a peaceful tribe, and were not armed, and even if they had been they would rather not have fought. It was such a cowardly thing for the government to do! They sold the land which belonged to the Poncas to the Sioux, without the knowledge of the owners, and, as the Poncas were perfectly helpless and the Sioux well armed, the government was not afraid to move the friendly tribe.

The tribe has been robbed of thousands of dollars' worth of property, and the government shows no disposition to return what belongs to them. That property was lawfully theirs; they had worked for it; the annuities which were to be paid to them belong to them. It was money promised by the government for land they had sold to the government. I desire to say that all annuities paid to Indian tribes by the government are in payment for land sold by them to the government, and are not charity. The government never gave any alms to the Indians, and we all know that through the "kindness" of the "Indian ring" they do not get the half of what the government actually owes them. Its seems to us sometimes that the government treats us with less consideration than it does even the dogs.

---

[*] From Susette LaFlesche, "*The Plight of the* Ponca *Indians*," in *Daily Advertiser* (Boston) November 26, 1879, 4.

For the past hundred years the Indians have had none to tell the story of their wrongs. If a white man did an injury to an Indian he had to suffer in silence, or being exasperated into revenge, the act of revenge has been spread abroad through the newspapers of the land as a causeless act, perpetrated on the whites just because the Indian delighted in being savage. It is because I know that a majority of the whites have not known of the cruelty practiced by the "Indian ring" on a handful of oppressed, helpless and conquered people, that I have the courage and confidence to appeal to the people of the United States. I have said "a conquered people." I do not know that I have the right to say that. We are helpless, it is true; but at heart we do not feel that we are a conquered people. We are human beings; God made us as well as you; and are peculiarly his because of our ignorance and helplessness. I seem to understand why Christ came upon the earth and wandered over it, homeless and hated of all men. It brings him so much nearer to us to feel that he has suffered as we suffer, and can understand it all—suffered that we might feel that we belonged to him and were his own. . . .

Before the tribal relations were voluntarily broken up by the Omahas, my father was a chief. He helped make some of the treaties with the government. He had been acquainted with the last eighteen agents who have transacted the business for one tribe on the part of the government, and out of those eighteen agents four only were good and honest men. The following instance will show how these agents squandered the money of the tribe: about four years ago one of them, without counseling the tribe, had a large handsome house built at the cost of about five thousand dollars, at the expense of the Omaha tribe. The building was intended by the agent, he said, for an infirmary, but he could not get any Indian to go into it, and it has never been used for anything since. It is of no use to the tribe, but it was a good job for the contractors. The tribe is now endeavoring to have it altered, to use it as a boarding school for the Indian children.

I have been intimately acquainted with the affairs of the Poncas. The Poncas and the Omahas speak the same language and have always been friends, and thus I have known all their sorrows and troubles. Being an Indian, I, of course, have a deep interest in them. So many seem to think that Indians fight because they delight in being savage and are bloodthirsty. Let me relate one or two instances which serve to show how powerless we are to help ourselves. Some years ago an Omaha man was missed from one of our tribes. No one could tell what had become of him. Some of our people went to look for him. They found him in a pigpen, where he had been thrown to the hogs after having been killed by the white men. Another time a man of our tribe went to a settlement about ten miles distant from our reserve to sell potatoes. While he stood sorting them out two young men came along—they were white men, and one of them had just arrived from the East; he said to his companion, "I should like to shoot that Indian, just to say that I had shot one." His companion badgered him to do it. He raised his revolver and shot him. Four weeks ago, just as we were starting this trip, a young Indian boy of sixteen was stabbed by a white boy of thirteen. The stabbing took place near my house. The white people in the settlements around wondered that the

Indian allowed the white boy to stab him, when he was so much older and stronger. It was because the Indian knew, as young as he was, that if he struck a blow to defend himself, and injured the boy in defending himself, the whole tribe would be punished for his act; that troops might be sent for and war made on the tribe. I think there was heroism in that boy's act. For wrongs like these we have no redress whatever. We have no protection from the law. The Indians all know that they are powerless. Their chiefs and leading men had been to Washington, and have returned to tell their people of the mighty nation which fill the land once theirs. They know if they fight that they will be beaten, and they only fight when they are driven to desperation or are at the last extremity; and when they do at last fight, they have none to tell their side of the story, and it is given as a reason that they fight because they are bloodthirsty.

I have come to you to appeal for your sympathy and help for my people. They are immortal beings, for whom Christ died. They asked me to appeal to the churches, because they had heard that they were composed of God's people, and to the judges because they righted all wrongs. The people who were once owners of this soil ask you for their liberty, and law is liberty.

Ida Wells Barnett, *A Red Record* (1895)

An African-American journalist from Memphis, Tennessee, Ida Wells Barnett (1862–1931) witnessed the increased racial violence of the post-Reconstruction era. A leading civil rights advocate, she led a national crusade against lynching. In the following excerpt from her writings, Wells Barnett addressed the subject of interracial sexual relationships. She argued that these voluntary relationships served as the pretext for allegations of rape and subsequent lynching. What did Barnett mean by "true chivalry?" In what ways was white anxiety over interracial sexual relations linked to the colonial era Virginia statute that outlawed interracial sexual union?[*]

A word as to the charge itself. In considering the third reason assigned by the Southern white people for the butchery of blacks, the question must be asked, what the white man means when he charges the black man with rape. Does he mean the crime which the statutes of the states describe as such? Not by any means. With the Southern white man, any misalliance existing between a white woman and a colored

---

[*] From Ida Wells Barnett, *A Red Record* (Chicago: Donohue & Henneberry, 1895), 8–15.

man is a sufficient foundation for the charge of rape. The Southern white man says that it is impossible for a voluntary alliance to exist between a white woman and a colored man, and therefore, the fact of an alliance is a proof of force. In numerous instances where colored men have been lynched on the charge of rape, it was positively known at the time of lynching, and indisputably proven after the victim's death, that the relationship sustained between the man and the woman was voluntary and clandestine, and that in no court of law could even the charge of assault have been successfully maintained.

It was for the assertion of this fact, in the defense of her own race, that the writer hereof became an exile; her property destroyed and her return to her home forbidden under penalty of death, for writing the following editorial which was printed in her paper, the *Free Speech*, in Memphis, Tenn., May 21, 1892:

"Eight Negroes lynched since last issue of the *Free Speech:* one at Little Rock, Ark., last Saturday morning where the citizens broke (?) into the penitentiary and got their man; three near Anniston, Ala., one near New Orleans; and three at Clarksville, Ga.; the last three for killing a white man, and five on the same old racket—the new alarm about raping white women. The same programme of hanging, then shooting bullets into the lifeless bodies was carried out to the letter. Nobody in this section of the country believes in the old threadbare lie that Negro men rape white women. If Southern white men are not careful, they will overreach themselves and public sentiment will have a reaction; a conclusion will then be reached which will be very damaging to the moral reputation of their women."

But threats cannot suppress the truth, and while the Negro suffers the soul deformity, resultant from two and a half centuries of slavery, he is no more guilty of this vilest of all vile charges than the white man who would blacken his name.

During all the years of slavery, no such charge was ever made, not even during the dark days of the rebellion. . . .While the master was away fighting to forge the fetters upon the slave, he left his wife and children with no protectors save the Negroes themselves. . . .

Likewise during the period of alleged "insurrection," and alarming "race riots," it never occurred to the white man that his wife and children were in danger of assault. Nor in the Reconstruction era, when the hue and cry was against "Negro Domination," was there ever a thought that the domination would ever contaminate a fireside or strike toward the virtue of womanhood. . . .

It is not the purpose of this defense to say one word against the white women of the South. Such need not be said, but it is their misfortune that the. . . .white men of that section. . . .to justify their own barbarism. . . .assume a chivalry which they do not possess. True chivalry respects all womanhood, and no one who reads the record, as it is written in the faces of the million mulattos in the South, will for a minute conceive that the southern white man had a very chivalrous regard for the honor due the women of his race, or respect for the womanhood which circumstances placed in his power. . . .Virtue knows no color line, and the chivalry which depends on complexion of skin and texture of hair can command no honest respect.

When emancipation came to the Negroes . . . from every nook and corner of the North, brave young white women . . . left their cultured homes, their happy associations and their lives of ease, and with heroic determination went to the South to carry light and truth to the benighted blacks. . . . They became the social outlaws in the South. The peculiar sensitiveness of the southern white men for women, never shed its protecting influence about them. No friendly word from their own race cheered them in their work; no hospitable doors gave them the companionship like that from which they had come. No chivalrous white man doffed his hat in honor or respect. They were "Nigger teachers"—unpardonable offenders in the social ethics of the South, and were insulted, persecuted and ostracized, not by Negroes, but by the white manhood which boasts of its chivalry toward women.

And yet these northern women worked on, year after year. . . .Threading their way through dense forests, working in schoolhouses, in the cabin and in the church, thrown at all times and in all places among the unfortunate and lowly Negroes, whom they had come to find and to serve, these northern women, thousands and thousands of them, have spent more than a quarter of a century in giving the colored people their splendid lessons for home and heart and soul. Without protection, save that which innocence gives to every good woman, they went about their work, fearing no assault and suffering none. Their chivalrous protectors were hundreds of miles away in their northern homes, and yet they never feared any "great dark-faced mobs." . . .They never complained of assaults, and no mob was ever called into existence to avenge crimes against them. Before the world adjudges the Negro a moral monster, a vicious assailant of womanhood and a menace to the sacred precincts of home, the colored people ask the consideration of the silent record of gratitude, respect, protection and devotion of the millions of the race in the South, to the thousands of northern white women who have served as teachers and missionaries since the war. . . .

These pages are written in no spirit of vindictiveness. . . .We plead not for the colored people alone, but for all victims of the terrible injustice which puts men and women to death without form of law. During the year 1894, there were 132 persons executed in the United States by due form of law, while in the same year, 197 persons were put to death by mobs, who gave the victims no opportunity to make a lawful defense. No comment need be made upon a condition of public sentiment responsible for such alarming results.

Mary Church Terrell, *What It Means to Be Colored in the Capital of the United States* (1906)

Throughout her long life, Mary Church Terrell (1863–1954) was one of the nation's most outspoken advocates for civil rights. College educated and affluent, Terrell personally experienced the indignities of racial segregation. Her description of how Jim Crow segregation circumscribed her life and demeaned her identity provides testimony that for African-American women racism—not gender discrimination—was their primary oppression. What specific examples of discrimination does Terrell discuss? Why was the discrimination based on race rather than on class or gender?*

Washington, D.C., has been called "The Colored Man's Paradise." Whether this sobriquet was given to the national capital in bitter irony by a member of the handicapped race, as he reviewed some of his own persecutions and rebuffs, or whether it was given immediately after the war by an ex-slaveholder who, for the first time in his life saw colored people walking about like freemen, minus the overseer and his whip, history saith not. It is certain that it would be difficult to find a worse misnomer for Washington than "The Colored Man's Paradise," if so prosaic a consideration as veracity is to determine the appropriateness of a name.

For fifteen years I have resided in Washington, and while it was far from being a paradise for colored people, when I first touched these shores it has been doing its level best ever since to make conditions for us intolerable. As a colored woman I might enter Washington any night, a stranger in a strange land, and walk miles without finding a place to lay my head. Unless I happened to know colored people who live here, or ran across a chance acquaintance who could recommend a colored boardinghouse to me, I should be obliged to spend the entire night wandering about. Indians, Chinamen, Filipinos, Japanese and representatives of any other dark race can find hotel accommodations, if they can pay for them. The colored man alone is thrust out of the hotels of the national capital like a leper.

As a colored woman I may walk from the Capitol to the White House, ravenously hungry and abundantly supplied with money with which to purchase a meal, without finding a single restaurant in which I would be permitted to take a morsel of food, if it was patronized by white people, unless I were willing to sit behind a screen. As a colored woman I cannot visit the tomb of the Father of this country, which owes its slavery existence to the love of freedom in the human heart, and which stands for

* From *The Independent*, January 24, 1907, 181–86.

equal opportunity for all, without being forced to sit in the Jim Crow section of an electric car, which starts from the very heart of the city, midway between the Capitol and the White House. If I refuse thus to be humiliated, I am cast into jail and forced to pay a fine for violating the Virginia laws. Every hour in the day Jim Crow cars, filled with colored people, may of whom are intelligent and well to do, enter and leave the national capital.

As a colored woman I may enter more than one white church in Washington without receiving that welcome which as a human being I have a right to expect in the sanctuary of God. Sometimes the color blindness of the usher takes on that particular form which prevents a dark face from making any impression whatsoever upon his retina, so that it is impossible for him to see colored people at all. If he is not so afflicted, after keeping a colored man or woman waiting a long time, he will ungraciously show these dusky Christians who have had the temerity to thrust themselves into a temple where only the fair of face are expected to worship God, to a seat in the rear, which is named in honor of a certain personage, well known in this country, and commonly called Jim Crow.

Unless I am willing to engage in a few menial occupations, in which the pay for my services would be very poor, there is no way for me to earn an honest living, if I am not a trained nurse or a dressmaker, or can secure a position as teacher in the public schools, which is exceedingly difficult to do. It matters not what my intellectual attainments may be or how great is the need for the services of a competent person, if I try to enter many of the numerous vocations in which my white sisters are allowed to engage, the door is shut in my face.

From one Washington theater I am excluded altogether. In the remainder certain seats are set aside for colored people, and it is almost impossible to secure others. I once telephoned to the ticket seller just before a matinee and asked if a neat-appearing colored nurse would be allowed to sit in the parquet with her little white charge, and the answer rushed quickly and positively through the receiver—NO. When I remonstrated a bit and told him that in some of the theaters colored nurses were allowed to sit with the white children for whom they cared, the ticket seller told me that in Washington it was very poor policy to employ colored nurses, for they were excluded from many places where white girls would be allowed to take children for pleasure.

If I possess artistic talent, there is not a single art school of repute which will admit me. A few years ago a colored woman who possessed great talent, submitted some drawings to the Concoran Art School of Washington, which were accepted by the committee of awards, who sent her a ticket entitling her to a course in this school. But when the committee discovered that the young woman was colored, they declined to admit her and told her that if they had suspected that her drawings had been made by a colored woman, they would not have examined them at all. The efforts of Frederick Douglass and a lawyer of great repute who took a keen interest in the affair were unavailing. In order to cultivate her great talent, this young woman was forced to leave her comfortable home in Washington and incur the expense of going to New

York. Having entered the Woman's Art School of Cooper Union, she graduated with honor, and then went to Paris to continue her studies, where she achieved signal success and was complimented by some of the greatest living artists in France.

With the exception of the Catholic University, there is not a single white college in the national capital to which colored people are admitted, no matter how great their ability, how lofty their ambition, how unexceptionable their character or how great their thirst for knowledge may be.

A few years ago the Columbia Law School admitted colored students, but in deference to the Southern white students the authorities have decided to exclude them altogether. . . .

Not only can colored women secure no employment in the Washington stores, department and otherwise, except as menials, and such positions, of course, are few, but even as customers they are not infrequently treated with discourtesy by both the clerks and the proprietor himself. Following the trend of the times, the senior partner of the largest and best department store in Washington, who originally hailed from Boston, once the home of Wm. Lloyd Garrison, Wendell Phillips and Charles Sumner, if my memory serves me right, decided to open a restaurant in his store. Tired and hungry after her morning's shopping, a colored schoolteacher, whose relation to her African progenitors is so remote as scarcely to be discernible to the naked eye, took a seat at one of the tables in the restaurant of this Boston store. After sitting unnoticed a long time the colored teacher asked a waiter who passed her by if he would not take her order. She was quickly informed that colored people could not be served in that restaurant, and was obliged to leave in confusion and shame, much to the amusement of the waiters and the guests who had noticed the incident. Shortly after that a teacher in Howard University, one of the best schools for colored youth in the country, was similarly insulted in the restaurant of the same store.

In one of the Washington theaters from which colored people are excluded altogether, members of the race have been viciously assaulted several times, for the proprietor well knows that colored people have no redress for such discriminations against them in the District courts. Not long ago a colored clerk in one of the departments, who looks more like his paternal ancestors who fought for the lost cause, than his grandmothers who were victims of the peculiar institution, bought a ticket for the parquet of this theater in which colored people are nowhere welcome, for himself and mother, whose complexion is a bit swarthy. The usher refused to allow the young man to take the seats for which his tickets called and tried to snatch from him his coupons. A scuffle ensued and both mother and son were ejected by force. A suit was brought against the proprietor, and the damages awarded the injured man and this mother amounted to the munificent sum of one cent. One of the teachers in the Colored High School received similar treatment in the same theater.

8

Industrial Expansion and the Woman Worker: Gender and the Workplace

---

After the Civil War and through the early 1900s, rapid industrial and business expansion provided women with new opportunities to enter the workplace. Widening opportunity was not the same as equal opportunity: gender bias pervaded the workplace. Sex-segregated classifications limited choices, kept wages low and usually made advancement impossible. Race proved an even more formidable barrier and African-American women generally remained restricted to domestic and agricultural work. Although the west did not provide women with equal economic opportunity, labor scarcity and the need to increase population muted gender discrimination. In search of economic opportunity, single women as well as families made the hazardous journey west. Although teaching provided women with their most common employment opportunity, some single women became homesteaders. Mary Elizabeth Lease gained prominence as a Populist Party leader and countless other women also were actively involved in the agrarian protest movements of the late nineteenth century. Many white working-class women preferred factory work to domestic service and African American women filled the need for domestic labor. Within segregated school systems, better educated women found their best employment opportunity in teaching.

Educated white women entered the expanding fields of office work and retail sales as typists, secretaries and sales clerks. The invention of the telegraph and telephone opened additional areas of employment to women as telephone operators and telephone clerks. Expanded opportunity rarely translated into financial success. Segregated in low-paying fields, entry-level positions tended to remain permanent. Even when women performed work identical to that of men, their paychecks were approximately half that of their male counterparts.

The factory also was structured in accordance with cultural beliefs about gender. The garment industry was numerically dominated by women and, as was true even before the Civil War, paid women only a subsistence wage. Garment factories of the late nineteenth and early twentieth centuries undervalued woman's work. Throughout the industry, skills were divided up based on sex. Men entered skilled fields like tailoring and pattern making. Denied choice, women clustered in the lower paid area of sewing.

Labor protest and militancy drew sustenance from the ranks of native born and immigrant working-class women. Irish-born Leonora Barry criss-crossed the nation organizing for the Knights of Labor. From Mother Jones to Russian-Jewish garment workers like Rose Schneiderman, women played key roles in some of the era's most dramatic strikes. Labor militants' primary emphasis was on workplace activism and union organizing. Although the Knights of Labor had supported their efforts, the successor union, the American Federation of Labor resented women's presence in the workplace and generally refused assistance.

Although Susan B. Anthony lectured extensively on the link between the ballot, and economic independence, many women placed their faith in marriage and their husbands' ability to support and protect them. For such working-class women, the basic priority was to have their husbands secure a "family wage" that would allow them to devote their care to their families full time. Leonora Barry's deepest wish was that women would not have to practice a trade and could devote themselves completely to domestic roles. Dedicated to working-class men and children, Mother Jones was an outspoken opponent of suffrage. Not until the twentieth century would middle-class suffragists successfully cross class lines and forge an alliance with working-class women.

Susan B. Anthony, *Bread Not Ballots* (c. 1867)

Susan B. Anthony (1820–1906) led the suffragist effort to recruit working-class women during the post-Civil War era. She addressed these remarks to those women whose wages were their only means of survival. Anthony attempted to convince working women that the vote would give them a political voice and the means to greater economic security. What specific arguments did Anthony offer to prove that voting rights for working women would lessen capitalist abuse? Why did many working women believe "capital not the vote regulates labor"?[*]

---

[*] From Ida Harper, *The Life and Work of Susan B. Anthony* (Arno, 1969).

It is said women do not need the ballot for their protection because they are supported by men. Statistics show that there are 3,000,000 women in this nation supporting themselves. In the crowded cities of the East they are compelled to work in shops, stores and factories for the merest pittance. In New York alone, there are over 50,000 of these women receiving less than fifty cents a day. Women wage-earners in different occupations have organized themselves into trades unions, from time to time, and made their strikes to get justice at the hands of their employers just as men had done, but I have yet to learn of a successful strike of any body of women. The best organized one I ever knew was that of the collar laundry women of the city of Troy, N.Y., the great emporium for the manufacture of shirts, collars and cuffs. They formed a trades union of several hundred members and demanded an increase of wages. It was refused. So one May morning in 1867, each woman threw down her scissors and her needle, her starch-pan and flat-iron, and for three long months not one returned to the factories. At the end of that time they were literally starved out, and majority of them were compelled to go back, but not at their old wages, for their employers cut them down to even a lower figure.

In the winter following I met the president of this union, a bright young Irish girl, and asked her, "Do you not think if you had been 500 carpenters or 500 masons, you would have succeeded?" "Certainly," she said, and then she told me of 200 bricklayers who had the year before been on strike and gained every point with their employers. "What could have made the difference? Their 200 were but a fraction of that trade, while your 500 absolutely controlled yours." Finally she said, "It was because the editors ridiculed and denounced us." "Did they ridicule and denounce the bricklayers?" "No." "What did they say about you?" "Why, that our wages were good enough now, better than those of any other workingwoman except teachers; and if we weren't satisfied, we had better go and get married. . . . It must have been because our employers bribed the editors.". . . In the case of the bricklayers, no editor, either Democrat or Republican, would have accepted the proffer of a bribe, because he would have known that if he denounced or ridiculed those men, not only they but all the trades union men of the city at the next election would vote solidly against the nominees advocated by the editor. If those collar laundrywomen had been voters, they would have held, in that little city of Troy, the "balance of political power." . .

There are many women equally well qualified with men for principals and superintendents of schools, and yet, while three-fourths of the teachers are women, nearly all of them are relegated to subordinate positions on half or at most two-thirds the salaries paid to me . . .sex alone settles the question. . . .

And then again you say, "Capital, not the vote, regulates labor." Granted, for the sake of argument, that capital does control the labor of women. . . .but no one with eyes to see and ears to hear, will concede for a moment that capital absolutely dominates the work and wages of the free and enfranchised men of this republic. It is in order to lift the millions of our wage earning women into a position of as much power over their own labor as men possess, that they should be invested with the franchise. This ought to be done not only for the sake of justice to the women, but to the men with whom they compete; for, just so long as there is a degraded class of labor in the market, it always will be used by the capitalists to checkmate and undermine the superior classes.

Now that as a result of the agitation for equality of chances, and through the invention of machinery, there has come a great revolution in the world of economics, so that wherever a man may go to earn an honest dollar, a woman may go also, there is no escape from the conclusion that she must be clothed with equal power to protect herself. That power is the ballot, the symbol of freedom and equality, without which no citizen is sure of keeping even that which he hath, much less of getting that which he hath not.

Massachusetts Bureau of Statistics of Labor, *The Working Girls of Boston* (1884)

This document, part of a state of Massachusetts report on the conditions of labor, recounts the unhealthy living conditions of women workers, who barely made a subsistence wage. What factors led to the low wages of the vast majority of working-women? What were their living conditions like?[*]

The population of the city of Boston, according to the Tenth United States Census, in 1880, was 362,839; of this number 172,368 were males and 190,571 were females. The whole number of persons engaged in that year in all occupations was 149,194, the males numbering 110,313 and the females 38,881; out of this latter number of females employed in all occupations, there were, in round numbers, 20,000 employed in occupations other than domestic service, and these constitute the body of the working girls of Boston. . . .

In numerous cases. . . girls were found living for the sake of economy in very limited quarters, which could not be conducive to good sanitary conditions. In some instances, girls were found living in small attic rooms, lighted and ventilated by the skylight only; the furnishing generally consisted of a small single bed, bureau and chair, with no wardrobe, except one curtained in the corner. In other cases, girls were forced to content themselves with small side rooms without a chance for a fire, which in some cases was sadly needed. One girl had a small side room in the third story of a respectable house, but said she could not expect much more at the present cost of

---

[*] From "The Working Girls of Boston," in the Carroll Wright, *15th Annual Report of the Massachusetts Bureau of Statistics of Labor*, 1884, (Boston: 1889).

living; still others were reported as living together with other members of the family in a tenement of one back room and side bedroom; another, as one of 18 families in a single building with hardly the necessary articles of furniture; another, occupying the third story of a house which seemed the poorest on the street. On the other hand, girls were found living in large rooms, quite well and sometimes handsomely furnished, in some instances with side rooms adjoining, not perhaps because they could really afford such quarters, but because they preferred to economize in other ways, in order to have some of the comforts, in looks at least, of home.

In a few cases where girls reported their health as being poor, or not good, they also complained of the poor board provided, as well as of the unpleasant surroundings at home; one girl made the statement that her home was pleasant and healthy, but to the agent of the bureau, the reverse seemed to be the case, for the hall was dirty, the floor covered with a worn-out rag carpet, while the air was filled with disagreeable odors; the girl appeared to be in poor health, untidily dressed, and dirty. Another was found living in the upper story of a cheap tenement house, directly in the rear of a kerosene factory having a tall chimney that constantly puffed out thick black smoke, which, together with the offensive smell of the kerosene, forced the occupants always to have the kitchen windows closed. In another case, one of the girls said that she spent all her spare time and Sundays with her sister in another part of the city, as her home was very unpleasant and uncomfortable; she also said the Board of Health had visited the house last year and recommended many alterations, but she did not know whether they were attended to or not. Another girl was found living in four small rooms as one of a family of 12, in a house located very near a stable and having bad drainage. One other girl complained of the odor from the waterclosets in the halls, and said it was anything but agreeable.

In a house where a considerable number of girls are cared for, it was found that there was no elevator in the building, and some of the girls were obliged to go up five flights of stairs to reach their rooms, two or three girls being placed in each room; the upper story of the building was without heat, and in the winter was said to be like an ice house; radiators are placed at the ends of halls, and transoms open into the rooms, but these have no particular effect on the temperature of the rooms, and there are no other ways of heating; extra charge is made for rooms heated directly by the register, and even then such rooms are not always to be obtained, they being generally occupied, and there being but a few of them. . . .

Leonora Barry, *Investigator for the Knights of Labor* (1888)

The Knights of Labor was the nation's first major union. Established in 1869, the union began to organize women workers in 1881. Leonora Barry (1849–1930), a widow and former factory worker, led the effort to recruit women and reported to the Knights on the conditions of labor. Although dedicated to improving conditions for women, Barry's deepest commitment was not economic independence for women, but to have men earn an adequate family wage so their wives could assume full-time domestic roles.   What evidence does Barry provide about worsening conditions for women factory workers? *

During our stay at Minneapolis, I addressed two public meetings, visited the Woman's Local, whose numerical strength and progress in the work of Knighthood was sufficient evidence of the clear brain and honest heart of its members. From October 22 to 31, I filled an engagement under the auspices of D.A. 72 at Toledo, Ohio. There are two Locals of women in this city. A few are organized from the many industries in which they are employed, such as tailoring, knitting mills, box factories, pin factory, etc. The earnestness and activity of the officials of D.A. 72 will surely have its reward. After my address in Findlay, Ohio, a Woman's Local was organized. November 18 I delivered an address in Allentown, Pa. Here I found women employed in shoe, silk, shirt, stocking and cigar factories, none of which were organized, except about half of the three hundred employed in the silk mill. It is stated on good authority that of the eight hundred people employed in this factory, about one hundred and fifty are children under 14 years of age—another proof of the great need of a state factory inspection law in the Keystone State, many parts of which are known as the Europe of America by the products of its cheap labor. . . .

December 7 to 20—filled dates with D.A. 68 of Troy, N.Y. There is not a city in the Empire State, excepting New York City, which stands so much in need of thorough organization as Troy. Women are employed principally in manufacturing shirts, collars, cuffs and laundering, with one or two knitting mills. In the shirt industry, Troy has a governing influence throughout the State. This is also true of laundering. At the first inception of the Order in Troy, women flocked into the Order until their membership numbered thousands, but closely following their membership with the order, came the Ide's strike and lockout, with which all our members are familiar. Had the strike been successful, they might have remained members until disappointed in some other demand; its injudicious precipitation and consequent failure caused disruption in their ranks, although a faithful few still remain at the helm. . . .

On January 30 held a meeting of the hat workers in Brooklyn.

On February 10 held a public meeting in Harrisburg, Pa. One Woman's Local Assembly in the city, which was not as flourishing as it should be, owing, it was

---

* From "Report of the General Investigator," *Proceedings of the General Assembly of the Knights of Labor,* 1887.

claimed, to some injudicious and illegal action on the part of some men, officials at the time of its formation. . . .

On May 2 and 3 I was at Sandy Hill, N.Y., and from May 5 to 9 at Cohoes, N.Y. (D.A. 104). The unsuccessful termination of a strike in the Harmony Cotton Mills of that city caused the almost total disruption of the woman's organization; and it is a pity that such is the fact, as there is no city in the Union more in need of organized effort on the part of workingmen to protect themselves from wrongs that are suicidal to life, liberty and happiness. The effect of the employment of foreign labor, child labor, together with cutdowns and fines, the large number of married women who are obliged to seek employment to support their families owing to the inability, incapacity or dissipation of their husbands, is seen in the fact that in twelve years the reduction in the wages of the cotton operatives of Cohoes has been 45 percent by actual cut-downs—to say nothing of the injustice of holding back their earnings by shortage in measurement. And in these twelve years the amount of work required of the individual has been increased. The number of women employed in the six cotton mills, known as the Harmony Mills, and conducted by Garner & Co., is 1,617—married women, 500, single, 1,117—about 250 of whom as widow's children (321 from 11 years of age and upward). Notwithstanding the repeated and continuous efforts of the State Factory Inspector, through the conniving of parents and employers, the child-labor law is violated. The large number of women and children employed is owing chiefly to there being no work for men at living wages. Fines are reported to be excessively large. In the twenty-one woolen mills of Cohoes, the number of women employed is 2,449; children, from 12 years upward, 117.

The box-making industry of this city employs 100 women—married, 5; single 85; widows, 4; children, from 12 to 16 years; 25. In all three of these industries the prevalence of diseases among women is very great, being mostly of consumption and complaints peculiar to women only, brought on by constant confinement and close application to their work, defective sanitary condition and inability through small wages to secure sufficient home comforts. The effect of all this on future generations will be a progeny wanting in development and health of body and mind. . . .

Mary Elizabeth Lease, *Populist Crusader* (1892)

A political activist long before women received the vote, Mary Elizabeth Lease (1850–1933) was a leader in the populist farm-protest movement. In the Populist campaign of 1890, she traveled and lectured extensively throughout the state of Kansas. A fiery speaker, she was best known for her protest against capitalism's exploitation of farmers and laborers. Her views reflected the growing chasm between capital and labor that characterized late nineteenth-century industrial expansion. She was also a feminist with a strong commitment to voting rights for women. Why did Lease believe farm women joined the Alliance? What role did they play?

Yet, after all our years of toil and privation, dangers and hardships upon the Western frontier, monopoly is taking our homes from us by an infamous system of mortgage foreclosure, the most infamous that has ever disgraced the statutes of a civilized nation. It takes from us at the rate of five hundred a month the homes that represent the best years of our life, our toil, our hopes, our happiness. How did it happen? The government, at the bid of Wall Street, repudiated its contracts with the people; the circulating medium was contracted in the interest of Shylock from $54 per capita to less than $8 per capita; or, as Senator Plumb tells us, "Our debts were increased, while the means to pay them was decreased;" or as grand Senator Steward puts it, "For twenty years the market value of the dollar has gone up and the market value of labor has gone down, till today the American laborer, in bitterness and wrath, asks which is the worst—the black slavery that has gone or the white slavery that has come?"

Do you wonder the women are joining the Alliance? I wonder if there is a woman in this broad land who can afford to stay out of the Alliance. Our loyal, white-ribbon women should be heart and hand in this Farmers' Alliance movement, for the men whom we have sent to represent us are the only men in the councils of this nation who have not been elected on a liquor platform; and I want to say here, with exultant pride, that the five farmer Congressmen and the United States Senator we have sent up from Kansas—the liquor traffic, Wall Street, "nor the gates of hell shall not prevail against them."

It would sound boastful were I to detail to you the active, earnest part the Kansas women took in the recent campaign. A Republican majority of 82,000 was reduced to less than 8,000, when we elected 97 representatives, 5 out of 7 Congressmen, and a United States Senator, for to the women of Kansas belongs the credit of defeating John J. Ingalls. He is feeling badly about it yet, too, for he said today that "women and Indians were the only class that would scalp a dead man." I rejoice that he realizes that he is politically dead.

I might weary you to tell you in detail how the Alliance women found time from cares of home and children to prepare the tempting, generous viands for the Alliance picnic dinners; where hungry thousands and tens of thousands gathered in the forests and groves to listen to the words of impassioned oratory, oftentimes from woman's lips, that nerved the men of Kansas to forget their party prejudice and vote for "Mollie and the babies." And not only did they find their way to the voters' hearts, through their stomachs, but they sang their way as well. I hold here a book of Alliance songs, composed and set to music by an Alliance woman, Mrs. Florence Olmstead of Bulter

County, Kan., that did much toward molding public sentiment. Alliance Glee Clubs composed of women, gave us such stirring melodies as the nation has not heard since the Tippecanoe and Tyler campaign of 1840. And while I am individualizing, let me call your attention to a book written also by an Alliance woman. I wish a copy of it could be placed in the hands of every woman in this land. "The Fate of a Fool" is written by Mrs. Emma G. Curtis of Colorado. This book in the hands of women would teach them to be just and generous toward women, and help them to forgive and condemn in each other the sins so sweetly forgiven when committed by men.

Let no one for a moment believe that this uprising and federation of the people is but a passing episode in politics. It is a religious as well as a political movement, for we seek to put into practical operation the teachings and precepts of Jesus of Nazareth. We seek to enact justice and equity between man and man. We seek to bring the nation back to the constitutional liberties guaranteed us by our forefathers. The voice that is coming up today from the mystic chords of the American heart is the same voice that Lincoln heard blending with the guns of Fort Sumter and the Wilderness, and it is breaking into a clarion cry today that will be heard around the world.

Crowns will fall, thrones will tremble, kingdoms will disappear, the divine right of kings and the divine right of capital will fade away like the mists of the morning, when the Angel of Liberty shall kindle the fires of justice in the hearts of men. "Exact justice to all, special privileges to none." No more millionaires, and no more paupers; no more gold kings, silver kings and oil kings, and no more little waifs of humanity starving for a crust of bread. No more gaunt faced, hollow-eyed girls in the factories, and no more little boys reared in poverty and crime for the penitentiaries and the gallows. But we shall have the golden age of which Isaiah sang and the prophets have so long foretold; when the farmers shall be prosperous and happy, dwelling under their own vine and fig tree; when the laborer shall have that for which he toils; when occupancy and use shall be the only title to land, and everyone shall obey the divine injunction, "In the sweat of thy face shalt thou eat bread." When men shall be just and generous, little less than gods, and women shall be just and charitable toward each other, little less than angels; when we shall have not a government of the people by capitalists, but a government of the people, by the people.

Mother Jones, *The March of the Mill Children* (1903)

This is an excerpt from Mother Jones' autobiography. A labor radical, but neither a feminist nor a suffrage advocate, Mother Jones (1830–1930) spent much of her life actively involved in some of the nation's most dramatic strikes. Her deepest concern was to end the exploitation of children. To publicize the victimization of mill children, many of whom had missing fingers and other work-caused deformities, she led a march of child laborers from Philadelphia to President Theodore Roosevelt's home in Long Island, New York. Her activism contributed to protective legislation for children in Pennsylvania. Why did Jones hold capitalism responsible for the evils of child labor? In what ways does her criticism of capitalism express views similar to those of Lease?*

In the spring of 1903 I went to Kensington, Pennsylvania, where seventy-five thousand textile workers were on strike. Of this number at least ten thousand were little children. The workers were striking for more pay and shorter hours. Every day little children came into Union Headquarters, some with their hands off, some with the thumb missing, some with their fingers off at the knuckle. They were stooped little things, round shouldered and skinny. Many of them were not over ten years of age, although the state law prohibited their working before they were twelve years of age.

The law was poorly enforced and the mothers of these children often swore falsely as to their children's age. In a single block in Kensington, fourteen women, mothers of twenty-two children all under twelve, explained it was a question of starvation or perjury. That the fathers had been killed or maimed at the mines.

I asked the newspapermen why they didn't publish the facts about child labor in Pennsylvania. They said they couldn't because the mill owners had stock in the papers.

"Well, I've got stock in these little children," said I, "and I'll arrange a little publicity."

We assembled a number of boys and girls one morning in Independence Park, and from there were arranged to parade with banners to the courthouse where we would hold a meeting.

A great crowd gathered in the public square in front of the city hall. I put the little boys with their fingers off and hands crushed and maimed on a platform. I held up their mutilated hands and showed them to the crowd, and made the statement that Philadelphia's mansions were built on the broken bones, the quivering hearts and drooping heads of these children. That their little lives went out to make wealth for others. That neither state nor city officials paid any attention to these wrongs. That they did not care that these children were to be the future citizens of the nation. . . .

I called upon the millionaire manufacturers to cease their moral murders, and I cried to the officials in the open windows opposite, "Someday the workers will take possession of your city hall, and when we do, no child will be sacrificed on the altar of profit."

---

* From *The Autobiography of Mother Jones*, 3d ed. (Chicago: Charles H. Kerr Publishing Company, 1977).

The reporters quoted my statement that Philadelphia mansions were built on the broken bones and quivering hearts of children. The Philadelphia papers and the New York papers got into a squabble with each other over the question. The universities discussed it. Preachers began talking. That was what I wanted. Public attention on the subject of child labor.

The matter quieted down for a while and I concluded the people needed stirring up again. . . . I asked some of the parents if they would let me have their little boys and girls for a week or ten days, promising to bring them back safe and sound. They consented. A man named Sweeny was marshall for our "army." A few men and women went with me to help with the children. They were on strike and I thought they might as well have a little recreation.

The children carried knapsacks on their backs in which was a knife and fork, a tin cup and a plate. We took along a wash boiler in which to cook the food on the road. One little fellow had a drum and another had a fife. That was our band. We carried banners that said, "We want more schools and less hospitals." "We want time to play." "Prosperity is here. Where is ours!"

We started from Philadelphia where we held a great mass meeting. I decided to go with the children to see President Roosevelt to ask him to have Congress pass a law prohibiting the exploitation of childhood. I thought that President Roosevelt might see these mill children and compare them with his own little ones who were spending the summer on the seashore at Oyster Bay. . . .

The children were very happy, having plenty to eat, taking baths in the brooks and rivers every day. I thought when the strike is over and they go back to the mills, they will never have another holiday like this. All along the line of the march the farmers drove out to meet us with wagon loads of fruit and vegetables. Their wives brought the children clothes and money. The interurban trainmen would stop their trains and give us free rides.

We were on the outskirts of New Trenton, New Jersey, cooking our lunch.in the wash boiler, when the conductor on the interurban car stopped and told us the police were coming to notify us that we could not enter the town. There were mills in the town and the mill owners didn't like our coming.

I said, "All right, the police will be just in time for lunch."

Sure enough, the police came and we invited them to dine with us. They looked at the little gathering of children with their tin plates and cups around the wash boiler. They just smiled and spoke kindly to the children, and said nothing at all about not going into the city.

We went in, held our meeting, and it was the wives of the police who took the little children and cared for them that night, sending them back in the morning with a nice lunch rolled up in paper napkins.

Everywhere we had meetings, showing up with living children, the horrors of child labor. . . .

I called on the mayor of Princeton and asked for permission to speak opposite the campus of the University. I said I wanted to speak on higher education. The mayor gave me permission. A great crowd gathered, professors and students and the people; and I told them that the rich robbed these little children of any education of the lowest order, that they might send their sons and daughters to places of higher education. . . . And I showed those professors children in our army who could scarcely read or write because they were working ten hours a day in the silk mills of Pennsylvania.

"Here's a text book on economics," I said, pointing to a little chap, James Ashworth, who was ten years old and who was stooped over like an old man from carrying bundles of yarn that weighed seventy-five pounds. "He gets three dollars a week." . . .

I sent a committee over to the New York Chief of Police, Ebstein, asking for permission to march up Fourth Avenue to Madison Square, where I wanted to hold a meeting. The chief refused and forbade our entrance to the city.

I went over myself to New York and saw Mayor Seth Low. The mayor was most courteous but he said he would have to support the police commissioner. I asked him what the reason was for refusing us entrance to the city, and he said that we were not citizens of New York.

"Oh, I think we will clear that up, Mr. Mayor," I said. "Permit me to call your attention to an incident which took place in this nation just a year ago. A piece of rotten royalty came over here from Germany, called Prince Henry. The Congress of the United States voted $45,000 to fill that fellow's stomach for three weeks and to entertain him. His brother was getting $4,000,000 in dividends out of the blood of the workers in this country. Was he a citizen of this land?"

"And it was reported, Mr. Mayor, that you and all the officials of New York and the University Club entertained that chap." And I repeated, "Was he a citizen of New York?"

"No, Mother," said the mayor, "he was not." . . .

"Well, Mr. Mayor, these are the little citizens of the nation and they also produce its wealth. Aren't we entitled to enter your city?" . . .

We marched to Twentieth Street. I told an immense crowd of the horrors of child labor in the mills around the anthracite region, and I showed them some of the children. I showed them Eddie Dunphy, a little fellow of twelve, whose job it was to sit all day on a high stool, handing in the right thread to another worker. Eleven hours a day he sat on the high stool with dangerous machinery all about him. All day long, winter and summer, spring and fall, for three dollars a week.

And then I showed them Gussie Rangnew, a little girl from whom all the childhood had gone. Her face was like an old woman's. Gussie packed stockings in a factory, eleven hours a day for a few cents a day.

We raised a lot of money for the strikers, and hundreds of friends offered their homes to the little ones while we were in the city.

The next day we went to Coney Island at the invitation of Mr. Bostick, who owned the wild animal show. The children had a wonderful time such as they never had in all their lives. After the exhibition of the trained animals, Mr. Bostick let me speak to the audience. . . .Right in front were the empty iron cages of the animals. I put my little children in the cages and they clung to the iron bars while I talked. . . .

"Fifty years ago there was a cry against slavery, and men gave up their lives to stop the selling of black children on the block. Today the white child is sold for two dollars a week to the manufacturers. Fifty years ago the black babies were sold C.O.D. Today the white baby is sold on the installment plan. . . .

"The trouble is that no one in Washington cares. I saw our legislators in one hour pass three bills for the relief of the railways, but when labor cries for aid for the children they will not listen.

"I asked a man in prison once how he happened to be there, and he said he had stolen a pair of shoes. I told him if he had stolen a railroad he would be a United States Senator.

"We are told that every American boy has the chance of being president. I tell you that these little boys in the iron cages would sell their chance any day for good square meals and a chance to play."

The next day we left Coney Island for Manhattan Beach to visit Senator Platt, who had made an appointment to see me at nine o'clock in the morning. The children got stuck in the sandbanks and I had a time cleaning the sand off the littlest ones. So we started to walk on the railroad track. I was told it was private property and we had to get off. Finally a saloon keeper showed us a shortcut into the sacred grounds of the hotel, and suddenly the army appeared in the lobby. The little fellows played "Hail, hail, the gang's all here" on their fifes and drums, and Senator Platt, when he saw the little army, ran away through the back door to New York.

I asked the manager if he would give the children breakfast, and charge it up to the Senator, as we had an invitation to breakfast that morning with him. He gave us a private room and he gave those children a breakfast as they had never had in all their lives. I had breakfast too, and a reporter from one of the Hearst papers and I charged it all up to Senator Platt.

We marched down to Oyster Bay, but the President refused to see us and he would not answer my letters. But our march had done its work. We had drawn the attention of the nation to the crime of child labor. And while the strike of the textile workers in Kensington was lost and the children driven back to work, not long afterward the Pennsylvania legislature passed a child labor law that sent thousands of children home from the mills, and kept thousands of others from entering the factory until they were fourteen years of age.

Rose Schneiderman, *A Cap Maker's Story* (1905)

In this document, Rose Schneiderman (1882–1972) recounted her youthful experiences as a factory cap maker. A Jewish immigrant from Russia-controlled Poland, Schneiderman played a central role in the leadership of the National Women's Trade Union League. Having entered the factory at thirteen, Scheiderman had firsthand knowledge of and sympathy for the hardships immigrant workers endured in the garment industry. How did family circumstances propel Schneiderman into child labor? What does she mean by the remark that "I knew nothing about the country, so it was not so bad for me . . ."? *

My name is Rose Schneiderman, and I was born in some small city of Russian Poland. I don't know the name of the city, and have no memory of that part of my childhood. When I was about five years of age my parents brought me to this country and we settled in New York.

So my earliest recollections are of living in a crowded street among the East Side Jews, for we also are Jews.

My father got work as a tailor, and we lived in two rooms on Eldridge Street, and did very well, though not so well as in Russia, because mother and father both earned money, and here father alone earned the money, while mother attended to the house. There were then two other children besides me, a boy of three and one of five.

I went to school until I was nine years old, enjoying it thoroughly and making great progress, but then my father died of brain fever and mother was left with three children and another one coming. So I had to stay at home to help her and she went out to look for work.

A month later the baby was born, and mother got work in a fur house, earning about $6 a week, and afterward $8 a week, for she was clever and steady.

I was the house worker, preparing the meals and looking after the other children—the baby, a little girl of six years and a boy of nine. I managed very well, tho the meals were not very elaborate. I could cook simple things like porridge, coffee and eggs, and mother used to prepare the meat before she went away in the morning, so that all I had to do was to put it in the pan at night. . . .

I was a serious child, and cared little for children's play, and I knew nothing about the country, so it was not so bad for me as it might have been for another. . . .

* From Rose Schneiderman, "A Cap Maker's Story," *The Independent* LVIII, no. 2943, (April 27, 1905), 935–36.

Rose Schneiderman, *The Triangle Fire* (1911)

Rose Schneiderman made the following speech after the disastrous Triangle garment factory fire in which an estimated 146 immigrant women lost their lives. She expressed her outrage and dismay that the lives of factory workers were so unimportant that the owners had neglected to provide even minimal fire safety precautions. Why did she advocate collective action? How was her anger similar to that of Mother Jones?[*]

I would be traitor to these poor burned bodies if I came here to talk good fellowship. We have tried you good people of the public, and we have found you wanting. The old Inquisition had its rack and its thumbscrews and its instruments of torture with iron teeth. We know what these things are today: the iron teeth are our necessities, the thumbscrews the high-powered and swift machinery close to which we must work, and the rack is here in the "fireproof" structures that will destroy us the minute they catch on fire.

This is not the first time girls have been burned alive in the city. Each week I must learn of the untimely death of one of my sister workers. Every year thousands of us are maimed. The life of men and women is so cheap and property is so sacred. There are so many of us for one job it matters little if 143 of us are burned to death.

We tried you, citizens; we are trying you now, and you have a couple of dollars for the sorrowing mothers and daughters and sisters by way of a charity gift. But every time the workers come out in the only way they know to protest against conditions which are unbearable, the strong hand of the law is allowed to press down heavily upon us. Public officials have only words of warning to us—warning that we must be intensely orderly and must be intensely peaceable, and they have the workhouse just back of all their warnings. The strong hand of the law beats us back when we rise into the conditions that make life bearable.

I can't talk fellowship to you who are gathered here. Too much blood has been spilled. I know from my experience it is up to the working people to save themselves. The only way they can save themselves is by a strong working-class movement.

[*] From "Triangle Memorial Speech," in Rose Schneiderman and Lucy Goldmaite, *All for One*, (New York: Paul Erickson, 1967).

9

Progressive Era: Maternal Politics, Protective Legislation, and Suffrage Victory

Well-educated middle-class white women played a central role in molding progressive reforms. In part, their activism evolved from the women's clubs that were involved in community improvement and outreach to the poor. Reform impetus also sprang from women in the newly established settlement house movement. Sustained by a network of female friends, and committed to making social reform—not marriage—the central focus of their lives, settlement leaders became the caregivers of the nation's urban immigrants—they "settled" immigrants into their new environments and provided services from child care to citizenship classes. Settlement houses enabled college-educated women to participate in social work at a time when professional employment opportunities were limited.

Key settlement house leaders like Jane Addams, Florence Kelley, and Lillian Wald made advocacy of protective legislation for working women and children a major priority. In an era of unbridled capitalism and rampant industrialization, protective legislation sought to mitigate exploitation. With a background in factory inspection and settlement work, Florence Kelley supplied the data on women's working conditions that led to the landmark 1908 Supreme Court decision *Muller* v. *Oregon,* that upheld the right of states to pass protective legislation for women. Settlement house women also lobbied the federal government on behalf of child welfare. The result was the establishment of the Children's Bureau in 1912. Headed by Julia Lathrop, who lived at Hull House for many years, the bureau focused on achieving a ban on child labor and increasing federal funding for maternal and infant care.

Progressive reformers and affluent suffragists also promoted the unionization of working women. Recognizing common needs and areas of concern, some of the nation's wealthiest women, like Alva Belmont, crossed class lines to join immigrant women workers in an effort for the ballot, unionization, and improved factory conditions. Wealthy women helped to organize and support the Women's Trade

Union League (WTUL). The cross-class commitment to protective legislation helped transform a laissez-faire government into a government that assumed social responsibility.

Maternal politics and social reform were the dominant but not the sole current of women's activism. More radical women advocated alternatives to the centrality of motherhood and domesticity. To provide mothers with the time for more "meaningful" work, Charlotte Perkins Gilman promoted communal kitchens and nursery schools. Margaret Sanger began her crusade to make birth control available to the poor, and liberate women from unwanted pregnancies.

Progress toward voting rights inched along during the early 1900s. Increasingly, women gained the right to vote in school and municipal elections. As a region, the west proved most receptive to women's suffrage, and some state governments granted the vote in national elections. However, in general, women could not vote in national elections until 1920. Progressive-era female reformers struggled for the ballot as the means to gain social and moral reform, rather than as an expression of equal rights. Suffrage leaders no longer argued for the vote as a way to confront male political dominance. Leaders now described the vote as an extension of maternal concern, female moral authority, and women's traditional community involvement.

Suffragists, such as Anna Garlin Spencer, and male proponents of the vote, such as Eugene Hecker, both discredited and utilized the nineteenth-century assumption of women's separate domestic sphere. They emphasized that the expanding functions of government had entered the private realm of the home, making the older notion of a separate sphere obsolete. Yet, they also advocated voting rights for women on the grounds that their domestic and maternal roles made them ideally suited to participate in a government that was assuming the functions of child welfare, food and water safety, and educational and recreational needs.

The nineteenth-century feminists' equal rights agenda had continually provoked the outrage of advocates of women's domestic identity. The new argument for voting rights tied it to women's mission to better society and protect the vulnerable, and it attracted increasing support. Even the cautious Confederation of Women's Clubs could identify with the new emphasis on community-oriented priorities, and in 1914 endorsed suffrage.

During the 1900s, middle-class and elite suffragists successfully crossed class lines and recruited native-born and immigrant working-class women. Like Harriet Stanton Blatch, the daughter of Elizabeth Cady Stanton, they dropped the rhetoric of limiting the ballot to the educated. Within New York State, Blatch organized the Equality League of Self-Supporting Women. Working-class women like Mollie Schepps became part of an activist political coalition, concerned with voting rights and economic independence.

In direct contrast to this inter-class support, white suffragists distanced themselves from African-American women's effort to achieve the vote, in part because they were unwilling to alienate southern support. Jim Crow legislation blanketed the South, and the entire nation supported segregated social and economics institutions. Progressive reform had little to offer black women. African-American women who left the rural South for cities in the Northeast and Midwest, found that racial barriers excluded them fromoffice work and most types of factory work. Generally confined to domestic service, they benefited neither from protective legislation nor labor organizations. Although Mary Church Terrell and Ida Wells Barnett, two of the era's most prominent African-American spokeswomen, joined white supporters in a rare effort at interracial cooperation to organize the NAACP; the redress of racial injustice remained for the future.

The final phase of the suffrage movement occurred during the effort in World War I to make the world "safe for democracy." During the war, women worked in munitions plants, as street car conductors, and as postal workers. Nontraditional employment dramatically demonstrated the ability and willingness of women to move beyond their prescribed gender roles. The heightened emphasis on democracy and female participation in the war effort, helped create a conducive environment for the suffrage victory. President Wilson supported the Nineteenth Amendment in part in recognition of the female contribution to the war. However, peace was also a women's issue. Jeanette Rankin, the nation's first congresswoman from the pro-suffrage state of Montana, voted against the United States' entry into World War I. Despite criticism, Jane Addams also retained her commitment to pacifism. Carrie Chapman Catt joined Addams and other pacifist women in the organization of the Women's Peace Party. Unlike Addams, Catt put aside her pacifist convictions and supported the war. In 1931, Addams shared the Nobel prize for peace.

In the closing years of the struggle, suffragists waged extensive campaigns on both the state and national levels. Under Carrie Chapman Catt's leadership, membership in the National American Women's Suffrage Association (NAWSA) increased to two million, and NAWSA leaders secured President Wilson's support in 1916. The formation of a new suffrage organization, the National Woman's Party (NWP), in 1916, further drew national attention to the suffrage crusade. Led by Alice Paul, who borrowed from the protest strategies of the militant British suffragettes, NWP staged massive demonstrations, picketed the White House, hung banners to embarrass President Wilson. When arrested the women endured hunger strikes in prison. NWP's militance gained enormous media attention, and served to make the NAWSA appear more ladylike and acceptable in contrast. Suffrage gained congressional approval in 1919 and the requisite number of states ratified the Nineteenth Amendment in 1920.

Anna Garlin Spencer, *Women Citizens* (1898)

Anna Garlin Spencer (1831–1931) was a suffragist and an ordained minister. Anti-suffragists repeatedly argued that women's private domestic lives made them unsuitable for the ballot. Suffragists responded by demonstrating how government and the home (the public and private spheres) overlapped. What evidence does Spencer offer that women's domestic lives give them an ideal background for voting?[*]

Government is not now merely the coarse and clumsy instrument by which military and police forces are directed; it is the flexible, changing and delicately adjusted instrument of many and varied educative, charitable and supervisory functions, and the tendency to increase the functions of government is a growing one. Prof. Lester F. Ward says: "Government is becoming more and more the organ of the social consciousness and more and more the servant of the social will." The truth of this is shown in the modern public school system; in the humane and educative care of dependent, defective and wayward children; in the increasingly discriminating and wise treatment of the insane, the pauper, the tramp and the poverty-bound; in the provisions for public parks, baths and amusement places; in the bureaus of investigation and control, and the appointment of officers of inspection to secure better sanitary and moral conditions; in the board of arbitration for the settlement of political and labor difficulties; and in the almost innumerable committees and bills, national, State and local, to secure higher social welfare for all classes, especially for the weaker and more ignorant. Government can never again shrink and harden into a mere mechanism of military and penal control.

It is, moreover, increasingly apparent that for these wider and more delicate functions a higher order of electorate, ethically as well as intellectually advanced, is necessary. Democracy can succeed only by securing for its public service, through the rule of the majority, the best leadership and administration the State affords. Only a wise electorate will know how to select such leadership, and only a highly moral one will authoritatively choose such. . . .

When the State took the place of family bonds and tribal relationships, and the social consciousness was born and began its long travel toward the doctrine of "equality of human rights" in government, and the principle of human brotherhood in social organization; man, as the family and tribal organizer and ruler, of course took command of the march. It was inevitable, natural and beneficent so long as the State concerned itself with only the most external and mechanical of social interests. The

[*]From Anna Garlin Spencer, "The Fitness of Women to Become Citizens from the Standpoint of Moral Development," in Susan B. Anthony, ed. *History of Woman Suffrage,* (Indianapolis: Hollenbeck Press, 4: 1902), 308–309.

instant, however, the State took upon itself any form of educative, charitable or personally helpful work, it entered the area of distinctive feminine training and power, and therefore became in need of the service of woman. Wherever the State touches the personal life of the infant, the child, the youth, or the aged, helpless, defective in mind, body or moral nature, there the State enters the "woman's peculiar sphere," her sphere of motherly succor and training, her sphere of sympathetic and self-sacrificing ministration to individual lives. If the service of women is not won to such governmental action (not only through "influence or the shaping of public opinion," but through definite and authoritative exercise), the mother-office of the State, now so widely adopted, will be too often planned and administered as though it were an external, mechanical and abstract function, instead of the personal, organic and practical service which all right helping of individuals must be.

Insofar as motherhood has given to women a distinctive ethical development, it is that of sympathetic personal insight respecting the needs of the weak and helpless, and of quick-witted, flexible adjustment of means to ends in the physical, mental and moral training of the undeveloped. And thus far has mother-hood fitted women to give a service to the modern State which men cannot altogether duplicate. . . .

Whatever problems might have been involved in the question of woman's place in the State when government was purely military, legal and punitive, have long since been antedated. Whatever problems might have been involved in that question when women were personally subject to their families or their husbands, are well-nigh outgrown in all civilized countries, and entirely so in the most advanced. Woman's nonentity in the political department of the State is now an anachronism and inconsistent with the prevailing tendencies of social growth. . . .

The earth is ready, the time is ripe, for the authoritative expression of the feminine as well as the masculine interpretation of that common social consciousness which is slowly writing justice in the State and fraternity in the social order.

Jane Addams, *The Clubs of Hull House* (1905)

Jane Addams (1860–1935) pioneered the settlement house movement. She co-founded Hull House in an immigrant Chicago neighborhood in 1889. The clubs of Hull House provided social services and educational opportunities to working-class immigrant families. Living within the settlement house, college educated, affluent women like Addams gained firsthand knowledge of immigrant workers. Despite their elite backgrounds, these women were more open than most of their contemporaries to the needs and cultural backgrounds of immigrant working-class women and children. In what ways did the Hull House clubs promote the

Americanization of the immigrants? How did the clubs address the
needs of working women and children? *

The two original residents of Hull House are entering upon their sixth year of
settlement in the nineteenth ward. They publish this outline that the questions daily
asked by neighbors and visitors may be succinctly answered. . . . It aims not so much
to give an account of what has been accomplished, as to suggest what may be done by
and through a neighborhood of working people, when they are touched by a common
stimulus, and possess an intellectual and social centre about which they may group
their various organizations and enterprises.

The original residents came to Hull House with a conviction that social
intercourse could best express the growing sense of the economic unity of society.
They wished the social spirit to be the undercurrent of the life of Hull House, whatever
direction the stream might take. All the details were left for the demands of the
neighborhood to determine, and each department has grown from a discovery made
through natural and reciprocal social relations. . . .

The Jane Club

The Jane Club, a cooperative boarding-club for young workingwomen, had the
advice and assistance of HullHouse in its establishment. The original members of the
club, seven in number, were a group of trades union girls accustomed to organized
and cooperative action. The club has been from the beginning self-governing, without
a matron or outside control, the officers being elected by the members from their own
number, and serving for six months gratuitously. . . .

The club now numbers fifty members, and the one flat is increased to five. The
members do such share of the housework as does not interfere with their daily
occupations. There are various circles within the club for social and intellectual
purposes; and while the members are glad to procure the comforts of life at a rate
within their means, the atmosphere of the club is one of comradeship rather than
thrift. The club holds a monthly reception in the Hull House gymnasium.

The Phalanx Club

A similar cooperative club has been started by nine young men at 245 West Polk
Street, most of the members of which are members of the Typographical Union. The
club has made a most promising beginning.

The Labor Movement

The connection of the House with the labor movement may be said to have begun
on the same social basis as its other relations. Of its standing with labor unions, which
is now "good and regular," it owes the foundation to personal relations with the
organizer of the Bingery Girls' Union, who lived for some months in the House as a

*From Jane Addams and Ellen Gates Starr, "Hull House: A Social Settlement," in *Hull House Maps and Papers*, (Boston: Thomas Y. Crowell and Co., 1895), 207–230.

guest. It is now generally understood that Hull House is "on the side of the unions." Several of the women's unions have held their regular meetings at the House, two have been organized there, and in four instances men and women on strike against reduction in wages met there while the strike lasted. In one case, a strike was successfully arbitrated by the House. It is most interesting to note that a number of small and feeble unions have, from the very fact of their weakness, been compelled to a policy which has been their strength, and has made for the strength of their cause. In this policy it has been the privilege of Hull House to be of service to them.

Eight-Hour Club

After the passage of the factory and workshop bill, which includes a clause limiting women's labor to eight hours a day, the young women employees in a large factory in the near neighborhood of Hull House, formed an Eight-Hour Club for the purpose of encouraging women in factories and workshops to obey the eight-hour law.

The Working-People's Social Science Club

was formed during the first year of residence at Hull House, and has met weekly every since, with the exception of the two summer months. In the summer of 1893, however, owing to the number of interesting speakers to be secured from the World's Fair Congresses, the club met without interruption. The purpose of the club is the discussion of social and economic topics.

The Arnold Toynbee Club

meets at Hull House. The objects of the club are: (1) To offer lectures on economic subjects, (2) to ascertain and make known facts of interest to working people in the fields of economics and legislation, (3) to promote legislation for economic and social reform, especially to secure greater public control over natural monopolies.

The Chicago Question Club

meets in the Hull House Art Gallery at two o'clock every Sunday afternoon. The club was fully formed before it asked for the hospitality of Hull House. It is well organized, and each meeting is opened by presentation of two sides of a question. Occasionally, the various economic clubs meet for a common discussion. One of the most successful was led by Father Huntington, on the subject, "Can a Freethinker believe in Christ?" An audience of four hundred people followed closely the two hours' discussion, which was closed by Mr. Henry George.

The Nineteenth Ward Improvement Club

The Nineteenth Ward Improvement Club meets at Hull House the second Saturday evening of each month. The president is the district representative in the Illinois State Legislature, and one of the ward aldermen is an active member. The club is pledged to the improvement of its ward in all directions. It has standing committees on streetcleaning, etc., and was much interested in the efforts of the Municipal Order league to secure public baths.

The Hull House Women's Club

which now numbers ninety of the most able women in the ward, developed from a social meeting for purposes of tea-drinking and friendly chat. Several members of this club have done good work in street and alley inspecting through the Municipal Order League. The club has also presented to a public school in the neighborhood a fine autotype of Millet's *Knitting Shepherdess*, and hopes to do more in future for the art-in-schools movement. They have been active in the visiting and relief work which has taken so large a share of the energies of the settlement during the hard times. One winter they purchased a ticket to the lectures given to mothers in the Kindergarten College. One member attended each week, and reported to the club. They are in touch with some of the vigorous movements of the city, and have frequent lectures on philanthropic and reform questions.

Children's Clubs

Since its foundation, Hull House has had numerous classes and clubs for children. The fortunes and value of the clubs have varied, depending very much on the spirit of the leaders. An effort has always been made to avoid the school atmosphere. The children are received and trusted as guests, and the initiative and control have come from them as far as possible. Their favorite occupation is listening to stories. One club has had a consecutive course of legends and tales of chivalry. There is no doubt that the more imaginative children learn to look upon the house as a gateway into a magic land, and get a genuine taste of the delights of literature. One boy, after a winter of Charlemagne stories, flung himself half-crying, from the house, and said that "there was no good in coming anymore now that Prince Roland was dead." The boys' clubs meet every Tuesday afternoon at four o'clock, and clubs of little girls come on Friday. The latter are the Schoolgirls' Club and the Pansy Club, the Storytelling Club and the Kindergarten Club. They sew, paint, or make paper chains during the storytelling, and play games in the gymnasium together before they go home at five o'clock. A club of Bohemian girls, called "Libuse," meets every Monday, and studies the heroic women in history. The little children meet one afternoon in the week for advanced kindergarten work. There are various children's classes for gymnastics and dancing; and two children's choruses, of two hundred and fifty each, meet weekly under the direction of Mr. William Tomlins. Dinners are served to schoolchildren, upon presentation of tickets which have been sold to their mothers for five cents each. Those children are first selected whose mothers are necessarily at work during the middle of the day; and the dinner started with children formerly in the Hull House *creche*. While it is desired to give the children nutritious food, the little diners care much more for the toys and books and the general good time, than they do for the dinners. It has been found, too, that the general attractiveness performs the function of the truant officer in keeping them at school; for no school implies no dinner. The House has had the sympathetic and enthusiastic cooperation of the principal of the Polk Street public school.

The Paderewski Club

A club of twenty children, calling themselves the Paderewski Club, has had a year of instruction on the piano, together with Sunday afternoon talks by their teacher on the lives of the great musicians. Six of the most proficient have obtained scholarships in the Chicago Conservatory.

The Hull House Men's Club

holds a reception there once a month, and an occasional banquet. This club, which rents a room in the front of the building, is composed of one hundred and fifty of the abler citizens and more enterprising young men of the vicinity. Their constitution commits them, among other things, to the "cultivation of sobriety and good-fellowship."

Florence Kelley, *The Child, the State, and the Nation* (1905)

Affluent and highly educated, Florence Kelley (1859–1932) graduated from Cornell in 1882 and also studied in Europe. Active in the settlement house movement, Kelley was also one of the nation's foremost advocates of protective legislation for women and children. She lectured and wrote extensively on the need to end child labor, and also compiled extensive documentation of factory conditions. Arguing that childhood was the time for education and leisure, as was the case with other middle-class reformers, Kelley found it difficult to understand that child labor frequently was necessary for the immigrant family's survival. Aside from parental "greed," what other arguments are given for the abuse of child labor?[*]

It has been shown that children are working in their homes, in the streets, in commerce, and in manufacture; and it appears that there are divers economic and social causes for their work.

Chief among these causes of child labor is the greed of parents, due largely but not exclusively to poverty. Two cases out of the writer's acquaintance may illustrate the false ideals which underlie much parental exploitation of young children.

An Italian immigrant arrived in this country possessed of nothing beyond his wife, little son and daughter, and railroad fare to Chicago. In that city he rented one dark room in a tenementhouse and proceeded to pick up rags in the streets. His wife

---

[*]From Florence Kelley, *Some Ethical Gains Through Legislation* (New York, 1905), 58–66.

sorted the rags in the court of the tenementhouse with the help of the daughter; and the boy became a bootblack as soon as he was strong enough to make leather shine. The children never attended school, the compulsory attendance law being, at that time, wholly illusory. The father prospered, placed money in the savings bank, and in an incredibly short time began to buy, under a third mortgage, the house in which he lived. The court of the tenementhouse becoming too small for his work, he rented a vacant lot on which he stored rags, old iron and junk of all sorts. He never ceased to pick rags, and transferred the labors of his wife and daughter from their court to the new place of business, which he surrounded with a high fence. He completed the payments for all the mortgages upon the tenementhouse; continuing to the time of his death to live, with all his family, in the dark room which he had occupied on his arrival. He paid for the cornerlot upon which he conducted his business and made other investments. It was his ideal to leave his children a large fortune. But one day he trod upon a rusty nail, and with characteristic niggardliness, bound up his bleeding foot with one of his own rags. Lockjaw followed and he died, leaving to his now grown-up, illiterate son and daughter, one hundred and forty thousand dollars. This son, by drinking and gambling, dissipated the fortune in a few months, and the daughter disappeared into the sad obscurity of the Levee.

In the case of the second family, a young Bohemian, able-bodied and eager to work, brought his bride to this country, both filled with the hope of earning and owning a home. When the eldest child was eleven years old, the father was killed on the railroad, where he was at work as a section hand, and the home, half paid for, was lost by the widow. But she never wavered from the early ideal, and sent her eldest boy at once to work in a cutlery, were he riveted the wooden handles of knives, performing an entirely mechanical task adapted to his feeble intellect. The child was hunchbacked, feeble-minded and consumptive. When the mother was remonstrated with for exposing him to the fatigue and danger attending his work among wood-dust and steel filings, her reply was: "Him no good. Him work, send Valeria and Bocumil school, buy house, them some good." For years, the factory inspectors of the state, and the local school officer, after the enactment of the compulsory attendance law, endeavored to free the unfortunate boy from his deadly occupation. The mother made whatever affidavits might be necessary from time to time, to enable him to continue, and relentlessly sent his brother and sister to work at the earliest moment possible. When last seen, she was rising at three o'clock in the morning to dig onions for a pickle factory in the outskirts of the city; the daughter Valeria, ten years old, was working from dawn to dusk throughout the summer, sorting onions; the cripple was dying of overwork and neglect; and the other boy, Bocumil, originally healthy, had become deformed from beginning too early to carry boards on his back in a furniture factory.

The widow, however, regarded herself and was regarded by her approving pastor as a model of thrift, because she had bought and partially paid for a tiny frame cottage, on the prairie, far from any school, in the immediate neighborhood of the pickle factory. She will ever know that she has lost for her children all the best things that America offers to the immigrant child, in the life of the public schools. Fortunately, the recently enacted stringent laws will make it impossible for other children coming to Chicago to be deprived, by the false ideals of their parents, of those precious possessions of child life in America: leisure and school.

A second cause of child labor is the greed of employers for cheap labor, enhanced by every improvement in machinery of the kind that makes the work of children available; and enhanced, also, by the very cheapness of the children, to such an extent as to delay the introduction of new machinery if its installation is costly. This greed is exhibited in its most odious form in the glass industry, the textile industry, and the sweating system. It knows no restraints except those of effective legislation enforced by enlightened public opinion, as is shown by the action of those Northern cotton mill men who obey the laws of Massachusetts and New York in their mills in those states, but in Georgia fall to the level of their local competitors, employing children ten years old and less, throughout eleven hours a day.

A third cause of child labor is the greed of the community in desiring to keep down the cost of maintenance of its dependent class. This greed disguises itself under the form of solicitude for the moral welfare of the children. Just as the managers of the worst so-called reformatories insist that children must work under the contract system, "because they must be kept busy to keep them from being bad," so this solicitude for childish morals insists that "children must not be habituated to dependence," quite forgetting that dependence is the quality bestowed upon childhood as its distinguishing characteristic. . . .

The insistent plea that children must work in order that they may acquire habits of thrift and attain prosperity for themselves and their families, is uttered with greatest persistence by the employers who profit by the labor of the children. It is the glass manufacturers who voice this tender solicitude for the moral well-being of the wage-earning children in New Jersey and Pennsylvania, when there is a growing movement in those states for prohibiting night work, as it has been prohibited in Illinois. In the South, it is the cotton mill owners and their legal advisors who insist that little children from the mountain farms must toil eleven hours in the mills of Georgia, working throughout the night whenever it may be useful to their employers to have them do so.

These pleas are heard with willing ears by communities which begrudge money for the maintenance of schools and the assistance of dependent widows and orphans; and not without good reason. No sooner had the new law of New Jersey required children to attend school to the fourteenth birthday, and prohibited boys under that age from working in manufacture, than it became necessary to build a new schoolhouse in a suburb of Millville, to accommodate the boys turned out of the glassworks. In Alton the enforcement of the child labor law of 1893 led to the immediate construction of a new schoolhouse for the children freed from the glassworks, and to the reopening of a building which had long been out of use. Wherever children are freed from work, the community must provide for them schools, teachers, attendance agents, factory inspectors and all those officials and provisions which are essential to the care and defense of childhood under the pressure of the competitive system. . . .

Muller v. Oregon (1908)

In this landmark decision, the U.S. Supreme Court upheld the right of the state of Oregon to establish the maximum hours for women employees. Florence Kelley helped gather the data about factory conditions used by attorney Louis Brandeis (later appointed to the Supreme Court by Woodrow Wilson). A major victory for protective legislation, the decision later stirred enormous controversy. Feminist critics charged that "protection" caused women more damage than good. Social reformers and many workingwomen argued the reverse. What factors influenced the court's decision? What role did women's maternal function play? Given the exploitive conditions of the early twentieth century, and the hostile or indifferent attitude of the American Federation of Labor toward women workers, was protective legislation necessary or were there other viable solutions? *

Delivered by Mr. Justice Brewer, February 24, 1908

That woman's physical structure and the performance of maternal functions place her at a disadvantage in the struggle for subsistence is obvious. This is especially true when the burdens of motherhood are upon her. Even when they are not, by abundant testimony of the medical fraternity, continuance for a long time on her feet at work, repeating this from day to day, tends to injurious effects upon the body, and as healthy mothers are essential to vigorous offspring, the physical well-being of women becomes an object of public interest and care in order to preserve the strength and vigor of the race.

Still again, history discloses the fact that woman has always been dependent upon man. He established his control at the outset by superior physical strength, and this control in various forms, with diminishing intensity, has continued to the present. As minors, though not to the same extent, she has been looked upon in the courts as needing especial care that her rights may be preserved. Education was long denied her, and while now the doors of the schoolroom are opened and her opportunities for acquiring knowledge are great, yet even with that and the consequent increase of capacity for business affairs, it is still true that in the struggle for subsistence she is not an equal competitor with her brother. Though limitations upon personal and contractual rights may be removed by legislation, there is that in her disposition and habits of life which will operate against a full assertion of those rights. She will still be where some legislation to protect her seems necessary to secure a real equality of

---

*From *Muller v. State of Oregon*, Supreme Court of the United States, 1907, 208 U.S. 412.

right. Doubtless there are individual exceptions, and there are many respects in which she has an advantage over him; but looking at it from the viewpoint of the effort to maintain an independent position in life, she is not upon an equality. Differentiated by these matters from the other sex, she is properly placed in a class by herself, and legislation designed for her protection may be sustained, even when like legislation is not necessary for men and could not be sustained. It is impossible to close one's eyes to the fact that she still looks to her brother and depends upon him. Even though all restrictions on political, personal, and contractual rights were taken away, and she stood, so far as statutes are concerned, upon an absolutely equal plane with him, it would still be true that she is so constituted that she will rest upon and look to him for protection; that her physical structure and a proper discharge of her maternal functions—having in view not merely her own health, but the well-being of the race—justify legislation to protect her from the greed as well as the passion of man. The limitations which this statute places upon her contractual powers, upon her right to agree with her employer as to the time she shall labor, are not imposed solely for her benefit, but also largely for the benefit of all. Many words cannot make this plainer. The two sexes differ in structure of body, in the functions to be performed by each, in the amount of physical strength, in the capacity for long-continued labor, particularly when done standing, the influence of vigorous health upon the future well-being of the race, the self-reliance which enables one to assert full rights, and in the capacity to maintain the struggle for subsistence. This difference justifies a difference in legislation and upholds that which is designed to compensate for some of the burdens which rest upon her.

We have not referred in this discussion to the denial of the elective franchise in the State of Oregon, for while that may disclose a lack of political equity in all things with her brother, that is not of itself decisive. The reason runs deeper, and rests in the inherent difference between the two sexes, and in the different functions in life which they perform.

For these reasons, and without questioning in any respect the decision in *Lochner v. New York*, we are of the opinion that it cannot be adjudged that the act in question is in conflict with the Federal Constitution, so far as it respects the work of a female in a laundry, and the judgment of the Supreme Court of Oregon is

Affirmed.

National Women's Trade Union League, *Legislative Goals* (1911)

The following document outlines the protective legislation goals of the National Women's Trade Union League (WTUL). Affluent female reformers helped factory women organize the WTUL in

1903, during an American Federation of Labor (AFL) convention. Although AFL leaders recognized the WTUL, they offered little assistance to women workers. To further protect women workers, WTUL leaders promoted the establishment of the Women's Bureau of the Department of Labor. How would the second objective of WTUL's legislative goals affect women employees in ways that could be damaging as well as helpful? *

1. The eight hour day.

2. Elimination of night work.

3. Protected machinery.

4. Sanitary workshops.

5. Separate toilet rooms.

6. Seats for women and permission for their use when the work allows.

7. Prohibition of the employment of pregnant women two months before and after child-birth.

8. Pensions for working mothers during the lying-in period.

9. Factory inspection laws which make possible the enforcement of labor laws. An increased number of women inspectors. . . . and the inspectors to be men and women with a practical knowledge of the work, under civil service.

10. In the states where women workers are to be examined for physical fitness, women physicians to be employed.

11. A minimum wage commission to create wage boards for each industry; having an equal representation of employers and workers and representation from the public.

12. To provide adequate fire protection in factories, stores and offices, including compulsory fire drills.

13. Employers' Liability Law and compensation for industrial accidents.

14. Banking laws for the protection of the savings of workers. Weekly payment of wages, and prohibition of payment of wages by check.

15. Control and supervision of employment agencies, and abolition of the vampire system.

---

*From Gladys Boone, *The Women's Trade Union Leagues in Great Britain and the United States of America* (New York: Columbia University Press, 1911), 113–14.

16. The enactment of a law making it compulsory . . . when advertising for employees in time of strike, to state in such advertisement that a strike is going on.

17. The initiative, referendum and recall.

18. Amendment to the child labor law that the certificate of employment shall not be granted unless the child has passed an examination in the labor laws of the State.

Eugene Hecker, *General Considerations on Women's Rights* (1910)

From the inception of the organized women's movement at Seneca Falls, some men supported women's rights. Without the support of male voters the suffrage victory could not have occurred. The excerpt here is from Eugene Hecker's book written on behalf of women's rights. How did Hecker dismiss the argument that participation in politics would degrade women? What evidence did he offer that the role of the home and government overlapped? Why would this be an important pro-suffrage point? *

"The home is woman's sphere." This shibboleth is the logical result of the attitude mentioned. Doubtless, the home is women's sphere; but the home includes all that pertains to it—city, politics and taxes, laws relating to the protection of minors, municipal rottenness which may corrupt children, schools and playgrounds and museums which may educate them. Few doctrines have been productive of more pain than the "woman's sphere" argument. It is this which has, for a thousand years, made the unmarried woman, the *Old Maid*, the butt of the contemptible jibes of Christian society, whereof you will find no parallel in pagan antiquity. Dramatic writers have held her up to ridicule on the stage, on account of the peculiarities of character which are naturally acquired when a person is isolated from participation in the activities of life. It is the doctrine which has made women glad to marry drunkards and rakes, to bring forth children tainted with the sins of their fathers, and to suffer hell on earth rather than incur the ridicule of the Christian gentleman, who may, without incurring the protest of society, remain unmarried and sow an unlimited quantity of wild oats. It is this doctrine which was indirectly responsible for the hanging and burning of

---

*From Eugene A. Hecker, *A Short History of Women's Rights* (New York: The Knickerbocker Press, 1910), 246–47.

eccentric old women on the charge that they were witches. As men found a divine sanction for keeping women in subjugation, so in those days of superstition did they blaspheme their Creator by digging out of the Old Testament as a justification for their brutality, the text, "Thou shall not suffer a witch to live."

"Politics will degrade women"—this naive confession that politics are rotten is a fairly strong argument that some good influence is needed to make them cleaner. Generally speaking, it is difficult to imagine how politics could be made any worse. If a woman cannot get to the polls or hold office without being insulted by the rowdies, her vote will be potent to elect officials who should be able to secure for the community a standard of reasonable civilization. There is no case in which more sentimentality is wasted. A lovely woman is urged not to allow her beauty, her gentleness, her tender submissiveness to become the butt of the lounger at the street corner; and in most instances a lovely woman, like the celebrated Maitre Corbeau, is cajoled effectively. Meanwhile the brothel and the sweatshop continue on their prosperous way. By a curious inconsistency, man will permit woman to help him out of a political dilemma, and will then suavely remark that suffrage will degrade her.

During the Civil War, Anna Dickinson, by her remarkable lecture entitled, "The National Crisis," saved New Hampshire and Connecticut for the Republicans; Anna Carroll not only gave such a crushing rejoinder to Breckinridge's secession speech that the government printed and distributed it, but she also, as is now generally believed, planned the campaign which led to the fall of Forts Henry and Donelson and opened the Mississippi to Vicksburg. How many men realize these facts?

Anna Howard Shaw, *NAWSA Convention Speech* (1913)

In addition to playing a central role in the suffrage movement and serving as NAWSA president from 1904 to 1915, Anna Howard Shaw (1847–1919) was also a medical doctor and Protestant minister. In the following speech, she ridiculed gender stereotyping. Anti-suffrage advocates repeatedly argued that men were born leaders, purposeful and rational in contrast to women who were too emotional to vote. Shaw described the behavior of men at the Democratic National Convention. What evidence does Shaw provide of men's hysterical and emotional behavior? *

---

*From Anna Howard Shaw, "Remarks on Emotionalism in Politics Given at the National American Women Suffrage Association Convention in 1913," in *History of Woman Suffrage*, Susan B. Anthony, ed. (Indianapolis: Hollenbeck Press: 1920), 5.

By some objectors women are supposed to be unfit to vote because they are hysterical and emotional, and of course men would not like to have emotion enter into a political campaign. They want to cut out all emotion and so they would like to cut us out. I had heard so much about our emotionalism that I went to the last Democratic National Convention, held at Baltimore, to observe the calm repose of the male politicians. I saw some men take a picture of one gentleman whom they wanted elected, and it was so big they had to walk sidewise as they carried it forward; they were followed by hundreds of other men screaming and yelling, shouting and singing the "Houn' Dawg;" then, when there was a lull, another set of men would start forward under another man's picture, not to be outdone by the "Houn' Dawg" melody, whooping and howling still louder. I saw men jump up on the seats and throw their hats in the air and shout: "What's the matter with Champ Clark?" Then when those hats came down, other men would kick them back in the air, shouting at the top of their voices: "He's all right!!" Then I heard others howling for "Underwood, Underwood, first, last and all the time!!" No hysteria about it—just patriotic loyalty, splendid manly devotion to principle. And so they went on and on until 5 o'clock in the morning—the whole night long. I saw men jump up on their seats and jump down again and run around in a ring. I saw two men turn towards another man to hug him both at once, and they split his coat up the middle of his back and sent him spinning around like a wheel. All this with the perfect poise of the legal male mind in politics!

I have been to many women's conventions in my day, but I never saw a woman leap up on a chair and take off her bonnet and toss it up in the air and shout: "What's the matter with" somebody. I never saw a woman knock another woman's bonnet off her head as she screamed: "She's all right!" I never heard a body of women whooping and yelling for five minutes when somebody's name was mentioned in the convention. But we are willing to admit that we are emotional. I have actually seen women stand up and wave their handkerchiefs. I have even seen them take hold of hands and sing, "Blest be the tie that binds." Nobody denies that women are excitable. Still, when I hear how emotional and how excitable we are, I cannot help seeing in my mind's eye the fine repose and dignity of this Baltimore and other political conventions I have attended!

Mollie Schepps, *Senators v. Working Women* (1912)

Working-class women like Mollie Schepps increasingly supported the suffrage effort. In the following address Schepps responded to the New York legislature's refusal to amend state suffrage requirements to include women. For Schepps and other poorly paid women workers, the vote represented the key to political recognition and the means to achieve higher wages and safer working conditions. What evidence does Schepps cite about working women's political powerlessness? Why does she believe the Triangle fire disaster would have been averted if women had been granted the vote? *

Mollie Schepps, Shirtwaist Maker, answers the New York Senator who says:

"Now there is nobody to whom I yield in respect and admiration and devotion to the sex."

We want man's admiration, but we do not think that it is all there is to live for. Since economic conditions force us to fight our battle side by side with man in the industrial field, we do not see why we should not have the same privileges in the political field, in order to better the conditions under which we must work. . . . We demand a voice as to how politics shall be conducted. Yes, we want man's admiration, but not the kind that looks well on paper or sounds good when you say it. (Applause.) What we want men to do is to practice, to stop talking of the great comforts that they have provided for us; we know in most the cases we are the providers; we also want them to know that in these days they will have to try to win our admiration. . . .

Don't you gentlemen worry, our minds are already made up as to what we are going to do with our vote when we get it. Another reason is given against woman suffrage; it is said that equal say will enable the women to get equal pay, and equal pay is dangerous. Why? Because it would keep the women from getting married. Well, then, if long, miserable hours and starvation wages are the only means man can find to encourage marriage, it is a very poor compliment to themselves. In the name of a purer marriage we must have equal voice in making the laws, for we have found out from experience that it is not only men who have to get married.

There are a few facts from the shirtwaist strike I would like to call to your attention. . . . When the bosses hired thugs to break our ranks and create riots, the police arrested the girls; when the girls were brought before the judge, he showed his *devotion* by sending a sixteen-year-old girl, Rose Perr, to the workhouse for six days. And for what crime, on what evidence? Simply that a thug accused her of violating the law while picketing. The word of the thug was taken in preference every time to the innocent girl's. Again when we sent a committee to Mayor McCellan to speak for protection for 30,000 women on strike in the shirtwaist industry, and to protest against the brutality of the police, what answer did the Mayor give the committee? This. He could not be bothered with any striking shirtwaist makers. Had that same committee represented 30,000 men, men who would have a vote at the next election, you can bet that the committee would have received a different answer, for it would mean 30,000 votes at the next election. This is the kind of respect, admiration and devotion we receive from our admirers the politicians when we fight for a better condition and a decent wage.

*From Mollie Schepps, "Senators vs. Working Women," Wage Earner's Suffrage League of New York, 1912. From the Leonora O'Reilly Collection, Schlesinger Library, Radcliffe College.

One year later, when we had the terrible disaster of the Triangle Shirtwaist Factory, where our bodies were burned by the wholesale, and many jumped from the tenth floor and smashed their poor bodies rather than be roasted. Then again those very same gentlemen, that a year ago tried to break our ranks when we fought for a safer place to work in, shed tears over the bodies on the sidewalk crushed to pieces. . . We cannot, and must not, wait until our sisters that live in comfort get the votes for us.

NAWSA, *A Letter to Clergymen* (1912)

Although NAWSA women paraded and held suffrage rallies, the organization upheld the norms of the middle-class. In the following letter, what justification did the NAWSA provide for religious support for the ballot? *

Dear Sir:

"Mother's Day" is becoming more and more observed in the churches of our land, and many clergymen on that day are delivering special sermons, calling attention to the Mother's influence in the Home. . . .

In view of the fact that in the moral and social reform work of the churches, the Mothers and Women of the churches are seeking to correct serious evils that exist in our cities as a menace to the morals of their children outside the home, and in view of the fact that churchwomen are finding that much of their effort is ineffective and of no value, because they are denied the weapon of Christian warfare, the ballot . . . we ask of you, will you not in justice to the Mothers of your church choose for your topic on "Mother's Day" some subject bearing on "The need of the Mother's influence in the State?"

Women are recognized as the most religious, the most moral and the most sober portion of the American people. Why deny them a voice in public affairs when we give it for the asking to every ignorant foreigner who comes to our shores?

The women have always been the mainstay and chief supporters of the churches, and in their struggle for their civil liberty. Should not their clergymen or Christian brothers sympathize with them and "Remember those in bonds as bound with them" and help them in their struggle? On behalf of the church work committee representing Christian Mothers in every State in the Union, I would be pleased to know if you will

---

*From "Report of the Church Work Committee," *Proceedings of the Forty-Fourth Annual Convention of the National American Woman Suffrage Association* (New York: National American Woman Suffrage Association, 1912), 55–57.

be one to raise your voice on "Mother's Day" in favor of the extension of the Mother's influence in our land "to help those women that labored with you in the Gospel?"

Carrie Chapman Catt, *Mrs. Catt Assails Pickets* (1917)

> Under Carrie Chapman Catt's (1859-1947) leadership the NAWSA achieved suffrage victory. Catt grew up on an Iowa farm and became a superindent of schools, a position rarely opened to women in the East. Under Catt's energetic leadership, suffrage became a well-organized protest movement that still paid attention to the norms of ladylike behavior. Concerned about propriety, Catt distinguished NAWSA from the unladylike tactics of the militant NWP, in this case their heckling of President Wilson. What mistake did she believe the NWP made? [*]

Mrs. Carrie Chapman Catt, President of the National American Woman Suffrage Association, said yesterday that the women who were doing the picketing in Washington had made a psychological mistake.

"The pickets," Mrs. Catt said, "make the psychological mistake of injecting into this stage of the suffrage campaign tactics which are out of accord with it. Every reform, every change of idea in the world passes through three stages—agitation, argument, and surrender. We have passed through the first two stages and entered into the third. The mistake of the pickets is that they have no comprehensive idea of the movement, and are trying to work this first stage in the third. We stand on the threshold of final victory, and the only contribution these women make to it is to confuse the public mind.

Alice Paul, *Why the Suffrage Struggle Must Continue* (1917)

> Alice Paul (1885–1977) received a Ph.D. from the University of Pennsylvania in 1912. She organized the National Woman's Party (NWP) in 1916. Having visited Britain and participated in the suffrage struggle there, she popularized the more radical strategy

---

[*]From "Mrs. Catt Assails Pickets," the *New York Times*, November 13, 1917.

and tactics of the British Suffragette Movement. NWP women continued to picket the White House and stage demonstrations during the U.S. involvement in World War I. Do you find Paul's linking suffrage to U.S. involvement in World War I persuasive? *

In our national convention in March, our members, though differing widely on the duty of the individual in war, were unanimous in voting that in event of war the National Woman's party, as an organization, should continue to work for political liberty for women and for that alone, believing, as the convention resolution stated, that in so doing the organization "serves the highest interest of the country." . . .

Never was there greater need of work for internal freedom in this country. At the very moment when democracy is increasing among nations in the throes of war, women in the United States are told that attempts at electoral reforms are out of place until war is over. The Democrats have decided in caucus that only war measures shall be included in their legislative program, and have announced that they will take up no new subjects, unless the President considers them of value for war purposes. Suffrage has not yet been included under this head. . . . No "war measure" that has been suggested would contribute more toward establishing unity in the country, than would the giving of suffrage to all the people. It will always be difficult to wage a war for democracy abroad while democracy is denied at home.

---

*From Alice Paul, "Why the Suffrage Struggle Must Continue," *The Suffragist*, April 21, 1917.

10

Post-Suffrage Trends and the Uneven Rate of Gender Change

In the history of women, the 1920s was a period of great contrasts as women began to liberate themselves from traditional social and sexual constraints. As growing numbers of women entered the workplace and college, changes in clothing and conduct gained momentum. Gender roles were in a state of flux, and sharply differentiated nineteenth-century assumptions about male and female sexuality were collapsing. Women were no longer considered passionless, they were now perceived sexual beings capable of sexual pleasure. With her bobbed hair, scanty clothing and more explicit sexuality, the flapper won popular attention as a symbol of women's greater freedom. Although flapper behavior had roots in young working women's nonconformist clothing and lifestyles of the late nineteenth century, with the flapper, social liberation entered the middle-class mainstream.

A quest for greater economic opportunity did not accompany the flapper's liberated behavior. Little had changed in the sex-segregated and gender-biased workplace. Except for a small group of feminists, economic independence was not a central issue. Acknowledgement of sexuality coexisted with a reassertion that womanly fulfillment depended on marriage and domesticity. Heightened emphasis on marital fulfillment devalued women's friendships and support networks. For the majority of middle-class urban women and some rural women, laborsaving appliances and a vast array of consumer goods made domesticity appealing. In recognition of the resurgence of domestic values, even prominent women's colleges relaxed their rigorous academic standards and offered home economics courses.

The disbanding of the suffrage movement ended the era of women's nationwide collective political activism. For many women the suffrage victory provided a satisfactory conclusion to a struggle initiated more than seventy years earlier. For others, voting represented only an initial step in the struggle for full equality. What remained of the organized suffrage movement splintered into two major groups. Alice Paul led the National Woman's Party (NWP) in the struggle for an Equal Rights Amendment (ERA) to the Constitution, that would end gender inequities and allow women to compete equally with men. ERA advocates campaigned against protective as well as discriminatory legislation. Labor activists, like Elisabeth Christman, the conservative League of Women Voters under Carrie Chapman Catt, and women social reformers combated the ERA and supported protective legislation.

While significant numbers of African-American women had also supported the suffrage amendment, for them the right to vote remained illusory. Southern states prevented black women from voting as they had previously disenfranchised black men. Appeals made by African-American women to the white NWP were rejected. The NWP, intent on securing the ERA, asserted that the disenfranchisement of black women was a racial rather than a women's issue.

Although the ferment of reform that characterized the Progressive era declined, women's social reform networks retained their purposefulness and solidarity. On the federal level, social welfare networks forged during the Progressive era molded the agendas of both the Children's and Women's Bureaus; their welfare objectives would receive important support during the New Deal. Neither the Supreme Court nor the conservative Republican administrations of the 1920s, were hospitable to the Children's and Women's Bureau's objectives. In 1923, the court overturned the ban on child labor and minimum wage laws for women; Congress repealed the Sheppard-Towner Maternity bill in 1929. Passed in 1921, the Maternity bill made federal funds available to the states to establish clinics for prenatal and infant care.

Although the term feminism gained currency in the 1920s, women did not agree about what feminism meant. Dorothy Bromley spoke for many younger women who denied that they needed to identify with a collective group. To such women, feminism came to mean greater personal autonomy and the satisfaction of individual aspirations. They believed post-suffrage women would advance in the workplace on the basis of individual merit. Optimistic that women could combine careers with marriage and motherhood, they saw no reason to continue the older feminist generation's political activism.

U.S. Government, *Survey of Employment Conditions: The Weaker Sex* (1917)

After women employees complained about discrimination, the government surveyed its employees. The survey revealed that sex-based discrimination did not exist. Clerical work in the U.S. government became increasingly available to women after the Civil War. Sex-segregated positions for government work reflected the same gendered occupational structures that prevailed in factories. In fact, the very idea of "woman's work" is a gender definition, and is used in this survey to justify women's exclusion from most positions. How does the justification for exclusion relate to the *Muller* v. *Oregon* Supreme Court decision?[*]

Office of the Director

January 31, 1917

Mr. E. J. Ayers,
Chief Clerk,
Department of the Interior

My dear Mr. Ayers:

In reply to your notation on the copy of the letter from Senator Jones, requesting information as to whether any discrimination against women based solely upon the grounds of their sex, was made by the Geological Survey:

As you are doubtless aware, much of the work carried on by the Survey requires field ability for which it is necessary to employ men rather than women. In the field branches, therefore, women necessarily are unable to meet the strain attendant upon constant exposure in all kinds of weather, and in the strenuous physical exertions that are required of the geologists, topographers, and hydrographic engineers. There are on the rolls of the Survey 417 men, distributed as follows among the different field branches: geologists, 188; topographers, 49; water resources engineers, 74; Alaskan geologists, 15.

In the Division of Engraving and Printing, the work is necessarily of a man's type, requiring the handling of machinery, heavy lifting, dirty work and various trades to which men are especially adapted. The conditions under which much of the engraving and printing work is done is such as to preclude the employment of women. There are 126 men employed in the various nonclerical jobs in the division of Engraving and Printing and no women.

The force of laborers, messengers, mechanics, etc., consists of 130 men and one woman. The character of the work performed is such as to practically preclude the possibility of employing women for the various duties.

From the above it will be seen that there are 646 positions in which, from the character of the work, the employment of men is necessitated.

Turning to the distinctly clerical jobs, the following table shows the distribution among the sexes of the different clerks:

Branches	Males	Females
Field	28	111
Engraving	3	0
Administrative	53	28
Total	84	139

[*]From George Otis Smith to E. J. Ayers, January 31, 1917; in Record Group 48, "Records of the Department of the Interior," Office of the Secretary, Personnel Supervision and Management, 1907–1942, File 15–15–35, National Archives, Washington, D.C.

It should be noted in the above table that the great number of males in the administrative branch is due to the including of all the various administrative officers not attached to the field service, as for instance, the Chief Clerk, the Chief Disbursing Officer, the Chief of the Accounts Division, the Chief of the Executive Division, the Chief of the Division of Distribution, etc. . . .

I think the above tables will clearly show that women are chosen for the clerical positions, in general, in preference to the men at a rate of about two to one, and that so far as the Geological Survey is concerned, the spirit, as well as the letter of the law, regarding equal chance to both sexes is lived up to.

Yours very truly,

Director.

[George Otis Smith]

Women Streetcar Conductors Fight Layoffs (1921)

The involvement of the United States in World War I provided women with new employment opportunities. Their employment was based solely on the scarcity of male labor. As this government document reveals, many women wished to retain their jobs after the end of the war. However, unions and management pressured them to leave. Working women struggled against the effort to limit their work to their "appropriate" sphere. Why did the women want to keep their jobs? What role did the union play? Did women have the same right to work as men? *

Conspicuous among the occupations which were opened to women at the time of our entry into the war, was the work of conductor on street and elevated railways and subways. While women had been employed as ticket agents by various companies for many years, the woman streetcar conductor was a complete innovation, and about her employment in this capacity have centered much discussion and several bitter controversies. . . .

Having once been accepted as a successful participant in transportation work, there were two factors which were to influence the future employment of women in these occupations. First, Were the men employees going to accept women as fellow

---

*From "Controversies Regarding the Right of Women to Work as Conductors." *Women Streetcar Conductors and Ticket Agents* (Washington, D.C.: U.S. Government Printing Office, 1921).

workers? Second, Was it going to prove possible to provide such legal regulation as might be necessary for the protection of these women workers, and at the same time allow for the unusual difficulties with which a transportation company is faced in arranging the working hours of its employees?

The first question was soon answered in one way for the women conductors in Detroit and Cleveland, and in the opposite way in Kansas City. The history of the situation in Detroit and Cleveland, as it affected the employment of women, is extremely significant. The issue was a clear-cut one, between the men on the one hand who wished to maintain the work of streetcar conductors as strictly men's work, and on the other hand the women who had proved that they could do the work well, and who were not ready to accept their exclusion from an occupation where the pay was good, and the hours and working conditions no more unsatisfactory than in many other occupations considered to come within the sphere of women's activities.

Women were put on as conductors during the after part of August, 1918, in Cleveland, when the street railway company of that city claimed that it could not secure a sufficient number of men for this work. The men objected to the employment of women and threatened to strike if it continued. But a compromise was finally effected and the matter submitted to Department of Labor investigators, who were to decide whether the women should be retained during the investigation, and whether there was a sufficient shortage of men to require the continued employment of women. The decision to retain the women during the investigation was made almost immediately, but after the investigation it was decided that while there was still a scarcity of male labor, it was not sufficient to justify the continued employment of women. This decision was rendered by the investigators in spite of their statement that "It is true the company will have to lower its standards somewhat, owing to the extraction of the best men from civil life into the military service of the county." It was recommended that the women be discharged from the service by November 1. The women protested against this and brought the matter before the War Labor Board. They claimed that it was illegal for the company and the men employees to make the original agreement to submit to arbitration the question of whether the women should be kept, as the company had engaged the women to work during good behavior and to be discharged only for incompetency, insubordination, or other unsatisfactory service. The company expressed itself as completely satisfied with the work of the women, who claimed that the contracts between them and the company were still valid, and that they had not been consulted in any of the negotiations or investigations relative to their dismissal. They also claimed that the agreement to arbitrate was in disregard of their right to be employed and to hold employment as long as their work was satisfactory, and was an abridgment of their constitutional right to work.

The men claimed that the question of the employment of women was a matter between the company and the union. The union had an agreement with the company that no women should be employed, therefore the women had been engaged in disregard of this contract and were not parties to the discussion . . . On December 2, the union formally demanded that the women be discharged, and threatened to go on strike immediately if this were not done. The strike began on December 3 and the War

Labor Board was hurriedly appealed to by the Mayor of Cleveland, and immediately handed down the decision that the company should hereafter employ no more women, and that within the next 30 days all women should be replaced by competent men. This decision was not mandatory and the men refused to abide by it. The strike was finally settled by the following agreement between the union and the company:

It is hereby agreed by and between the undersigned that on and after this date there will be no more women employed as conductors; that the Cleveland Railway Co. will remove and displace the women that are now in its service as rapidly as possible.

This agreement was made by the officers of the union and the company without including the women at any stage of the negotiations. Vigorous protests by various women's organizations, as well by the women conductors themselves, followed this settlement, as it seemed to be a very dangerous precedent to deny women the right to work in any occupation, for no other reason than that their dismissal was demanded by the men, and without even giving the women a hearing so that they might present their case.

Ann Martin, *We Couldn't Afford a Doctor* (1920)

This excerpt from a magazine article written in support of the Sheppard-Towner Maternity bill describes how poor women received inadequate prenatal care and gave birth to sickly babies. Women progressives like Florence Kelly advocated government funding for prenatal and maternity care. In an effort to appeal to newly enfranchised women, Congress passed the Maternity bill in 1921. However, with the collapse of the mass based women's movement, the effort to provide poor women with free medical services lost its political clout. Under increasing pressure from the male medical profession, Congress repealed the legislation in 1929. What evidence is offered that poor and rural women needed government-funded care?[*]

She went into the textile mills in Providence when she was twelve. She had worked there ever since, first to increase her father's and then her husband's insufficient wages. Her hours were from five in the afternoon till one in the morning. Her work was done standing at a machine during the whole eight hours, except for half an hour off for some food. She went home at one o'clock and slept till six, when she rose to cook breakfast and get her husband off to the mills and her children off to school.

---

[*]From Ann Martin, "We Couldn't Afford a Doctor," *Good Housekeeping*, April 1920, 19–20.

"I always feel tired," she said. She looked it. Her hair was gray; she was thin and undersized and seemed fifty instead of thirty-five. She had borne six children, and another was coming very soon. With stoicism she told how she had always worked in the mill up to the last day, and had usually managed to return within a few days after the birth of her baby, so as to continue earning money. One baby was stillborn; three were too feeble at birth to live more than a few days; two had managed to survive. Owing to her rundown condition, she could not nurse any of them, she said, but could not have nursed them anyway, as she had to keep on at the mill.

She worked at night because it enabled her to "see the children some in the daytime," and to do the family washing, cooking, and sewing. She made over, for both the children and herself, old clothes which were sent by a relative. She had not had a new dress in eight year, or a vacation in twelve. The family earnings barely sufficed for the most meager supply of food and a place in which to live.

"I do not see how we can pay the doctor for coming for the next baby," she said. "He charges fifteen dollars and only comes once. The midwife will come eight times for eight dollars, but of course she doesn't know as much as the doctor. The housework always goes to pieces, though my husband cooks and does the best he can. But the children always get sick when I am sick, and everything in the house gets dirty, and we get in debt, so having babies is getting to be a horror to me."

The wife of a homesteader in Montana left the ranch with her husband in December, two weeks before confinement, and after a seventy-mile automobile drive to the railroad, traveled over one hundred miles by train to the nearest hospital. They started back before the baby was three weeks old, in bitter winter weather. They knew this was unwise, but the hospital expenses were heavy and the mother was worried about the other children, who had been left alone on the ranch. Owing to bad roads and a snowstorm, they were four days and nights driving the last seventy miles. One night they had to spend in the open.

"We intended to get to the hospital again for my next baby," said this Montana mother, "but the terrible expense of my last baby got us into debt, and then I couldn't get away in time because all the autos in the neighborhood were being used for sheepshearing."

She was attended only by a midwife in this next confinement, and suffered serious complications which caused the death of the baby.

These stories, as told to representatives of the Federal Children's Bureau, are typical of many thousands of others in the industrial cities and rural districts of the United States. Is it surprising that we have one of the highest infant death-rates in the word, that more babies die every year in he United States, under normal conditions and in proportion to the number born, than in almost any other county, great or small?

The facts are simple and tragic. Of the 2,500,000 babies born yearly in this country, at least a quarter of a million—one out of every ten babies born—die within the first twelve months of birth. Foreign countries long ago adopted government measures to save the lives of babies, and have thereby lowered the death rate. France loses only one out of thirteen babies born; Australia and Sweden one out of fourteen; Norway, one out of seventeen; New Zealand, which through its care for the mother before and after childbirth, has achieved the lowest baby death rate of any country in the world, loses only one out of twenty.

The Farmer's Wife, *The Labor Savers I Use* (1923)

For housewives in general and farm women in particular, the technological developments that first made their appearance in rural areas during the 1920s revolutionized housework. In the following letters farm wives applaud the way in which indoor plumbing, furnaces and running water were not only laborsavers but "lifesavers." To what appliances and technological developments did women give the greatest praise? How did these lighten the burden of housework?[*]

Saving Every Minute

First comes my kitchen cabinet, standing five feet from and in front of the stove, and containing everything that is needed for baking. I can prepare anything for the oven without taking a step, till the cake, or pies or biscuits are ready to slip into the oven.

Next comes my built-in woodbox that can be filled from the shed and forms a nest in my kitchen beside the firebox end of the stove.

With my five babies all under five and one-third years of age, the bathroom on our first floor is a blessing. Two springs piped into a concrete reservoir supply the house and barn. The hot water tank is connected with my range.

And my laundry tubs! Such backache and time savers as they are. Mine are in the kitchen and covered as a table when not in use for washing. With no tubs to fill and empty, washing does not seem like washing. I had rather be without my hand-power washer than the tubs.

My husband had acetylene lights put in, so all the time I once used cleaning and filling oil lamps is now used for other work. With the outfit is the hot plate, which makes summer cooking more comfortable.

I have an ironing board on a standard and a gasoline iron so I can iron when and where I choose.

One year I spent almost a day pitting cherries but never again! I bought a pitter and an apple parer. They not only do better and much quicker work, but my five-year-old boy can operate them as well as I. Doing every bit of my own work, sewing for all of us, even to the making of the children's coats, I must plan to save every minute I can so as to have a little time for reading and other things I enjoy.

---

[*] From "The Labor Savers I Use" in *The Farmer's Wife*, February 1923, p. 301.

By using my bread-mixer, it takes seven minutes to knead bread and have it set to rise.

I must also mention my mop wringer, dust mop and sweeper.

Winter used to mean spending a goodly share of each day carrying "chunks" from the woodshed to keep two heaters going. Now we have a pipeless furnace, all wood for it in the cellar and a much warmer house. Mrs. L. L. S., N.Y.

Quartette of Life-Savers

When our laundry bill steadily mounted higher till we were paying two dollars every week for clothes not always well washed, we decided something had to be done. We had a gasoline engine but no washroom just a back porch too small for the engine and washing machine.

A washing machine with engine directly beneath the tub settled that problem, as it occupied no more space than an ordinary tub. Less than a year's laundry bill bought it. It not only took the drudgery out of washing but gave us *clean* clothes and saved money.

An old piano stool and a gasoline iron made the combination I thought-out, that saves so much time and energy and money on ironing days. I found that I could iron as well sitting as standing; the iron was always the right temperature; and no time was lost going to the stove for hot irons. One pint of gasoline is sufficient for a big ironing; making the fuel cost almost nothing.

The Home Economics Clubs of this country have formed testing circles for trying out a number of laborsaving devices. I am using the wheeled table or kitchen jitney and have found it such an efficient maid that my boy is going to make me one at school.

The dishes and silver and all the food can be wheeled in at one trip, and at the close of the meal one load of used dishes goes back to the kitchen, instead of four or five as usual. Counting ten steps from kitchen to dining room (both are small) and at least five trips from one to the other, there is a saving of three hundred steps in one day in the preparation and clearing away of meals.

On ironing day this jitney is close at hand, and as the clothes are ironed they are piled on it, then wheeled to their proper places.

My kitchen is so small that there is not room for a drain board at the sink, but why should I worry? I have a large dish dryer with galvanized dripping pan underneath so I can use it on my kitchen cabinet. I wipe glasses and silver, but dishes and cooking utensils are scalded and dried by evaporation. Counting just one-half hour saved in a day in one week's time I am three and one half hours to the good.

These four articles constitute my much prized quartette of labor savers. Since the foremost women specialists of the American Medical Association agree that a large percent of the women who die are the unnecessary victims of the strain of housework, I think I may call them lifesavers, for they eliminate so much of the wasted energy that is expended in housekeeping.—Mrs. J.E.T., Wash.

Blessed Water

The running water in the house! What a constant cause of thankfulness! What a joy to use all I need and want! And I cannot bear to waste it unnecessarily even yet, for memory of former days has left scars so deep. It is foolish for me to say, "I *could* not keep house without it" for I have; and I'll not say, "I *would* not," for circumstances alter cases. One does so much for love and for necessity. But I will say, "I would much *rather* not keep house without it!"

Have you ever, in utter need, heard the clank of the dipper against the sides of an empty water pail? I remember hearing that dismal sound when my little girl, sick and feverish, was crying for a drink. Not a drop of cold water in the house for a craving child! The men from the hayfield had drunk the last drop and left the empty pail. The spring was downhill, a long, long way in the hot sun. I could not leave the child, so I took an umbrella for shade, a can for the water and carried her down to the spring.

How delicious it must have tasted on that feverish tongue. Then came the long, slow walk back up the hill, with the water and the child, who fortunately was quieted enough to manage the umbrella.

The water from that same spring is in our pressure-tank now, but to me *water* is the most necessary, the biggest item in the country household for saving the time and strength of the whole family. Other things shrink into insignificance beside that all-important one.

There is my washing machine. It doesn't *seem* as if I could put through by hand the big washes I have done in the machine. I think I have succeeded where my friends have been disappointed in theirs, because I have followed implicitly the directions accompanying it.

My mop wringer! I can remember my mother scrubbing floors on hands and knees with the old scrub brush, or later wringing the heavy, wet mop. My heart is truly thankful, I hope, for the things I do not have to do. I only wish I could share with so many of my neighbors who have not.

I must mention one other labor saver—the Little Maid In The House. She amuses the baby; she runs upstairs and down on errands for me; she sets the table; she is dishwasher and drier. She is indeed a constant joy and interest. Could I keep house without her? I would much rather not!—Mrs. H.W., Maine.

National Woman's Party, *Declaration of Principles* (1922)

During the 1920s, Alice Paul, president of the National Woman's Party (NWP), attempted to mobilize support for an Equal Rights Amendment (ERA). The amendment sought to nullify the reams of gender-based legislation that constrained women's equality. The amendment would have negated protective legislation in pursuit of gender equity. Until the resurgence of feminism in the 1970s, the ERA had very limited appeal. The NWP defined its objectives in the following Declaration? How do these objectives relate to the Declaration of Sentiments (1848) in Chapter 5?[*]

That women shall no longer be the governed half of society, but shall participate equally with men in the direction of life. . . .

That women shall no longer be barred from the priesthood or ministry, or any other position of authority in the church, but equally with men shall participate in ecclesiastical offices and dignities.

That a double moral standard shall no longer exist, but one code shall obtain for both men and women.

That exploitation of the sex of women shall no longer exist, but women shall have the same right to the control of their persons as have men.

That women shall no longer be required by law or custom to assume the name of her husband upon marriage, but shall have the same right as a man to retain her own name after marriage.

That the wife shall no longer be considered as supported by the husband, but their mutual contribution to the family maintenance shall be recognized.

That the headship of the family shall no longer be in the husband alone, but shall be equally in the husband and wife. . . .

In short—that woman shall no longer be in any form of subjection to man in law or in custom, but shall in every way be on an equal plane in rights, as she has always been and will continue to be in responsibilities and obligations.

Elisabeth Christman, *What Do Working Women Say?* (c. 1912)

Elisabeth Christman was secretary of the International Glove Workers Union and from 1921 to 1951 was the secretary/treasurer of the Women's Trade Union League. Her negative response to the ERA was representative of the views of reformers and many working-class women who believed that passage of the amendment would nullify years of effort spent in gaining protective legislation. Fully aware that men still possessed economic and social advantages, Christman and other opponents of the ERA supported the legal protection of women. How did Christman

[*]From National Woman's Party, "Declaration of Principles," *Equal Rights*, February 17, 1923.

differentiate between legal and economic equality? Why did she believe women workers were in a weaker position than men? *

Would you say that, in order to give women in Ohio the right to be taxidrivers or open a shoe shining parlor, you ought to take away the 48-hour law for women in Massachusetts and the hour laws of 42 other states?

Would you say that in order to give the right to jury service to women in twenty states, you ought to throw into court the mother's pension laws of 39 states?

Would you go so far as to say that you would be justified in even taking the risk of such consequences to the millions of wage earning women and mothers, for the sake of a few prospective women taxi drivers, bootblacks, and jurors?

Especially when you could get what you want without taking such risk?

Where the Risk Lies

Yet it is exactly those risks—and many more—the National Woman's Party proposes to take in its constitutional amendment which reads:

"Men and women shall have equal rights throughout the United States and every place subject to its jurisdiction."

The risk is due to the fact, first, that this is an amendment to the United States Constitution and would invalidate automatically all laws in conflict with it, **without automatically replacing** most of them.

It is due, second, to the fact that blanket provisions in law, whether in the constitution or in status, require court interpretation in each case, and the term "rights" and "equal rights" are subject to diverse construction.

Legal Rights vs. Economic Rights

And, last but not least, the risk is due to the fact that legal rights and other rights are not by any means identical. Legal equality is not necessarily the same as economic equality. It may actually defeat economic equality.

For instance, a state may give the wife a right to sue her husband for non-support. The husband has not the same right to sue her. The proposed amendment would probably, lawyers say, give this man and this woman equal rights by taking away, automatically, the woman's right to sue.

Having thus achieved **legal equality**, however, the wife, whose best years have been spent caring for her home and children, now finds herself confronted with the necessity of earning her living and also of contributing to the support of her children. Untrained for business or industry, her life's experience totally different from her husband's, she is now faced with identical responsibilities and a handicap which only a superhuman could overcome.

Legal equality it may be.

Economic equality it is not.

---

*From Elizabeth Christman, "What do Working Women Say," *National Women's Trade League*, c. 1912.

Realty vs. Theory

Consider the woman in industry. She is working, say, in a state with an eight-hour law for women, passed because women had been working much longer hours. The man-employing industries of that sate, however, are probably on an eight-hour schedule established by their unions. The eight-hour law and the eight-hour trade agreement both limit the worker's freedom of contract. But the **law** would probably be destroyed by the so-called "equal rights" amendment, because the **legal** rights of women are restricted thereunder but not the **legal** rights of men. In other words, to give the women legal equality with the men, the amendment would take away the eight-hour day from the women but not from the men.

This may be legal equality.

Economic equality, decidedly not.

The Sensible Course

The risk involved in the National Woman's Party amendment is, moreover, a wholly gratuitous risk. The amendment is altogether unnecessary, because the things it purports to do can all be done, right now, exactly as most of them would have to be done in any case by Acts of Congress and the states, which already have the power this amendment would confer.

Not only **can** those things all be done, but they are actually being done—86 new laws or amendments to laws in 30 states since the federal woman suffrage amendment was passed.

Why take a gratuitous risk?

Letter to Margaret Sanger (1928)

Margaret Sanger spent her life in a crusade for birth control. In 1916 she opened a birth control clinic in an immigrant, working-class neighborhood in Brooklyn, New York, in violation of state laws, which outlawed birth control as a form of obscenity. She was soon arrested and the clinic closed. During the 1920s middle-class women began to use contraception on a wide scale. However, many poor women still lacked access to modern contraception. As the nation's foremost advocate of birth control, Sanger received letters, such as the following, from women desperate for advice on how to avoid unwanted pregnancies. How do these letters support

Sanger's belief that the ability to control pregnancy was women's most vital right?[*]

Please tell me what to do to keep from having any more babies. I am only twenty-six years old and the mother of five children the oldest eight years and the others six, four and two, and I have four living. The last time I had a six month's miscarriage and I have been weak ever since. It happened this past August. My husband is gone to try and find work and I have to support my children myself. I have to work so hard until I feel like it would kill me to give birth to another. I am nervous. My back and side give me a lot of trouble. I am not able to give my children the attention that I desire. I take in washing to support my children, I suffered this last time from the time I got that way until I lost it and am yet weak in my back. Please! for my sake tell me what to do to keep from having another. I don't want another child. Five is enough for me.

* * *

I don't care to bear any more children for the man I got he is most all the time drunk and not working and gone for days and nights and leave me alone most of the time. I'm sewing to support me and my baby that is two years old and one dead born so I know you don't blame me for not wanting any more children and he is always talking about leaving me he might as well for what he is doing but I am worried that I may get in wrong.

* * *

I was married when I was seventeen and seven months. After nine months married I had a miscarriage at eight months. After fourteen months I had a baby boy and he is living and is now seven years old. After three years I had another boy. He was born with consumption in the bones and would shake his head one side and another but doctors did not know what that was. Now I have them nervous spells myself. All through my married life I have been working in factories. I took my children to the day nursery. Two months before the birth of my last child my husband deserted me with my children. He had left home eleven time before that but always came back, but that night his mother gave him money to get out of town. I was then married five years to him. After four years I could not get no trace of him I got the divorce. I had to work hard to keep my furniture and pay the rent as I did not want to go boarding. Now as I was twenty-six and as I had no one to depend on I married again. He is good young man of twenty-five and he is not a lazy gambler like the other, but even with that I fear having any more children as they will not be healthy. We were married a few months ago and neither of us had any money and he is only a laborer and makes twenty-five dollars a week, so you see I have struggled with the first husband and I wish I will not struggle with this one, so please if you can help me.

---

[*] From Margaret Sawyer, *Motherhood in Bondage* (New York: Brentano, 1928).

Dorothy Dunbar Bromley, *Feminist: New Style* (1927)

Dorothy Dunbar Bromley believed that women could compete with men on an even playing field in which individual merit alone would determine success. Her argument was an individualistic brand of feminism. She placed major emphasis on fulfillment through work and the determination of "new style" feminists to combine marriage, motherhood, and work. How do these "new style" objectives differ from the Seneca Falls Declaration of Sentiments? How are they similar? In what ways were Bromley's views overly optimistic?*

Is it not high time that we laid [bare] the ghost of the so-called feminist?

"Feminism" has become a term of opprobrium to the modern young woman. For the word suggests the old school of fighting feminists who wore flat heels and had very little feminine charm. Indeed, if a blundering male assumes that a young woman is a feminist simply because she happens to have a job or a profession of her own, she will, be highly—and quite justifiably insulted. Yet she and her kind can hardly be dubbed "old-fashioned" women. What *are* they, then?

The pioneer feminists were hard-hitting individuals, and the modern young woman admires them or their courage—even while she judges them for their zealotry and their inartistic methods. Furthermore, she pays all honor to them, for they fought her battle. But *she* does not want to wear their mantle, and she has to smile at those women who wear it today.

The constantly increasing group of young women in their twenties and thirties, the truly modern ones, admit that a full life calls for marriage and children, as well as a career. These women, if they launch upon marriage, are keen to make a success of it and an art of child rearing. But *at the same time* they are moved by an inescapable inner compulsion to be individuals in their own right. And in this era of simplified housekeeping they see their opportunity, for it is obvious that a woman who plans intelligently can salvage some time for her own pursuits. Furthermore, they are convinced that they will be better wives and mothers for the breath they gain from functioning outside the home. In short, they are highly conscious creatures who felt obliged to plumb their own resources to the very depths, despite the fact that they are under no delusions as to the present inferior status of their sex in most fields of endeavor.

Since men must have things pointed out to them in black and white, we beg to enunciate the tenets of the modern woman's credo. Let us call her "Feminist—New Style."

First Tenet. Our modern young woman freely admits that American women have so far achieved but little in the arts, sciences, and professions as compared with men. So far as the arts are concerned, it cannot be stated categorically that women lack creative power, in view of their original work in fiction, poetry, and the plastic arts. As of their status in the professions, it might fairly be claimed that they have scarcely had time to get a running start. And their limited success in business would prove that they have not yet cast off their age-old habit of over-emphasizing detail and, as a consequence, they have not yet learned to grasp the larger issues.

But it remains true that a small percentage of women have proved the capacity, even the creative power of the feminine mind.

Second Tenet. Why, then, does the modern woman care about a career or a job if she doubts the quality and scope of women's achievement to date? There are three good reasons why she cares immensely: first, she may be of that rare and fortunate breed of persons who find a certain art, science, or profession as inevitable a part of their lives as breathing; second, she may feel the need of a satisfying outlet for her energy, whether or not she may possess creative ability; third, she may have no other means of securing her economic independence. And the latter she prizes above all else, for it spells her freedom as an individual, enabling her to marry or not to marry, as she chooses—to terminate a marriage that has become unbearable, and to support and educate her children if necessary.

In brief, Feminist—New Style reasons that if she is economically independent, and if she has, to boot, a vital interest in some work of her own, she will have given as few hostages to Fate as it is humanly possible to give. Love may die, and children may grow up, but one's work goes on forever.

Third Tenet. She will not, however, live for her job alone, for she considers that a woman who talks and thinks only shop has just as narrow a horizon as the housewife who talks and thinks only husband and children—perhaps more so, for the latter may have a deeper understanding of human nature. She will therefore refuse to give up all of her personal interests, year in and year out, for the sake of her work. In this respect she no doubt will fall short of the masculine ideal of commercial success, for the simple reason that she has never felt the economic compulsion which drives men on to build up fortunes for the sake of their growing families.

Yet she is not one of the many women who look upon their jobs as tolerable meal tickets or as interesting pastimes to be dropped whenever they may wish. On the contrary, she takes great pride in becoming a vital factor in whatever enterprise she has chosen, and she therefore expects to work long hours when the occasion demands.

Fourth Tenet. Nor has she become hostile to the other sex in the course of her struggle to orient herself. On the contrary, she frankly likes men and is grateful to more than a few for the encouragement and help they have given her.

In the business and professional worlds, for instance, Feminist—New Style has observed that more and more men are coming to accord women as much responsibility as they show themselves able to carry. She and her generation have never found it necessary to bludgeon their way, and she is inclined to think that certain of the pioneers would have got farther if they had relied on their ability, rather than on their militant methods. To tell the truth, she enjoys working with men, more than with women, for their methods are more direct and their view larger, and she finds that she can deal with them on a basis of frank comradeship.

Fifth Tenet. By the same corollary, Feminist—New Style professes no loyalty to women *en masse*, although she staunchly believes in individual women. Surveying her sex as a whole, she finds their actions petty, their range of interests narrow, their talk trivial and repetitious. As for those who set themselves up as leaders of the sex, they are either strident creatures of so little ability and balance that they have won no chance to "express themselves" (to use their own hackneyed phrase) in a man-made world; or they are brilliant, restless individuals who too often battle for women's rights for the sake of personal glory.

Sixth Tenet. There is, however, one thing which Feminist—New Style envies Frenchwoman, and that is their sense of "chic." Indeed, she is so far removed from the early feminists that she is altogether baffled by the psychology which led some of them to abjure men in the same voice with which they aped them. Certainly their vanity must have been anaesthetized, she tells herself, as she pictures them with their short hair, so different from her own shingle, and dressed in their own unflattering mannish clothes—quite the antithesis of her own boyish effects which are subtly designed to set off feminine charms.

Seventh Tenet. Empty slogans seem to Feminist—New Style just as bad taste as masculine dress and manners. They serve only to prolong the war between the sexes and to prevent women from learning to think straight. Take these, for instance, "Keep your maiden name." "Come out of the kitchen." "Never darn a sock." After all, what's in a name or in a sock? Madame Curie managed to become one of the world's geniuses even though she suffered the terrible handicap of bearing her husband's name, and it is altogether likely that she darned a sock or two of Monsieur Curie's when there was no servant at hand to do it.

Finally, Feminist—New Style proclaims that men and children shall no longer circumscribe her world, although they may constitute a large part of it. She is intensely self-conscious, whereas the feminists were intensely sex-conscious. Aware of possessing a mind, she takes a keen pleasure in using that mind for some definite purpose; and also in learning to think clearly and cogently against a background of historical and scientific knowledge. She aspires to understand the meaning of the twentieth century, as she sees it expressed in the skyscrapers, the rapid pace of city life, the expressionistic drama, the abstract conceptions of art, the new music, the Joycian novel. She knows that it is her American, her twentieth-century birthright to emerge from creature of instinct into a full-fledged individual who is capable of molding her own life. And in this respect she holds that she is becoming man's equal.

If this be treason, gentlemen, make the most of it.

11

The Impact of the Depression and the New Deal

Fueled by massive male unemployment, the right of married women to work became problematic during the Depression. Many married women lost their jobs. The government and private sector preferred to hire men. Gallup polls revealed that an overwhelming majority of Americans believed that married women should stay home, and that their employment took jobs away from men. Professional women, in particular, found diminished opportunity. Even women in traditionally female fields like teaching were affected as school districts fired married women and hired men instead.

The popular perception that working women deprived men of employment obscured the reality of the sex-segregated labor market. In most cases, men and women did not compete for the same jobs. The Depression hit the male preserve of heavy industry with extreme force. Many married women scrambled to find work because their husbands faced chronic unemployment. In fact, low paid "women's" service and clerical positions continued to grow despite the Depression. Among employed women the percentage of married women working rose.

As both Meridel Le Sueur and Louise Mitchell reported, millions of impoverished white and African-American women lived on the edge of disaster. Generally barred by race from factory work and other occupations, African-American domestic workers experienced some of the most desperate economic conditions during the period. For at least some of these impoverished women New Deal relief programs meant the difference between survival and starvation. However, class, race and gender biases also pervaded New Deal policies. Employed mainly as farm and domestic laborers, neither African- nor Mexican-American workers would benefit from the old age provisions of the Social Security Act, which failed to cover, as had the National Recovery Act, these types of work.

African-American women wrote letters to Eleanor Roosevelt protesting against the discriminatory provisions of New Deal legislation. They also sought to unionize domestic workers and in Harlem, New York staged a boycott against white storeowners who refused to hire African-Americans.

In contrast to the bleak conditions poor women faced, women social reformers found a welcome reception in the New Deal administration of Franklin Roosevelt. At the top level of government, a more significant female presence existed than in all previous administrations. With ties to the Progressive era reform, these women clustered around Eleanor Roosevelt and Frances Perkins, who, as Secretary of Labor became the first woman in U.S. history to receive a cabinet-level appointment. Compassionate and responsive, Eleanor Roosevelt personified the administration's concern for the victims of economic disaster. Active in the promotion of racial justice, Eleanor Roosevelt secured an administrave appointment for noted African-American educator Mary McLeod Bethune, who helped widen employment opportunities for minority youth. The commitment of New Deal women to ameliorate suffering, resulted in the Social Security Act's provision for aid to dependent women and their children. Democratic party activist and reformer Molly Dewson became the first woman to serve on the Social Security Board.

The government's commitment to welfare created new opportunities for women in the field of social work. In line with the earlier tradition of women's voluntary settlement house work, the female-designated area of social work widened employment opportunities without challenging a traditional male occupation. As in other women's fields, gender bias kept the status and pay scale in social work low.

Meridel Le Sueur, *The Despair of Unemployed Women* (1932)

Born in Iowa in 1900, LeSueur was a journalist, poet, and novelist. This document is an eyewitness account of the desperation of unemployed women seeking domestic work. New Deal legislation addressed the needs of unemployed men, but unemployed women who were responsible for their own survival were a forgotten segment of the population. What life experiences do these women share? Would they benefit from any New Deal programs?[*]

I am sitting in the city free employment bureau. It's the women's section. We have been sitting here now for four hours. We sit here every day, waiting for a job. There are no jobs. Most of us have had no breakfast. Some have had scant rations for over a year. Hunger makes a human being lapse into a state of lethargy, especially city hunger. Is there anyplace else in the world where a human being is supposed to go hungry amidst plenty without an outcry, without protest, where only the boldest steal

---

[*] From Meridel LeSueur, "Women on the Breadlines". Originally published in *New Masses*, January 1932. Reprinted by permission of Rachel Tilsen.

or kill for bread, and the timid crawl the streets, hunger like the beak of a terrible bird at the vitals?

We sit looking at the floor. No one dares think of the coming winter. There are only a few more days of summer. Everyone is anxious to get work to lay up something for that long siege of bitter cold. But there is no work. Sitting in the room we all know it. That is why we don't talk much. We look at the floor dreading to see that knowledge in each other's eyes. There is a kind of humiliation in it. We look away from each other. We look at the floor. It's too terrible to see this animal terror in each other's eyes.

So we sit hour after hour, day after day, waiting for a job to come in. There are many women for a single job. A thin sharp woman sits inside a wire cage looking at a book. For four hours we have watched her looking at that book. She has a hard little eye. In the small bare room there are half a dozen women sitting on the benches waiting. Many come and go. Our faces are all familiar to each other, for we wait here every day.

This is a domestic employment bureau. Most of the women who come here are middle-aged, some have families, some have raised their families and are now alone, some have men who are out of work. Hard times and the man leaves to hunt for work. He doesn't find it. He drifts on. The woman probably doesn't hear from him for a long time. She expects it. She isn't surprised. She struggles alone to feed the many mouths. Sometimes she gets help from the charities. If she's clever she can get herself a good living from the charities, if she's naturally a lickspittle, naturally a little docile and cunning. If she's proud then she starves silently, leaving her children to find work, coming home after a day's searching to wrestle with her house, her children.

Some such story is written on the faces of all these women. There are young girls, too, fresh from the country. Some are made brazen too soon by the city. There is a great exodus of girls from the farms into the city now. Thousands of farms have been vacated completely in Minnesota. The girls are trying to get work. The prettier ones can get jobs in the stores when there are any, or waiting on table, but these jobs are only for the attractive and the adroit. The others, the real peasants, have a more difficult time.

Bernice sits next to me. She is a Polish woman of thirty-five. She has been working in people's kitchens for fifteen years or more. She is large, her great body in mounds, her face brightly scrubbed. She has a peasant mind and finds it hard even yet to understand the maze of the city, where trickery is worth more than brawn. Her blue eyes are not clever but slow and trusting. She suffers from loneliness and lack of talk. When you speak to her, her face lifts and brightens as if you had spoken through a great darkness, and she talks magically of little things as if the weather were magic, or tells some crazy tale of her adventures on the city streets, embellishing them in bright colors until they hang heavy and thick like embroidery. She loves the city anyhow. It's exciting to her, like a bazaar. She loves to go shopping and get a bargain, hunting out the places where stale bread and cakes can be had for a few cents. She likes walking the streets looking for men to take her to picture shows. Sometimes she goes to five picture shows in one day, or she sits through one the entire day until she knows all the dialogue by heart.

She came to the city a young girl from a Wisconsin farm. The first thing that happened to her, a charlatan dentist took out all her good shining teeth and the fifty dollars she had saved working in a canning factory. After that she met men in the park who told her how to look out for herself, corrupting her peasant mind, teaching her to mistrust everyone. Sometimes now she forgets to mistrust everyone and gets taken in. They taught her to get what she could for nothing, to count her change, to go back if she found herself cheated, to demand her rights.

She lives alone in little rooms. She bought seven dollars' worth of secondhand furniture eight years ago. She rents a room for perhaps three dollars a month in an attic, sometimes a cold house. Once the house where she stayed was condemned and everyone else moved out, and she lived there all winter alone on the top floor. She spent only twenty-five dollars all winter.

She wants to get married but she sees what happens to her married friends, left with children to support, worn out before their time. So she stays single. She is virtuous. She is slightly deaf from hanging out clothes in winter. She had done people's washings and cooking for fifteen years and in that time saved thirty dollars. Now she hasn't worked steady for a year and she has spent the thirty dollars. She had dreamed of having a little house or a houseboat perhaps with a spot of ground for a few chickens. This dream she will never realize.

She has lost all her furniture now along with the dream. A married friend whose husband is gone gives her a bed for which she pays by doing a great deal of work for the woman. She comes here every day now, sitting bewildered, her pudgy hands folded in her lap. She is hungry. Her great flesh has begun to hang in folds. She has been living on crackers. Sometimes a box of crackers lasts a week. She has a friend who's a baker and he sometimes steals the stale loaves and brings them to her.

A girl we have seen every day all summer went crazy yesterday at the Y.W. She went into hysterics, stamping her feet and screaming.

She hadn't had work for eight months. "You've got to give me something," she kept on saying. The woman in charge flew into a rage that probably came from days and days of suffering on her part, because she is unable to give jobs, having none. She flew into a rage at the girl and there they were facing each other in a rage, both helpless, helpless. This woman told me once that she could hardly bear the suffering she saw, hardly hear it, that she couldn't eat sometimes and had nightmares at night.

So they stood there, the two women in a rage, the girl weeping and the woman shouting at her. . . .

Ruth Shallcross, *Shall Married Women Work?* (1936)

As this document reveals, a majority of Americans believed that married women should not work. Both government and the private sector developed employment policies that excluded married female workers. In part, this discriminatory treatment expressed the traditional view that married women belonged at home taking care of their families. However, many married women sought work because their unemployed husbands could no longer provide for their families. In what fields did married women face the greatest discrimination?[*]

Legislative Action

Within the last few years, bills have been introduced in the legislatures of twenty-six states against married woman workers. Only one of these passed. This was in Louisiana, and it was later repealed. Six other states have either joint resolutions or governors' orders restricting married women's right to work. Three other states have made a general practice of prohibiting married women from working in public employment . . .

Extent of Discrimination

The National Federation of Business and Professional Women's Clubs made a survey early in 1940 of local employment policies. This was part of a general study which assembled all materials relating to the employment of married women. The survey shows that married women are most likely to find bars against them if they seek jobs as school teachers, or as office workers in public utilities or large manufacturing concerns. Only a very small number of department stores refuse jobs to married women. However, in 1939, the *Department Store Economist* reported that the sentiment against married women "is growing stronger." Opposition, it was found, came from customers, labor organizations, women's clubs, and miscellaneous groups of the unemployed. Despite this opposition, "nearly all stores are either doubtful whether it would be a wise plan to announce publicly a policy against hiring or retaining married women, or believe it would not be helpful to public relations." This attitude may reflect the fact that married women's employment has been advantageous to department stores because the necessary part-time arrangements suited both parties

---

[*]From Ruth Shallcross, "Shall Married Women Work?" National Federation of Business and Professional Women's Clubs, Public Affairs Pamphlet No. 40, New York, 1936.

well. Single women usually want full-time employment, but many married women prefer to work only a few hours each day. . . .

Kinds of Bars

The bars against married women are of different kinds—all of which exist for some school teachers. They may take the form of refusal to hire married women (the most frequent), of dismissal upon marriage, delay in granting promotion, or actual demotion, and either permanent or temporary dismissal when pregnant. Discrimination is often difficult to detect; a married woman may assume that her marriage is the cause of her inability to hold a job, or to get a new one, when the real reason may lie in her lack of ability, personality, or training.

The National Education Association has from time to time made surveys of employment policies in local communities with respect to married women teachers. Its material is more complete than any other. Its survey, made in 1931, revealed that 77 percent of the cities reporting made a practice of not employing married women as new teachers, and 63 percent dismissed women teachers upon marriage. Tenure acts protect married teachers from being dismissed in some states. But although tenure acts may protect teachers who marry after being employed, they do not assure a new teacher that marriage will not be a bar to getting a job. The National Education Association reported in 1939 that teachers in at least thirteen states are legally protected by court decisions from being dismissed for being married. Kentucky seems to be the only state where the contract of marriage is deemed "the very basis of the whole fabric of society" and hence is not an obstacle to employment. . . .

Studies show that men have been affected by unemployment to a much greater extent than have women, because unemployment has been more acute in the heavy industries (steel, oil, mining, etc.) where men are mostly employed. . . . The administrative and clerical jobs connected with these industries, which are partially filled by women, have not been eliminated to anything like the same degree as production jobs.

Consumer and service industries (textile, food, beauty parlors, telephone service, to name only a few), where women are mostly to be found, were not affected seriously as heavy industries by the Depression. The government's recovery measures, based on artificially increasing purchasing power, chiefly stimulated the consumer and service industries, thus opening up relatively more opportunities for women than men. As a result, women have fared better than men in getting new jobs. . . .

State and federal employment offices also give evidence of the relative ease with which women have obtained jobs compared with men, and indicate that men have been unemployed for longer periods of time than have women. One study of a community of 14,000 people in the West makes this point specific. Women's work in the town increased during the early years of the Depression in the needle trades and textiles, as well as in the service occupations, while men's work in glass declined sharply. Another study in a steel town showed much the same thing. Few of the people who oppose married women's employment seem to realize that a coal miner or steel worker cannot very well fill the jobs of nursemaids, cleaning women, or the factory and clerical occupations now filled by women. Unhappily, men accustomed to work in the heavy industries have not been able to fill the jobs in consumer and service industries. Retraining of these men has been practically negligible, and could not have been done in time to benefit them immediately. Expenditures for defense are now once more increasing opportunities in heavy industries, so we may expect to see a fundamental change in the situation in the coming months.

Letter to Eleanor Roosevelt (1934)

Eleanor Roosevelt's empathy for the victims of the Depression made her the social conscience of the New Deal. Hundreds of thousands of letters appealing for assistance were addressed to her. In this letter a California wife pleads with Roosevelt to find work for her husband. Although the letter addresses the family's desperation and her pregnancy, the writer promised to return to work when her baby was a year old. How does this letter provide evidence of married women's need for employment? *

Eureka, Calif.
June 14, 1934

Mrs. F. D. Roosevelt
Washington, D.C.

Dear Mrs. Roosevelt:

I know you are overburdened with requests for help and if my plea cannot be recognized, I'll understand it is because you have so many others, all of them worthy. But I am not asking for myself alone. It is as a potential mother and as one woman to another.

My husband and I are a young couple of very simple, almost poor families. We married eight years ago on the proverbial shoestring but with a wealth of love. We both wanted more than anything else to establish a home and maintain that home in a charming, quiet manner. I had a job in the County Court House before I married, and my husband was, and is, a surveyor. I kept my job as it seemed the best and only way for us to pay for a home as quickly as we could. His work was not always permanent, as surveyors, jobs seldom are, but we managed to build our home and furnish it

*From "Mrs. M. H. A. to Eleanor Roosevelt," June 14, 1934, in Robert S. McElvaine, *Down and Out in the Great Depression: Letters from the Forgotten Man* (Chapel Hill: University of North Carolina Press, 1983), 54–55. Copyright © by the University of North Carolina Press. Used by permission of the publisher.

comfortably. Perhaps we were foolish to put all our money into it but we felt it was not only a pleasure but a saving for the future.

Then came the depression. My work has continued and my salary alone has just been sufficient to make our monthly payments on the house and keep our bills paid. But with the exception of two and one-half months work with the U.S. Coast and Geodetic Survey under the C.W.A., my husband has not had work since August 1932.

My salary could continue to keep us going, but—I am to have a baby. We wanted one before but felt we should have more assurance for the future before we deliberately took such a responsibility. But now that it has happened, I won't give it up! I'm willing to undergo any hardship for myself, and I can get a leave of absence from my job for a year. But can't you, won't you do something so my husband can have a job, at least during that year? I realize there is going to be a lot of expense and we have absolutely nothing but our home, which still carries a mortgage of $2000. We can't lose that because our baby will need it. And I can't wait until the depression is over to have a baby. I will be 31 in October and I'll soon be too old.

We had such high hopes in the early spring that the Coast and Geodetic work would continue. Tommy, my husband, had a good position there, and we were so happy. We thought surely our dreams of a family could come true. Then the work ended and like "The best laid plans of mice and men" our hopes were crushed again. But now Fate has taken it into her own hands and left it to us to work it out somehow. I'm happy, of course, but Tommy is nearly out of his head. He has tried every conceivable prospect but you must know how even pick and shovel jobs do not exist.

If the Coast and Geodetic work could continue or if he could get a job with the Bureau of Public Roads—anything in the surveying line. A year is all I ask and after that I can go back to work and we can work out our own salvation. But to have this baby come to a home full of worry and despair, with no money for things it needs, is not fair. It needs and deserves a happy start in life.

As I said before, if it were only ourselves, or if there were something we could do about it, we would never ask for help. We have always stood on our own feet and been proud and happy. But you are a mother and you'll understand this crisis.

Tommy is competent and dependable. He has a surveyor's license and was level man for the U.S. Coast and Geodetic work in this (Humbolt) county. He will go away from home for work, if necessary, but, dear Mrs. Roosevelt, will you see if you can arrange for a job for him? It sounds impossible, I know, but I am at a point where I *ask* the impossible. I have to be selfish now.

I shall hope and pray for a reply and tell myself that you are the busiest woman in America, if I don't receive it. I am going to continue to work for as long as I can and then—an interval of waiting. God grant it will be serene and untroubled for my baby's sake.

Very sincerely yours,

Mrs. M. H. A.
Eureka, Humboldt County
California

Ann Marie Low, *Dust Bowl Diary* (1934)

Excerpts from Ann Marie Low's diary show the contribution young unmarried women made to the family economy. The constant dust storms added to Low's despair and increased the burden of household tasks. What employment opportunities did Low have? How vital was her household labor to her family's well-being? [*]

April 25, 1934, Wednesday

Last weekend was the worst dust storm we ever had. We've been having quite a bit of blowing dirt every year since the drought started, not only here, but all over the Great Plains. Many days this spring the air is just full of dirt coming, literally, for hundreds of miles. It sifts into everything. After we wash the dishes and put them away, so much dust sifts into the cupboards we must wash them again before the next meal. Clothes in the closets are covered with dust.

Last weekend no one was taking an automobile out for fear of ruining the motor. I rode Roany to Frank's place to return a gear. To find my way I had to ride right beside the fence, scarcely able to see from one fence post to the next.

Newspapers say the deaths of many babies and old people are attributed to breathing in so much dirt.

May 7, 1934, Monday

The dirt is still blowing. Last weekend Bud [her brother] and I helped with the cattle and had fun gathering weeds. Weeds give us greens for salad before anything in the garden is ready. We use dandelions, lamb's quarter, and sheep sorrel. I like sheep sorrel best. Also, the leaves of sheep sorrel, pounded and boiled down to a paste, make a good salve.

Still no job. I'm trying to persuade Dad I should apply for rural school #3 out here where we went to school. I don't see a chance of getting a job in a high school when so many experienced teachers are out of work.

He argues that the pay is only $60.00 a month out here, while even in a grade school in town I might get $75.00. Extra expenses in town would probably eat up that extra $15.00. Miss Eston, the practice teaching supervisor, told me her salary has been cut to $75.00 after all the years she has been teaching in Jamestown. She wants to get married. School boards will not hire married women teachers in these hard time because they have husbands to support them. Her fiancé is the sole support of his

---

[*]From Ann Marie Low, *Dust Bowl Diary* (Lincoln, Neb: University of Nebraska Press, 1984), 95–96. Reprinted by permission of University of Nebraska Press. Copyright © 1984 by the University of Nebraska Press.

widowed mother and can't support a wife, too. So she is stuck in her job, hoping she won't get another salary cut because she can scarcely live on what she makes and dress the way she is expected to.

Dad argues the patrons always stir up so much trouble for a teacher at #3; some teachers have quit in mid-term. The teacher is also the janitor, so the hours are long.

I figure I can handle the work, kids, and patrons. My argument is that by teaching here I can work for my room and board at home, would not need new clothes, and so could send most of my pay to Ethel [her sister] and Bud.

Louise Mitchell, *Slave Markets in New York City* (1940)

The journalist Louise Mitchell, who wrote this account, compared the exploitation of African-American domestics to that of slaves. For the majority of African-American women, domestic employment was their sole means of survival. In major cities throughout the nation, desperate women stood on sidewalks waiting for white women to employ them. The extremely low pay and long hours that characterized domestic employment illustrate how class and race have divided women. Why did Mitchell describe African-American women wage earners as the nation's "most oppressed group?"[*]

Every morning, rain or shine, groups of women with brown paper bags or cheap suitcases stand on street corners in the . . .bargain for their labor.

They come as early as 7 in the morning, wait as late as four in the afternoon with the hope that they will make enough to buy supper when they go home. Some have spent their last nickel to get to the corner and are in desperate need. When the hour grows later, they sit on boxes if any are around. In the afternoon their labor is worth only half as much as in the morning. If they are lucky, they get about 30 cents an hour scrubbing, cleaning, laundering, washing windows, waxing floors and woodwork all day long; in the afternoon, when most have already been employed, they are only worth the degrading sum of 20 cents an hour.

Once hired on the "slave market," the women often find after a day's backbreaking toil, that they worked longer than was arranged, got less than was promised, were forced to accept clothing instead of cash and were exploited beyond

---

[*] From Louise Mitchell, "Slave Markets Typify Exploitation of Domestics." Published in the *Daily Worker*, May 5, 1940. Reprinted by permission of People's Weekly World.

human endurance. Only the urgent need for money makes them submit to this routine daily.

Throughout the county, more than two million women are engaged in domestic work, the largest occupational group for women. About half are Negro women . . .

Though many Negro women work for as little as two dollars a week and as long as 80 hours a week . . . they have no social security, no workmens' compensation, no old age security. . . .

The Women's Bureau in Washington points out that women take domestic work only as a last resort. Largely unprotected by law, they find themselves at the mercy of an individual employer. Only two states, Wisconsin and Washington, have wage or hour legislation. But enforcement is very slack. . . .

The tradition of street corner markets is no new institution in this city. As far back as 1834, the statute books show a place was set aside on city streets, where those seeking work could meet with those who wanted workers. This exchange also functions for male workers . . . . At present, markets flourish in the Bronx and Brooklyn, where middle-class families live. However, this method of employment is also instituted in Greenwich Village, Richmond and Queens. . . .

The prosperity of the nation can only be judged by the living standards of its most oppressed group. State legislatures must pass laws to protect the health and work of the domestic. A world of education is still needed, both for employees and employers.

Many civic and social organizations are now working toward improving conditions of domestics. Outstanding among these is the Bronx Citizens Committee for Improvement of Domestic Employees. The YWCA and many women's clubs are interested in the problem. Mayor LaGuardia . . . must be forced to end these horrible conditions of auction block hiring with the most equitable solution for the most oppressed section of the working class—Negro women.

Mary McLeod Bethune, *A Century of Progress of Negro Women* (1933)

In this speech Mary McLeod Bethune (1875–1955) recounted the progress African-American women had made since emancipation. In stark contrast to impoverished domestic workers, upwardly mobile African-American women not only achieved middle-class status, but a few, despite enormous odds, even achieved national recognition. Bethune was one of those women. A child of freed slaves, Bethune established an elementary school for blacks that she later transformed into a college. An advisor to Franklin Roosevelt, she was the first African-American woman to receive a high-level New Deal appointment. How did Bethune define the "character" of African-American womanhood? How would you reconcile this account of "progress" with the miserable conditions of domestic workers described in the preceding document? *

To Frederick Douglass is credited the plea that, "the Negro be not judged by the heights to which he is risen, but by the depths from which he has climbed." Judged on that basis, the Negro woman embodies one of the modern miracles of the New World.

One hundred years ago she was the most pathetic figure on the American continent. She was not a person, in the opinion of many, but a thing—a thing whose personality had no claim to the respect of mankind. She was a household drudge—a means for getting distasteful work done; she was an animated agricultural implement to augment the service of mules and plows in cultivating and harvesting the cotton crop. Then she was an automatic incubator, a producer of human live stock, beneath whose heart and lungs more potential laborers could be bred and nurtured and brought to the light of toilsome day.

Today she stands side by side with the finest manhood the race has been able to produce. Whatever the achievement of the Negro man in letters, business, art, pulpit, civic progress and moral reform, he cannot but share them with his sister of darker hue. Whatever glory belongs to the race for a development unprecedented in history for the given length of time, a full share belongs to the womanhood of the race.

By the very force of circumstances, the part she has played in the progress of the race has been of necessity, to a certain extent, subtle and indirect. She has not always been permitted a place in the front ranks where she could show her face and make her voice heard with effect. But she has been quick to seize every opportunity which presented itself; to come more and more into the open and strive directly for the uplift of the race and nation. In that direction, her achievements have been amazing.

Negro women have made outstanding contributions in the arts. Meta V.W. Fuller and May Howard Jackson are significant figures in Fine Arts development. Angelina Grimké, Georgia Douglass Johnson and Alice Dunbar Nelson are poets of note. Jessie Fausett has become famous as a novelist. In the field of Music; Anita Patti Brown, Lillian Evanti, Elizabeth Greenfield, Florence Cole-Talbert, Marian Anderson and Marie Selika stand out pre-eminently.

Very early in the post-emancipation period, women began to show signs of ability to contribute to the business progress of the Race. Maggie L. Walker, who is outstanding as the guiding spirit of the Order of Saint Luke, in 1902 went before her Grand Council with a plan for a Saint Luke Penny Savings Bank. This organization started with a deposit of about eight thousand dollars and twenty-five thousand in paid up capital, with Maggie L. Walker as the first Woman Bank President in America. For twenty-seven years she has held this place. Her bank has paid dividends to stockholders; has served as a depository for gas and water accounts of the city of

---

*From Mary McLeod Bethune, "A Century of Progress of Negro Women," speech Chicago Women's Federation, June 30, 1933. The Mary McLeod Bethune Papers, The Armistad Research Center, Tulane University, New Orleans.

Richmond, and has given employment to hundreds of Negro clerks, bookkeepers and office workers.

With America's great emphasis on the physical appearance, a Negro woman left her washtub and ventured into the world of facial beautification. From a humble beginning, Madame C. J. Walker built a substantial institution that is a credit to American business in every way.

Mrs. Annie M. Malone is another pioneer in this field of successful business. The C. J. Walker Manufacturing Company and the Poro College do not confine their activities in the field of beautification to race. They serve both races and give employment to both.

When the ballot was made available to the Womanhood of America, the sister of darker hue was not slow to seize the advantage. In sections where the Negro could gain access to the voting booth, the intelligent, forward-looking element of the Race's women have taken hold of political issues with an enthusiasm and mental acumen that might well set worthy examples for other groups. Of times she has led the struggle toward moral improvement and political record, and has compelled her reluctant brother to follow her determined lead.

In time of war as in time of peace, the Negro woman has ever been ready to serve for her people's and the nation's good. During the recent World War she pleaded to go in the uniform of the Red Cross nurse, and was denied the opportunity only on the basis of racial discrimination.

Addie W. Hunton and Kathryn M. Johnson gave yeoman service with the American Expeditionary Forces with the Y.M.C.A. group.

Negro women have thrown themselves whole-heartedly into the organization of groups to direct the social uplift of their fellow men, one of the greatest achievements of the race.

Perhaps the most outstanding individual social worker of our group today is Jane E. Hunter, founder and executive secretary of the Phillis Wheatley Association, Cleveland, Ohio.

In November, 1911, Miss Hunter, who had been a nurse in Cleveland for only a short time, recognizing the need for a Working Girls' Home, organized the Association and prepared to establish the work. Today the Association is housed in a magnificent structure of nine stories, containing one hundred thirty-five rooms, offices, parlours, a cafeteria and beautify parlour. It is not only a home for working girls but a recreational center and ideal hospice for the young Negro woman who is living away from home. It maintains an employment department and a fine, up-to-date camp. Branches of the activities of the main Phillis Wheatley are located in other sections of Cleveland, special emphasis being given to the recreational facilities for children and young women of the vicinities in which the branches are located.

In no field of modern social relationship has the hand of service and the influence of the Negro woman been felt more distinctly than in the Negro orthodox church. It may be safely said that the chief sustaining force in support of the pulpit and the various phases of missionary enterprise, has been the feminine element of the membership. The development of the Negro church since the Civil War has been another of the modern miracles. Throughout its growth the untiring effort, the unflagging enthusiasm, the sacrificial contribution of time, effort and cash earnings of the black woman have been the most significant factors, without which the modern Negro church would have no history worth the writing.

Both before and since emancipation, by some rare gift, she has been able to hold on to the fires of family unity and keep the home one unimpaired whole. In recent years it has become increasingly the case where in many instances the mother is the sole dependence of the home, and single-handed, fights the wolf from the door, while the father submits unwillingly to enforced idleness and unavoidable unemployment. Yet in myriads of instances she controls home discipline with a tight rein and exerts a unifying influence that is the miracle of the century.

The true worth of a race must be measured by the character of its womanhood.

As the years have gone on the Negro woman has touched the most vital fields in the civilization of today. Wherever she has contributed, she has left the mark of a strong character. The educational institutions she has established and directed have met the needs of her young people; her cultural development has concentrated itself into artistic presentation accepted and acclaimed by meritorious critics; she is successful as a poet and a novelist; she is shrewd in business and capable in politics; she recognizes the importance of uplifting her people through social, civic and religious activities; starting at the time when as a "mammy" she nursed the infants of the other race and taught him her meager store of truth, she has been a contributing factor of note to interracial relations. Finally, through the past century she has made and kept her home intact—humble though it may have been in many instances. She has made and is making history.

12

World War II and Postwar Trends: Disruption, Domestic Restoration, and Emergent Protest

During the war years the number of women workers grew from 12 million to 16.5 million. The war enabled women to participate in male-designated fields such as munitions manufacture, shipbuilding, and the automobile and airplane industries. Women worked within steel mills, in coke plants and tended blast furnaces. The demand for labor made possible African-American women's entry into positions previously denied them on the basis of race and gender. Even though women performed formerly forbidden work, sex-linked job classifications and lower pay perpetuated the customary bias against women's work. Women's assumption of nontraditional work was a response to wartime needs. At no time did the government, corporations or unions intend to restructure gender roles or permanently alter workplace patterns. For those women who were mothers responsible for the care of young children, neither the U.S. government nor private industry made adequate provision for day care. Approximately two hundred thousand women joined military auxiliaries. At war's end, women who wanted to continue working confronted the determination of both the government and the private sector to resume sex-segregated patterns of work and return women, particularly married women, to full-time domestic roles. In fact, a complete reversal of propaganda occurred with regard to women workers. During the war women were told it was selfish and unpatriotic to stay at home. After the war the argument was reversed: patriotic women relinquished their positions regardless of their own needs.

Identified as potential subversives, Japanese Americans were herded into internment camps. Denied civil liberties, relcoation entailed the loss of property and homes. Within this dismal context, parental bonds weakened and younger women gained a greater degree of self assertion.

With the veterans' return marriages proliferated and the birth rate soared. Veterans and their families fueled the massive postwar suburban expansion. By the 1950s the suburban lifestyle was the cultural norm. Women's magazines, educators, and psychologists popularized beliefs that fulfillment depended on marriage, home, and family care. To choose an alternative lifestyle was to be labelled "unfeminine" and "unnatural," and in need of psychological help. The national concern with the Cold War and the increasing belief that Communism menaced domestic security, intensified support for traditional family values. In a postwar world of international tension, the suburban home and family unity represented stability.

Yet, by the mid-1950s, undercurrents of social dissatisfaction whirled beneath the images of domestic bliss. Civil rights activism, in which African-American women played a central role, shattered white complacency about the racist status quo. Jo Ann Gibson Robinson recounts how Rosa Parks' refusal to give her seat to a white passenger launched the Montgomery, Alabama bus boycott, and the first of a series of mass-based civil rights demonstrations. Ann Moody describes her role in the effort to end segregated lunch counters. By the early 1960s, Mexican-American Dolores Huerta was involved in community and civil rights activism. She joined César Chávez in the formation of the United Farm Worker's Union. Huerta's activism undermined cultural norms of womanly subordination. Women's participation in civil rights protest facilitated the development of the feminist movement.

As Cold War tensions escalated, women organized peace demonstrations and protested nuclear proliferation and atomic testing. The mother of the modern environmental movement, Rachel Carson, exposed the lethal effects of pesticides on the environment and challenged the multibillion dollar chemical industry. In a flight from conventional domestic roles, some young women joined the beatnik subculture. With Betty Friedan's 1963 publication of *The Feminine Mystique*, evidence also began to appear that for many white middle-class wives and mothers all-enveloping domesticity produced more discontent than fulfillment.

Richard Jefferson, *African-American Women Factory Workers* (1941)

World War II provided African-American women with a rare opportunity for industrial employment. Approximately 6,000 black women were employed in war-related civilian jobs. In search of work, African-American women left their impoverished lives as sharecroppers. This document records conditions in St. Louis, where pervasive racial discrimination added to the burden of gender restriction.[*]

In July 1942, the Curtiss-Wright Company and the U.S. Cartridge Company announced that they would accept Negro applicants for training for skilled and semiskilled operators. By August the Curtiss-Wright Company had approximately 500 Negro workers in a segregated building in a variety of skilled jobs, including welders, riveters, assemblers and inspectors.

Simultaneously, the U.S. Cartridge Company provided a segregated plant identical with other production units and employed a complete force of Negro production workers. . . .

At peak production the company employed a total of 4,500 Negroes, many of whom held jobs as machine operators, millwrights, inspectors and adjusters.

If this form of segregation in industry can be looked upon with favor, it might be said that these firms made a reasonable effort to use the available Negro labor supply. However, other large industries attempted to restrict the number of Negroes to the population ratio of one to ten. Further, they made little or no effort to upgrade Negroes, according to seniority or skills. This flat refusal to comply with the spirit and letter of the Executive Order has precipitated a very unsatisfactory situation, and has caused numerous strikes and work stoppages among dissatisfied Negro workers. The prejudices of white workers in the area is unusually blamed for the failure to upgrade Negroes. In at least 100 important war production plants no Negro workers have been employed.

The employment of Negro women in St. Louis industries presents a more discouraging picture, as might be expected. Stronger resistance to their use except as maids and cleaners, or in segregated workshops, has been encountered in almost every instance. With the exception of the Curtiss-Wright Company, which employs about 200 women as riveters, assemblers, and inspectors, and the U.S. Cartridge Company, which used almost 1,000 women as operators and inspectors, few plants in the area have attempted to use them. The lack of separate toilet facilities and the prejudices of white women workers are the main barriers to the wider use of Negro women, according to officials of many of 200 plants that refuse to employ them.

Perhaps the one bright spot in this picture is the development in the garment industry, although the policy of segregation has been followed even in this field, despite our efforts to eliminate it. Since 1930 the Urban League of St. Louis has worked to secure employment opportunities for Negro women in some of the numerous textile plants. In the Spring of 1941 the Acme Manufacturing Company opened an all-Negro plant employing 28 operators, a packer and a foreman. . . .

Until March, 1943, no other manufacturer would consider the employment of Negro women. With depleted labor reserves and mounting war orders, several plants were forced to look elsewhere for workers, and the Portnoy Garment Company was

---

[*]From Richard R. Jefferson, "Negro Employment in St. Louis War Production," *Opportunity 22*, 3, July–September 1944.

one of the first to consider the use of Negroes. While not willing to integrate Negroes in the plant, the Portnoy Company agreed to open an all-Negro plant, if a suitable building could be obtained and qualified workers were available. Because of the exclusion of Negroes from the trade, there were few if any experienced operators except those employed by the Acme Co. However, the St. Louis and East St. Louis N.Y.A. projects had given training to approximately 300 girls, and a few had been trained at the Washington Technical School. From these groups, it was possible to recruit a sufficient number of operators to open the new plant on May 10, 1943. By the end of the year 60 women were employed, and by May 1, 1944 the factory had 90 workers and was planning an expansion to accommodate an additional 40 operators.

Negro workers in the St. Louis area have not accepted the discrimination against them without protest. Through mass meetings and petitions they have expressed their disapproval of the situation even after they have secured employment. No less than a half dozen all-Negro strikes have occurred in protest to discriminatory hiring or working policies. In June, 1943, Negroes struck because the company would not upgrade qualified Negroes to jobs as foremen. The company finally agreed to comply with their demands. A few weeks later the workers in the segregated Curtiss-Wright building staged a sit-down strike protesting the lack of adequate cooling equipment. In August, 1943, 600 Negro workers in the General Steel Casting plant in Madison, Illinois, struck because of a number of grievances, including differentials in the pay rate and discrimination against Negro women workers. After several weeks of negotiations in which the Urban League took an active part, 61 or the 62 grievance cases were satisfactorily adjusted.

In November, 1943 and March, 1944, 380 Negro employees of the Monsanto Chemical Company staged a series of work stoppages, one of which lasted 10 days. Long-standing grievances against both the company the union were responsible for the difficulties, but the refusal to upgrade Negro workers was the major complaint. The League was instrumental in placing their grievances before company and union officials and an acceptable settlement was finally negotiated. Minor incidents involving the introduction and integration of Negro workers in the industries in this area have been too frequent to enumerate, and they have served to further confuse a very tense and unsettled war production center. . . .

Postwar Plans of Women Workers (1946)

Government surveys provide explicit evidence that the majority of women employees wanted to continue working after the war. The following survey revealed that seventy-five percent of female workers planned to keep their wartime positions. Among this group, eighty-four percent alleged that they had no other means of support. Yet, government and the private sector ignored the expressed needs of women, and many lost their jobs. What reasons did women give for wanting to keep their work? How did the post-World War II situation relate to the experience confronted by the women streetcar conductors after World War I?[*]

That very large numbers of wartime women workers intend to work after the war is evidenced by their statements to interviewers. On the average, about 75 percent of the wartime-employed women in the 10 areas expected to be part of the postwar labor force. . . .

These prospective postwar women workers did not, for the most part, contemplate out-migration from their areas of wartime employment. Over 90 percent of them, in most areas, looked forward to continued employment after the war in the same areas where they had worked during the war period. . . .

In each area, the number of wartime-employed women who intended to work in the same area after the war, greatly exceeded the number of women employed in the area in 1940. In the Detroit area, for example, for every 100 women who were working in 1940, excluding household employees, 155 women will want postwar jobs. About two and one-half times as many women wanted to continue working in the Mobile area as were employed in 1940. . . .

The highest percentage of prospective postwar workers in most areas came from the group of women who had been employed before Pearl Harbor, rather than from those who had been in school or engaged in their own housework at that time. On average, over four-fifths of the women who had been employed both before Pearl Harbor and in the war period, intended to keep on working after the war. Among the war-employed women who had not been in the labor force the week before Pearl Harbor, over three-fourths of the former students expected to continue working, while over half of those formerly engaged in their own housework had such plans. . . .

Very large proportions of the migrant women workers planned to continue work in the areas where they had been employed during the war. Although in comparison to resident women employed in the war period smaller proportions of the in-migrants planned to remain in the labor force, the bulk of the in-migrants who did expect to work wanted to do so in the same area where they had been employed during the war. Consequently, in the areas where in-migrants were important during the war, they also constituted a substantial proportion of the women who intended to work in the area after the war. In four of the seven areas where in-migrants were important, in-migrants constituted between 32 and 44 percent of the total group of women who planned to continue work; and in the other three areas where in-migrants were important, they represented between 10 and 26 percent of the women who planned to continue.

---

[*]From *Women Workers in Ten War Production Areas and Their Postwar Employment Plans.* Washington, D.C.: US Government Printing Office, 1946 (Women's Bureau, Bulletin 209).

The nature of postwar employment problems is influenced not only by the number of wartime workers who expect to remain in the labor force, but also by their expressed desire for work in particular industries and occupations. Postwar job openings as cafeteria bus girls, for example, are not apt to prove attractive to women who are seeking work as screw-machine operators.

The bulk of the prospective postwar workers interviewed in this survey, or 86 percent, wanted their postwar jobs in the same industrial group as their wartime employment, and about the same proportion wanted to remain in the same occupational group. Postwar shifts to other industries were contemplated on a somewhat larger scale, however, among the wartime employees in restaurants, cafeterias, and similar establishments, as well in the personal service industries in certain areas. In the Dayton area, for example, among the war-employed women who expected to remain in the labor force, fully 36 percent of those in eating and drinking places, and 30 percent of those in personal service industries said they wanted jobs in other industries after the war. . . .

In the Mobile area almost a third of the women employed in the war period were Negro. Four areas, between 10 and 19 percent inclusive, were non-white (including some non-white in San Francisco). In the remaining five areas less than 10 percent of the war-employed women were Negro or of other non-white races.

In each of the nine areas where there were enough non-white employed women to make comparison valid, a much higher proportion of the Negro women planned to continue work than of the white women. In six areas 94 percent or more of the Negro or other non-white women who were employed in the war period, planned to continue after the war. . . .

Responsibility for the support of themselves, or themselves and others, was the outstanding reason given by war-employed women for planning to continue work after the war. As already pointed out, about three-fourths of the wartime-employed women in the ten areas (excluding household employees) planned to keep on working after the war. Fully 84 percent of them had no other alternative, as this was the proportion among them who based their decision on their need to support themselves and often, other persons as well. Eight percent offered special reasons for continuing at work, such as buying a home or sending children to school; and only eight percent reported they would remain in the labor force because they liked working, or liked having their own money.

Virtually all of the single women and those who were widowed or divorced (96 and 98 percent, respectively) who intended to remain in gainful employment after the war stated they would do so in order to support themselves, or themselves and others, whereas 57 percent of the married wartime workers who expected to remain at work gave this reason. The remaining married prospective postwar workers interviewed offered reasons of the special purpose type, such as buying a home, about as often as those of the "like-to-work" type. Because married women differed so much on this issue from women in other marital status groups, differences from area to area in the proportions of prospective postwar workers, who offered each of the three sets of reasons, reflect largely the relative concentration of married women in each area. . . .

That the need to work is just as pressing among some married women as among some single women was highlighted by the replies from the war-employed women on the number of wage earners in the family group. Out of every 100 married women who were living in family groups of two or more persons, 11 said they were the only wage earner supporting the family group. This was almost identical to the proportion of sole supporting wage earners among single women living with their families. The state of marriage, therefore, does not, in itself, always mean there is a male provider for the family.

Jo Ann Gibson Robinson, *The Montgomery Bus Boycott* (1955)

African-American women such as Rosa Parks and Jo Ann Gibson Robinson played key leadership roles against racist oppression. In the following document, Jo Ann Robinson, a college professor and community activist (b. 1912), recounts the unfolding of the Montgomery, Alabama, bus boycott. In addition to being a seamstress, Rosa Parks also was secretary of the Montgomery NAACP. What role did these women play in launching the boycott? [*]

In the afternoon of Thursday, December 1, [1955] a prominent black woman named Mrs. Rosa Parks was arrested for refusing to vacate her seat for a white man. Mrs. Parks was a medium-sized, cultured mulatto woman; a civic and religious worker; quiet unassuming, and pleasant in manner and appearance; dignified and reserved; of high morals and a strong character. She was—and still is, for she lives to tell the story—respected in all black circles. By trade she was a seamstress, adept and competent in her work.

Tired from work, Mrs. Parks boarded a bus. The "reserved seats" were partially filled, but the seats just behind the reserved section were vacant, and Mrs. Parks sat down in one. It was during the busy evening rush hour. More black and white passengers boarded the bus, and soon all the reserved seats were occupied. The driver demanded that Mrs. Parks get up and surrender her seat to a white man, but she was tired from her work. She remained seated. In a few minutes, police summoned by the driver appeared, placed Mrs. Parks under arrest and took her to jail.

[*]From Jo Ann Gibson Robinson, *The Montgomery Bus Boycott and the Women who Started: The Memoir of Jo Ann Gibson Robinson*, ed. by David J. Garrow (Knoxville: University of Tennessee Press, 1987), 43–45.

It was the first time the soft-spoken, middle-aged woman had been arrested. She maintained her decorum and poise, and the word of her arrest spread. Mr. E. D. Nixson, a longtime stalwart of our NAACP branch, along with liberal white attorney Clifford Durr and his wife Virginia, went to the jail and obtained Mrs. Parks's release on bond. Her trial was scheduled for Monday, December 5, 1955.

The news traveled like wildfire into every black home. Telephones jangled; people congregated on street corners and in homes and talked. But nothing was done. A numbing helplessness seemed to paralyze everyone. Very few stayed off the buses the rest of that day or the next. There was fear, discontent, and uncertainty. Everyone seemed to wait for someone to *do* something, but nobody made a move. For that day and a half, black Americans rode the buses as before, as if nothing had happened. They were sullen and uncommunicative, but they rode the buses. There was a silent, tension-filled waiting. For blacks were not talking loudly in public places—they were quiet, sullen, waiting. Just waiting!

Thursday evening came and went. Thursday night was far spent, when, at about 11:30 P.M., I sat in my peaceful, single-family dwelling on a side street. I was thinking about the situation. Lost in thought, I was startled by the telephone's ring. Black attorney Fred Gray, who had been out of town all day, had just gotten back and was returning the phone message I had left him about Mrs. Parks's arrest. Attorney Gray, though a very young man, had been one of my most active colleagues in our previous meetings with bus company officials and Commissioner Birmingham. A Montgomery native who had attended Alabama State and been one of my students, Fred Gray had gone on to law school in Ohio before returning to his hometown to open a practice with the only other black lawyer in Montgomery, Charles Langford.

Fred Gray and his wife Bernice were good friends of mine, and we talked often. In addition to being a lawyer, Gray was a trained, ordained minister of the gospel, actively serving as assistant pastor of Holt Street Church of Christ.

Tonight his voice on the phone was very short and to the point. Fred was shocked by the news of Mrs. Parks's arrest. I informed him that I already was thinking that the WPC [Women's Political Council] should distribute thousands of notices calling for all bus riders to stay off the buses on Monday, the day of Mrs. Parks's trial. "Are you ready?" he asked. Without hesitation, I assured him that we were. With that he hung up, and I went to work.

I made some notes on the back of an envelope: "The Women's Political Council will not wait for Mrs. Parks's consent to call for a boycott of city buses. On Friday, December 2, 1955, the women of Montgomery will call for a boycott to take place on Monday, December 5."

Anne Moody, *The Movement* (1963)

African-American women played key roles in the mass-based civil rights movement of the 1960s. In the following source, Anne Moody (b. 1940), a Mississippi college student, provides an eyewitness account of the effort to end segregated lunch counters at Woolworth's. What role did Moody and other women play in this event?[*]

I had counted on graduating in the spring of 1963, but as it turned out, I couldn't, because some of my credits still had to be cleared with Natchez College. A year before, this would have seemed like a terrible disaster, but now I hardly even felt disappointed. I had a good excuse to stay on campus for the summer and work with the Movement, and this was what I really wanted to do. I couldn't go home again anyway, and I couldn't go to New Orleans—I didn't have money enough for bus fare.

During my senior year at Tougaloo, my family hadn't sent me one penny. I had only the small amount of money I had earned at Maple Hill. I couldn't afford to eat at school or live in the dorms, so I had gotten permission to move off campus. I had to prove that I could finish school, even if I had to go hungry every day. I knew Raymond and Miss Pearl were just waiting to see me drop out. But something happened to me as I got more and more involved with the Movement. It no longer seemed important to prove anything. I had found something outside myself that gave meaning to my life.

I had become very friendly with my social science professor, John Salter, who was in charge of NAACP activities on campus. All during the year, while the NAACP conducted a boycott of the downtown stores in Jackson, I had been one of Salter's most faithful canvassers and church speakers. During the last week of school, he told me that sit-in demonstrations were about to start in Jackson and that he wanted me to be the spokesman for a team that would sit-in at Woolworth's lunch counter. The two other demonstrators would be classmates of mine, Memphis and Pearlena. Pearlena was a dedicated NAACP worker, but Memphis had not been very involved in the Movement on campus. It seemed that the organization had had a rough time finding students who were in a position to go to jail. I had nothing to lose one way or the other. Around ten o'clock the morning of the demonstrations, NAACP headquarters alerted the news services. As a result, the police department was also informed, but neither the policemen nor the newsmen knew exactly where or when the demonstrations would start. They stationed themselves along Capitol Street and waited.

To divert attention from the sit-in at Woolworth's, the picketing started at J.C. Penney's a good fifteen minutes before. The pickets were allowed to walk up and down in front of the store three or four times before they were arrested. At exactly 11 a.m., Pearlena, Memphis, and I entered Woolworth's from the rear entrance. We separated as soon as we stepped into the store, and made small purchases from various counters. Pearlena had given Memphis her watch. He was to let us know when it was 11:14. At 11:14 we were to join him near the lunch counter and at exactly 11:15 we were to take seats at it.

Seconds before 11:15 we were occupying three seats at the previously segregated Woolworth's lunch counter. In the beginning the waitresses seemed to ignore us, as if they really didn't know what was going on. Our waitress walked past us a couple of times before she noticed we had started to write our orders down and realized we wanted service. She asked us what we wanted. We began to read to her from our order slips. She told us that we would be served at the back counter, which was for Negroes.

"We would like to be served here," I said.

The waitress started to repeat what she had said, then stopped in the middle of the sentence. She turned the lights out behind the counter, and she and the other waitresses almost ran to the back of the store, deserting all their white customers. I guess they thought that the violence would start immediately after the whites at the counter realized what was going on. There were five or six other people at the counter. A couple of them just got up and walked away. A girl sitting next to me finished her banana split before leaving. A middle-aged white woman who had not yet been served rose from her seat and came over to us. "I'd like to stay here with you," she said, "but my husband is waiting."

The newsmen came in just as she was leaving. They must have discovered what was going on shortly after some of the people began to leave the store. One of the newsmen ran behind the woman who spoke to us and asked her to identify herself. She refused to give her name, but said she was a native of Vicksburg and a former resident of California. When asked why she had said what she said to us, she replied, "I am in sympathy with the Negro movement." By this time a crowd of cameramen and reporters had gathered around us taking pictures and asking questions, such as Where were we from? Why did we sit-in? What organization sponsored it? Were we students? From what school? How were we classified?

I told them that we were all students at Tougaloo College, that we were represented by no particular organization, and that we planned to stay there even after the store closed. "All we want is service," was my reply to one of them. After they had finished probing for about twenty minutes, they were almost ready to leave.

At noon, students from a nearby white high school started pouring in to Woolworth's. When they first saw us they were sort of surprised. They didn't know how to react. A few started to heckle and the newsmen became interested again. Then the white students started chanting all kinds of anti-Negro slogans. We were called a little bit of everything. The rest of the seats, except the three we were occupying, had been roped off to prevent others from sitting down. A couple of the boys took one end of the rope and made it into a hangman's noose. Several attempts were made to put it around our necks. The crowds grew as more students and adults came in for lunch.

We kept our eyes straight forward and did not look at the crowd except for occasional glances to see what was going on. All of a sudden I saw a face I remembered—the drunkard from the bus station sit-in. My eyes lingered on him just long enough for us to recognize each other. Today he was drunk too, so I don't think he remembered where he had seen me before. He took out a knife, opened it, put it in his pocket, and then began to pace the floor. At this point, I told Memphis and Pearlena what was going on. Memphis suggested that we pray. We bowed our heads, and all hell broke loose. A man rushed forward, threw Memphis from his seat, and slapped my face. Then another man who worked in the store threw me against an adjoining counter.

Down on my knees on the floor, I saw Memphis lying near the lunch counter with blood running out of the corners of his mouth. As he tried to protect his face, the man who'd thrown him down kept kicking him against the head. If he had worn hard-soled shoes instead of sneakers, the first kick probably would have killed Memphis. Finally a man dressed in plain clothes identified himself as a police officer, and arrested Memphis and his attacker. Pearlena had been thrown to the floor. She and I got back on our stools after Memphis was arrested. There were some white Tougaloo teachers in the crowd. They asked Pearlena and me if we wanted to leave. They said that things were getting too rough. We didn't know what to do. While we were trying to make up our minds, we were joined by Joan Trumpauer. Now there were three of us and we were integrated. The crowd began to chant, "Communists, Communists, Communists." Some old man in the crowd ordered the students to take us off the stools.

"Which one should I get first?" a big husky boy said.

"That white nigger," the old man said.

The boy lifted Joan from the counter by her waist and carried her out of the store. Simultaneously, I was snatched from my stool by two high school students. I was dragged about thirty feet toward the door by my hair when someone made them turn me loose. As I was getting up off the floor, I saw Joan coming back inside. We started back to the center of the counter to join Pearlena. Lois Chaffee, a white Tougaloo faculty member, was now sitting next to her. So Joan and I just climbed across the rope at the front end of the counter and sat down. There were now four of us, two white and two Negroes, all women. The mob started smearing us with ketchup, mustard, sugar, pies, and everything on the counter. Soon Joan and I were joined by John Salter, but the moment he sat down he was hit on the jaw with what appeared to be brass knuckles. Blood gushed from his face and someone threw salt into the open wound. Ed King, Tougaloo's chaplain, rushed to him.

Betty Friedan, *The Problem That Has No Name* (1963)

Betty Friedan's *The Feminine Mystique* described the cultural context and collective significance of why many women felt their lives lacked meaning. Although Friedan (b. 1921) based her critique on surveys of Smith College graduates, and students who were mainly of upper middle-class backgrounds, the book was widely read. Women identified with the message that their despair was not a personal psychological problem, but rather the result of a "feminine mystique" that pushed women into full-time domestic roles and disregarded their other needs. How does Friedan describe the mystique of feminine fulfillment?"*

The problem lay buried, unspoken, for many years in the minds of American women. It was a strange stirring, a sense of dissatisfaction, a yearning that women suffered in the middle of the twentieth century in the United States. Each suburban wife struggled with it alone. As she made the beds, shopped for groceries, matched slipcover material, ate peanut butter sandwiches with her children, chauffeured Cub Scouts and Brownies, lay beside her husband at night—she was afraid to ask even of herself the silent question—"Is this all?"

For over fifteen years there was no word of this yearning in the millions of words written about women and for women, in all the columns, books and articles by experts telling women their role was to seek fulfillment as wives and mothers. Over and over women heard in voices of tradition and Freudian sophistication, that they could desire no greater destiny than to glory in their own femininity. Experts told them how to catch a man and how to keep him, how to breastfeed children and handle their toilet training, how to cope with sibling rivalry and adolescent rebellion; how to buy a dishwasher, bake bread, cook gourmet snails, and build a swimming pool with their own hands; how to dress, look, and act more feminine and make marriage more exciting; how to keep their husbands from dying young and their sons from growing into delinquents. They were taught to pity the neurotic, unfeminine, unhappy women who wanted to be poets or physicists or presidents. They learned that truly feminine women do not want careers, higher education, political rights—the independence and the opportunities that the old-fashioned feminists fought for. Some women, in their forties and fifties, still remembered painfully giving up those dreams, but most of the younger women no longer even thought about them. A thousand expert voices applauded their femininity, their adjustment, their new maturity. All they had to do

*From Betty Friedan, *The Feminine Mystique* (New York: Norton, 1963), 11–16, 21–22, 27. Reprinted by permission of W. W. Norton & company, Inc. Copyright © 1974, 1973, 1963 by Betty Friedan.

was devote their lives from earliest girlhood to finding a husband and bearing children. . . .

The suburban housewife—she was the dream image of the young American women and the envy, it was said, of women all over the world. The American housewife—freed by science and labor-saving appliances from the drudgery, the dangers of childbirth and the illnesses of her grandmother. She was healthy, beautiful, educated, concerned only about her husband, her children, her home. She had found true feminine fulfillment. As a housewife and mother, she was respected as a full and equal partner to man in his world. She was free to choose automobiles, clothes, appliances, supermarkets; she had everything that women ever dreamed of.

In the fifteen years after World War II, this mystique of feminine fulfillment became the cherished and self-perpetuating core of contemporary American culture. Millions of women lived their lives in the image of those pretty pictures of the American suburban housewife, kissing their husband goodbye in front of the picture window, depositing their station wagonsful of children at school, and smiling as they ran the new electric waxer over the spotless kitchen floor. They baked their own bread, sewed their own and their children's clothes, kept their new washing machines and dryers running all day. They changed the sheets on the beds twice a week instead of once, took the rug-hooking classes in adult education, and pitied their poor frustrated mothers, who had dreamed of having a career. Their only dream was to be perfect wives and mothers; their highest ambition to have five children and a beautiful house, their only fight to get and keep their husbands. They had no thought for the unfeminine problems of the world outside the home; they wanted the men to make the major decisions. They gloried in their role as women, and wrote proudly on the census blank: "Occupation: housewife."

For over fifteen years, the words written for women, and the words women used when they talked to each other, while their husbands sat on the other side of the room and talked shop or politics or septic tanks, were about problems with their children, or how to keep their husband happy, or improve their children's school, or cook chicken or make slipcovers. Nobody argued whether women were inferior or superior to men; they were simply different. Words like "emancipation" and "career" sounded strange and embarrassing; no one had used them for years. When a Frenchwoman named Simone de Beauvoir wrote a book called *The Second Sex*, an American critic commented that she obviously "didn't know what life was all about," and besides, she was talking about French women. The "woman problem" in America no longer existed.

Gradually I came to realize that the problem that has no name was shared by countless women in America. As a magazine writer I often interviewed women about problems with their children, or their marriages, or their houses, or their communities. But after a while I began to recognize the telltale signs of this other problem. I saw the same signs in suburban ranch houses and split-levels on Long Island and in New Jersey and Westchester County; in colonial houses in a small Massachusetts town; on patios in Memphis; in suburban and city apartments; in living rooms in the Midwest. Sometimes I sensed the problem, not as a reporter, but as a suburban housewife, for during this time I was also bringing up my own three children in Rockland County, New York. I heard echoes of the problem in college dormitories and semi-private maternity wards, at PTA meetings and luncheons of the League of Women Voters, at suburban cocktail parties, in station wagons waiting for trains, and in snatches of conversation overheard at Schrafft's. The groping words I heard from other women, on quiet afternoons when the children were at school, or on quiet evenings when husbands worked late, I think I understood first as a woman long before I understood their larger social and psychological implications.

Just what was this problem that has no name? What were the words women used when they tried to express it? Sometimes a woman would say "I feel empty somehow . . . incomplete." Or she would say, "I feel as if I don't exist." . . .

It is no longer possible to ignore that voice, to dismiss the desperation of so many American women. This is not what being a woman means, no matter what the experts say. For human suffering there is a reason; perhaps the reason has not been found because the right questions have not been asked, or pressed far enough. I do not accept the answer that there is no problem because American women have luxuries that women in other times and lands never dreamed of; part of the strange newness of the problem is that it cannot be understood in terms of the age-old material problems of man: poverty, sickness, hunger, cold. The women who suffer this problem have a hunger that food cannot fill. It persists in women whose husbands are struggling interns and law clerks, or prosperous doctors and lawyers; in wives of workers and executives who make $5,000 a year or $50,000. It is not caused by lack of material advantages; it may not even be felt by women preoccupied with desperate problems of hunger, poverty or illness. And women who think it will be solved by more money, a bigger house, a second car, moving to a better suburb, often discover it gets worse.

It is no longer possible today to blame the problem on loss of femininity; to say that education and independence and equality with men have made American women unfeminine. I have heard so many women try to deny this dissatisfied voice within themselves because it does not fit the pretty picture of femininity the experts have given them. I think, in fact, that this is the first clue to the mystery: the problem cannot be understood in the generally accepted terms by which scientists have studied women, doctors have treated them, counselors have advised them, and writers have written about hem. Women who suffer this problem, in whom this voice is stirring, have lived their whole lives in the pursuit of feminine fulfillment. They are not career women (although career women may have other problems); they are women whose greatest ambition has been marriage and children. For the oldest of these women, these daughters of the American middle-class, no other dream was possible. The ones in their forties and fifties who once had other dreams gave them up and threw themselves joyously into life as housewives. For the youngest, the new wives and mothers, this was the only dream. They are the ones who quit high school and college to marry, or marked time in some job in which they had no real interest until they married. These women are very "feminine" in the usual sense, and yet they still suffer the problem. . . .

If I am right, the problem that has no name stirring in the minds of so many American women today, is not a matter of loss of femininity or too much education, or the demands of domesticity. It is far more important than anyone recognizes. It is the key to these other new and old problems that have been torturing women and their husbands and children, and puzzling their doctors and educators for years. It may well be the key to our future as a nation and a culture. We can no longer ignore that voice within women that says: "I want something more than my husband and my children and my home."

13

Feminist Revival and Women's Liberation

Despite the resurgent cult of domesticity during the 1950s, married women with children were entering the workforce in ever greater numbers. Demographic change undermined traditional roles even as popular culture emphasized them. The advent of the birth control pill and increasing societal acceptance of contraception furthered the separation between sex and motherhood. The 1965 Supreme Court decision *Griswold* v. *Connecticut* severed the remaining prohibition against the dissemination of contraceptives. The baby boom peaked in 1957. Lengthening lifespans and fewer children combined to produce an "empty nest" syndrome among middle-aged women. Growing numbers of older women entered the workforce and joined younger married women who also sought employment to supplement family incomes and to achieve personal fulfillment.

By 1960 signs of federal interest in women's issues appeared within the Kennedy administration. Disappointed by Kennedy's minimal number of federal appointments for women, Eleanor Roosevelt, Esther Petersen, the head of the Women's Bureau, and other prominent women active in Democratic politics, pressured the administration to express a greater commitment to women's issues. Of particular concern were employment opportunities and equitable pay for the growing numbers of working women. The result was the appointment of a Presidential Commission on the Status of Women that successfully promoted the congressional passage of an Equal Pay Act (1963). Although the legislation promised women pay scale equity with men, due to the concept of women's work that resulted in sex-typed designations and a gendered workplace, it was difficult, if not impossible, to determine whether male and female jobs actually were equal.

Title VII of the 1964 Civil Rights Act was a far more significant advance for gender equity. The Civil Rights Act prohibited discrimination in employment on the basis of sex as well as race, color, religion or national origin. The inclusion of sexual discrimination in the act was a result of the efforts of Alice Paul and a small group of politically active feminists, who had unsuccessfully promoted the Equal Rights Amendment. Now they effectively linked sexual discrimination to civil rights legislation. To deal with discrimination, Title VII established the Equal Employment Opportunity Commission (EEOC); however, the EEOC's sluggish efforts to address women's grievances about employment discrimination helped spark the revival of women's rights activism.

The women's rights movement that developed in the late 1960s was formed by two diverse groups of women. Educated, white middle-class women who had reached maturity during the postwar period, formed the National Organization for Women (NOW) in 1966. Demanding a massive reconstruction of gender roles, they stressed the need for women to have equal employment opportunity with men, and for married couples to create a truly equal partnership in home and family care. Under the leadership of Betty Friedan, the founder and first president of NOW, women also used the organization as a forum to express their discontent with the restrictions of domesticity.

Although they did not establish one official organization, younger women who had been active in anti-war and civil rights protest spoke on behalf of women's liberation, and directly confronted the issue of sexism that they maintained caused as much harm to women as racism did to African-Americans. They alleged that sexism pervaded language as well as institutional structures, creating male privilege and preferential treatment in all areas of life. Calling for a united sisterhood, liberation advocates met in small groups dedicated to raising their consciousness that women needed to view their personal problems in a political context. Liberationists also called for collective action to deal with issues concerning male power and also its abuse: male violence toward women. Because of the liberationist effort, spousal abuse, workplace harassment and rape—that had either remained unacknowledged or blamed on the victim—began to receive national attention.

Despite their greater militancy, liberationist groups shared major objectives with NOW. Both upheld a commitment to the dynamic expansion of female opportunity and gender equity. Both campaigned for the right of women to obtain medically safe abortions and the passage of the ERA. NOW also adopted the liberationist perspective on the destructive impact of sexism and supported consciousness raising groups.

Educated, white women from middle-class and professional backgrounds played the dominant role in the resurgence of feminism. In their fundamental concern with gender inequity, sexism, and the widespread societal and cultural acceptance of male privilege, they believed that they spoke in a universal voice for all women living in the United States. During the 1970s their universalist assumptions came under attack. African-American, Chicana, working class, and lesbian women denounced NOW for indifference to issues of oppression that sprang more from race and class than sexism. African-American women asserted that the issue of gender intersected with that of race and class for black women, and could be addressed only in the context of what it meant to be black in white America.

Minority and working class women accused NOW of being too concerned with the career issues of professional women. They charged the women's movement with indifference to the problems of single, working-class mothers and the limited options of poor women. Briefly stated, they asserted that gender was just one and not necessarily the most abusive oppression women faced.

In response to allegations that NOW was too white, too privileged, and too heterosexual, the organization widened its objectives and addressed issues that departed from the mainstream. From its inception, traditional women had rejected the feminist effort to strip away their primary identity as wives and mothers. As NOW moved further left, conservatives found the organization's validation of lesbian and single mother lifestyles an even more extreme example of the feminist determination to undermine women's traditional roles as wives and mothers.

National Organization for Women, *Statement of Purpose* (1966)

The National Organization for Women (NOW) envisioned that a transformation of gender roles would enable men and women to share domestic and child-care tasks. NOW also proposed child-care institutions that would enable women to combine full-time motherhood and a career. In what ways did NOW follow in the path of the Declaration of Sentiments? In what ways did their objectives differ?*

We, men and women who hereby constitute ourselves as the National Organization for Women, believe that the time has come for a new movement toward true equality for all women in America, and toward a fully equal partnership of the sexes, as part of the world-wide revolution of human rights now taking place within and beyond our national borders.

The purpose of NOW is to take action to bring women into full participation in the mainstream of American society now, exercising all the privileges and responsibilities thereof in truly equal partnership with men.

We believe the time has come to move beyond the abstract argument, discussion and symposia over the status and special nature of women, which has raged in America in recent years; the time has come to confront, with concrete action, the conditions that now prevent women from enjoying the equality of opportunity and freedom of choice which is their right as individual Americans, and as human beings.

NOW is dedicated to the proposition that women first and foremost are human beings, who, like all other people in our society, must have the chance to develop their fullest human potential. We believe that women can achieve such equality only by accepting to the full the challenges and responsibilities they share with all other

---

* Reprinted from the National Organization for Women "Statement of Purpose." It should be noted that this is a historical document and does not reflect all current NOW policies and priorities.

people in our society, as part of the decision-making mainstream of American political, economic and social life.

We organize to initiate or support action, nationally or in any part of this nation, by individuals or organizations, to break through the silken curtain or prejudice and discrimination against women in government, industry, the professions, the churches, the political parties, the judiciary, the labor unions; in education, science, medicine, law, religion and every other field of importance in American society. . . .

There is no civil rights movement to speak for women, as there has been for Negroes and other victims of discrimination. The National Organization for Women must therefore begin to speak.

WE BELIEVE that the power of American law, and the protection guaranteed by the U.S. Constitution to the civil rights of all individuals, must be effectively applied and enforced to isolate and remove patterns of sex discrimination, to ensure equality of opportunity in employment and education, and equality of civil and political rights and responsibilities on behalf of women, as well as for Negroes and other deprived groups.

We realize that women's problems are linked to many broader questions of social justice; their solution will require concerted action by many groups. Therefore, convinced that human rights for all are indivisible, we expect to give active support to the common cause of equal rights for all those who suffer discrimination and deprivation, and we call upon together organizations committed to such goals to support our efforts toward equality for women.

WE DO NOT ACCEPT the token appointment of a few women to high-level positions in government and industry as a substitute for a serious continuing effort to recruit and advance women according to their individual abilities. To this end, we urge American government and industry to mobilize the same resources of ingenuity and command with which they have solved problems of far greater difficulty than those now impeding the progress of women. . . .

WE REJECT the current assumptions that a man must carry the sole burden of supporting himself, his wife, and a family, and that a woman is automatically entitled to lifelong support by a man upon her marriage; or that marriage, home and family are primarily a woman's world and responsibility—hers, to dominate, his to support. We believe that a true partnership between the sexes demands a different concept of marriage, an equitable sharing of the responsibilities of home and children, and of the economic burdens of their support. We believe that proper recognition should be given to the economic and social value of homemaking and child care. To these ends, we will seek to open a reexamination of laws and mores governing marriage and divorce, for we believe that the current state of "half-equality" between the sexes discriminates against both men and women, and is the cause of much unnecessary hostility between the sexes.

WE BELIEVE that women must now exercise their political rights and responsibilities as American citizens. They must refuse to be segregated on the basis of sex into separate-and-not-equal ladies' auxiliaries in the political parties, and they must demand representation according to their numbers in the regularly constituted party committees—at local, state, and national levels—and in the informal power structure, participating fully in the selection of candidates and political decision-making, and running for office themselves.

IN THE INTERESTS OF THE HUMAN DIGNITY OF WOMEN, we will protest and endeavor to change the false image of women now prevalent in the mass media, and in the texts, ceremonies, laws and practices of our social institutions. Such images perpetuate contempt for women by society and by women for themselves. We are similarly opposed to all policies and practices—in church, state, college, factory or office—which, in the guise of protectiveness, not only deny opportunities but also foster in women self-denigration, dependence, and evasion of responsibility, undermine their confidence in their own abilities and foster contempt for women. . . .

Frances Sugre, *Diary of a Rent Striker* (1964)

In her diary, Frances Sugre, a Puerto Rican immigrant, recounts the daily struggle to survive in a rat-infested tenement. The behavior of this impoverished woman demonstrated that even women of limited resources have struggled for empowerment. Would a woman like Sugre benefit from the objectives of NOW? [*]

Wednesday, Feb. 5: I got up at 6:45. The first thing to do was light the oven. The boiler was broke so not getting the heat. All the tenants together bought the oil. We give $7.50 for each tenant. But the boiler is old and many things we don't know about the pipes, so one of the men next door who used to be superintendent is trying to fix. I make the breakfast for the three children who go to school. I give then orange juice, oatmeal, scrambled eggs, and Ovaltine. They have lunch in school and sometimes they don't like the food and won't eat, so I say you have a good breakfast. Miss Christine Washington stick her head in at 7:30 and say she go to work. I used to live on ground floor and she was all the time trying to get me move to third floor next door to her because this place vacant and the junkies use it and she scared the junkies break the wall to get into her place and steal everything because she live alone and go to work.

I'm glad I come up here to live because the rats so big downstairs. We all say the "rats is as big as cats." I had a baseball bat for the rats. It's lucky me and the children never got bit. The children go to school and I clean the house and empty the pan in the bathroom that catches the water dripping from pipe into the big hole in the ceiling. You have to carry umbrella to the bathroom sometimes. I got to the laundry place this afternoon and I wash again on Saturday because I change my kids' clothes every day because I don't want them dirty to attract the rats. . . .

After I go out to a rent strike meeting at night, I come home and the women tell me that five policemen came and broke down the door of the vacant apartment of the ground floor where we have meetings for the tenants in our building. They come looking for something—maybe junkies, but we got nothing in there only paper and some chairs and tables. They knocked them all over. The women heard the policemen laughing. When I came up to my place the children already in bed and I bathe myself and then I go to bed and read the newspaper until 11:30.

Thursday, Feb. 6: I wake up at six o'clock and I went into the kitchen to heat a bottle for my baby. When I put the light on in the kitchen I yelled so loud that I don't know if I disturbed the neighbors. There was a big rat coming out from the garbage pail.

Friday, Feb. 7: This morning I woke up a little early. The baby woke up at five o'clock. I went to the kitchen but this time I didn't see the rat.

After the girls left for school I started washing the dishes and cleaning the kitchen. I am thinking about their school. Today they ain't teaching enough. My oldest girl is 5.9 in reading. This is low level in reading. I go to school and English teacher tell me they ain't got enough books to read and that's why my daughter behind. I doesn't care about integration like that. It doesn't bother me. I agree with boycott for some reasons. To get better education and better teachers and better materials in school. I don't like putting them in buses and sending them away. I like to stay here and change the system. Some teachers has to be changed. My girl take Spanish in junior high school and I say to her, "Tell your teacher I'm going to be in school one day to teach him Spanish because I don't know where he learns to teach Spanish but it ain't Spanish."

I'm pretty good woman. I don't bother anyone. But I got my rights. I fight for them. I don't care about jail. Jail don't scare me. If I have to go to jail, I go. I didn't steal. I didn't kill nobody. There's no record for me. But if I have to go, I go.

Saturday, Feb. 8: A tenant called me and asked me what was new in the building because she works daytimes. She wanted to know about the junkies. Have they been on the top floor where the vacant apartment is? That's why I have leaking from the ceiling. The junkies on the top floor break the pipes and take the fixtures and the sink and sell them and that's where the water comes . . . I'm not ascared of the junkies. I open the floor and I see the junkies I tell them to go or I call the police. Many people scared of them, but they scared of my face. I got a baseball bat for the rats and the junkies. . . . I know my rights and I know my self-respect. After supper I played cards (casino) for two hours with the girls and later I got dressed and I went to a party for the rent strike. This party was to get funds for the cause. I had a good time. . . .

Sunday, Feb. 9: I dressed up in an hurry to got to church. When I got to church I pray for to have better house and have a decent living. I hope He's hearing. But I don't get discouraged on Him. I have faith. I don't care how cold I am I never lose my faith. When I come out of church I was feeling so good.

Monday, Feb. 10: At 9:30 a man came to fix the rat holes. He charged me only $3. Then one of the tenants came to tell me that we only had oil for today and every tenant would have to give $7.50 to send for more oil. I went to see some tenants to tell them there is no more oil. We all have to cooperate with money for the oil. . . .

Tuesday, Feb. 11: This morning was too cold in the house that I had to light the oven and heat hot water. We had no steam, the boiler is not running good. I feel miserable. You know when the house is cold you can't do nothing. When the girls left for school I went back to bed. I just got up at 11:30 and this house is so cold. Living in a cold apartment is terrible. . . .

Wednesday, Feb. 12: I wake up around 5 o'clock and the first thing I did was light the oven and the heater so when the girls wake up is a little warm. I didn't call them til 11 because they didn't have to got to school. It is still so cold they trembling. You feel like crying looking your children in this way.

I think if I stay a little longer in this kind of living I'm going to be dead duck. I know that to get into a project you have to have somebody prominent to back you up. Many people got to the projects and they don't even need them. I had been feeling applications I don't know since when. This year I feel another one. This year I *don't vote* for nobody. Maybe my vote don't count, but don't forget if you have fourteen cents you need another penny so you take the bus or the subway. At least I clean my house and you could eat on the floor. The rest of the day I didn't do nothing. I was so mad all day long. I cooked a big pot of soup. I leave it to God to help me. I have faith in Him.

Thursday, Feb. 13: I couldn't get up this morning. The house was so cold that I came out of bed at 7:15. . . . Later on, the inspector came. They were suppose to come to every apartment and look all violations. They knock at the door and asked if anything had been fixed. I think even the inspectors are afraid of this slum condition and that's why they didn't dare to come inside. I don't blame them. They don't want to take a rat or any bug to their houses or get dirty in this filthy houses. My little girl came from school with Valentine she made for me. Very pretty. At 8:30 I went downstairs to a meeting we had. We discuss about why there is no heat. We agreed to give $10 to fix the boiler for the oil. . . .

Friday, Feb. 14 I didn't write this about Friday in my book until this Saturday morning, because Friday night I sick and so cold. It is really hard to believe that this happens here in New York and richest city in the world. But such is Harlem and hope. Is this the way to live. I rather go to the Moon in the next trip.

Jean Smith, *Black Consciousness* (1967)

In this *Redbook* magazine article, Jean Smith (b. 1942) recounted the reasons for her loss of faith in civil rights and her transformation toward "black consciousness." How would the commitment of Smith and other young African-American women to black consciousness make it difficult for them to identify with the predominantly white women's rights movement? What did Smith mean by the statement "I became consciously black?"[*]

I think that once you knew me. It was a time not long past, about four years ago. I was the bright, well-mannered girl who lived down the street from you. My grandmother was always stopping you on your way to the grocery store; she would call you to the door to show you, proudly, college newspaper clippings about her granddaughter's winning a scholarship or achieving a place on the dean's list.

Or possibly you remember me from church. I was the girl who helped sustain the small, overambitious choir by appearing faithfully every Sunday to sing the praises of the Lord in songs that often were too difficult or out of my range. Sometimes you would stop and offer me a few words of encouragement because you said, you liked my spirit. . . .

Yes, I'm certain that you knew, if only superficially, that *something* in me which reached toward the American image. . . .

Thus my early personal experiences suggested that there was room for everybody. After all, I was nobody special and yet I was doing quite well. In fact, it was a long time before I became conscious that being a Negro made me different. I thought I was like everybody else.

It was in the context of my belief in our society's potential for making good on its promise of full men through freedom and democracy, that I responded to the urgings of some of my classmates at Howard University. They were members of the Students' Nonviolent Coordinating Committee (or SNCC, pronounced "Snick") and I joined the Movement. I truly felt, and I think that many SNCC workers then felt similarly, that most Americans believed in these principles, and that when confronted with our documentation that they were being violated in the South, Americans would move to support the rights of Negro citizens.

When I left Washington, D.C., in 1963 to go South with SNCC, you knew me. Now, four years later, I am a different person.

Essentially the difference is that I became consciously black. I came to understand that there wasn't room enough in the society for the mass of black people, that the majority of Americans are acting either in unbearably bad faith or in tragic ignorance when they project to their children the image of an American society where all men are free and equal.

Since, in a way, I was once a friend of yours, perhaps you'll invest a little time and emotional energy in trying to understand what happened.

I went South after the sit-ins that were aimed at desegregating eating places. In the summer of '63 I went to Georgia and then to Mississippi as a SNCC field worker. The focus of SNCC's activity in the Deep South then was voter registration. The logic of it seemed very clear to me. Negroes had a right to vote, to participate in our democracy. In fact, our society wanted everyone's participation. Because of some curious isolation from the rest of the country, the white Southerners had managed to deprive Negroes of this right. But the South was still part of the United States. What we had to do was to show the rest of the United States that democratic participation was being denied our people. Then the rest of the country would insist that the South allow Negroes to vote.

I saw the relationship between political representation and economic and social development: if Negroes could get the vote, then we could use it to attack the poverty and misery which plagued the Negro community. If we could vote, we would be well on our way to full economic and social participation in the larger society. And so I worked with the other SNCC staff people to show the rest of the country that Negroes in the South wanted to vote and couldn't.

We got our people to go down to the courthouse to try to register to vote. After they were turned away from the courthouse or were not allowed to "pass" the test of eligibility for voting, or were intimidated by threats of violence from whites, we appealed to the Justice Department, documenting carefully the instances of refusal and intimidation. Next we organized picket lines and marches to the courthouse to demonstrate to the rest of the country that Negroes *did* want to vote. The marches often ended in mass arrests and violence, but they were reported in the newspapers and on television and the Movement's case was made clear to the public. After there had been much marching and many protests, Congress passed the 1965 Voting Rights Act, which assured Negroes the right to vote. . . .

We found it was a shallow victory. After the earlier sit-ins, the Civil Rights movement had had us turn away from the preachings, assertions and principles of the larger white society and must turn inward to find the means whereby black people can lead full, meaningful lives. We must become conscious that our blackness calls for another set of principles, principles on whose validity we can depend because they come from our own experiences . . .

Redstockings Manifesto (1969)

Women's liberation groups such as Redstockings shared the view that male oppression represented society's major form of control over women. To oppose oppression, they called for a united sisterhood that crossed class, race and ethnic lines. Groups such as Redstockings emphasized that a woman's personal experience could be understood only in the context of unequal power relationships between men and women and sexist institutions. How did Redstockings support their allegation that men are the agents of women's oppression? What similarities exist between this manifesto and the Seneca Falls Declaration of Sentiments? What are the differences? *

I. After centuries of individual and preliminary political struggle, women are uniting to achieve their final liberation from male supremacy. Redstockings is dedicated to building this unity and winning our freedom.

II. Women are an oppressed class. Our oppression is total, affecting every facet of our lives. We are exploited as sex objects, breeders, domestic servants, and cheap labor. We are considered inferior beings, whose only purpose is to enhance men's lives. Our humanity is denied. Our prescribed behavior is enforced by the threat of physical violence.

Because we have lived so intimately with our oppressors, in isolation from each other, we have been kept from seeing our personal suffering as a political condition. This creates the illusion that a woman's relationship with her man is a matter of interplay between two unique personalities, and can be worked out individually. In reality, every such relationship is a *class* relationship, and the conflicts between individual men and women are *political* conflicts that can only be solved collectively.

III. We identify the agents of our oppression as men. Male supremacy is the oldest, most basic form of domination. All other forms of exploitation and oppression (racism, capitalism, imperialism, etc.) are extensions of male supremacy: men dominate women, a few men dominate the rest. All power structures throughout history have been male-dominated and male-oriented. Men have controlled all political, economic and cultural institutions, and backed up this control with physical force. They have used their power to keep women in an inferior position. *All men* receive economic, sexual and psychological benefits from male supremacy. *All men* have oppressed women.

IV. Attempts have been made to shift the burden of responsibility from men to institutions or to women themselves. We condemn these arguments as evasions. Institutions alone do not oppress; they are merely tools of the oppressor. To blame institutions implies that men and women are equally victimized, obscures the fact that men benefit from the subordination of women, and gives men the excuse that they are forced to be oppressors. On the contrary, any man is free to renounce his superior position, provided that he is willing to be treated like a woman by other men.

We also reject the idea that women consent to or are to blame for their own oppression. Women's submission is not the result of brainwashing, stupidity, or mental illness, but of continual, daily pressure from men. We do not need to change ourselves, but to change men.

---

*From "The Redstocking Manifesto," launched by the Redstockings of the Women's Liberation Movement, July 7, 1969. A catalogue and ordering information for this and other documents from the 1960s rebirth years of feminism, and writings by women and women's liberties organizers, is available from the Redstockings Liberation Archives Distribution Project, P.O. Box 2625, Gainsville, FL 32602.

The most slanderous evasion of all is that women can oppress men. The basis for this illusion is the isolation of individual relationships from their political context, and the tendency of men to see any legitimate challenge to their privileges as persecution.

V. We regard our personal experience, and our feelings about that experience, as the basis for an analysis of our common situation. We cannot rely on existing ideologies as they are all products of male supremacy culture. We question every generalization and accept none that are not confirmed by our experience.

Our chief task at present is to develop female class consciousness through sharing experiences and publicly exposing the sexist foundation of all our institutions. Consciousness-raising is not "therapy," which implies the existence of individual solutions and falsely assumes that the male-female relationship is purely personal, but the only method by which we can ensure that our program for liberation is based on the concrete realities of our lives.

The first requirement for raising class consciousness is honesty, in private and in public, with ourselves and other women.

VI. We identify with all women. We define our best interest as that of the poorest, most brutally exploited woman.

We repudiate all economic, racial, educational or status privileges that divide us from other women. We are determined to recognize and eliminate any prejudices we may hold against other women.

We are committed to achieving internal democracy. We will do whatever is necessary to ensure that every woman in our movement has an equal chance to participate, assume responsibities, and develop her political potential.

VII. We call on all our sisters to unite with us in struggle.

We call on all men to give up their male privileges and support women's liberation in the interest of our humanity and their own.

In fighting for our liberation we will always take the side of women against their oppressors. We will not ask what is "revolutionary" or "reformist," only what is good for women.

The time for individual skirmishes has passed. This time we are going all the way.

July 7, 1969

Gloria Steinem, *Statement to Congress* (1970)

Gloria Steinem (b. 1934), a publicist for women's rights and the founder of *Ms.* magazine, defended the ERA by minimizing the biological difference between men and women. She urged all women, regardless of class and racial background, to fight "outdated myths" that enforced both race and gender inequities. In the effort to achieve complete gender equity, advocates of the ERA advanced a legal identity for women that was not dependent on their roles as wives and mothers. Although the amendment received congressional approval, conservatives successfully mobilized to prevent states from ratifying it. What are the "outdated myths" that Steinem discusses?

My name is Gloria Steinem. I am a writer and editor, and I am currently a member of the policy council of the Democratic committee. And I work regularly with the lowest-paid workers in the country, the migrant workers, men, women and children both in California and in my own State of New York. . . .

During twelve years of working for a living, I have experienced much of the legal and social discrimination reserved for women in this country. I have been refused service in public restaurants, ordered out of public gathering places, and turned away from apartment rentals; all for the clearly stated, sole reason that I was a woman. And all without the legal remedies available to blacks and other minorities. I have been excluded from professional groups, writing assignments on so-called "unfeminine" subjects such as politics, full participation in the Democratic party, jury duty, and even from such small male privileges as discounts on airline fares. Most important to me, I have been denied a society in which women are encouraged, or even allowed, to think of themselves as first-class citizens and responsible human beings.

However, after two years of researching the status of American women, I have discovered that in reality, I am very, very lucky. Most women, both wage-earners and housewives, routinely suffer more humiliation and injustice than I do.

As a freelance writer, I don't work in the male-dominated hierarchy of an office. (Women, like blacks and other visibly different minorities, do better in individual professions such as the arts, sports, or domestic work; anything in which they don't have authority over white males.) I am not one of the millions of women who must support a family. Therefore, I haven't had to go on welfare because there are no day-care centers for my children while I work, and I haven't had to submit to the humiliating welfare inquiries about my private and sexual life, inquiries from which

---

*From "The Equal Rights Amendment: Hearings Before the Subcommittee on Constitutional Amendments of the Committee on Judiciary of the United States Senate," 91st Congress, May 5, 6, 7, 1970 (Washington, D.C.: U.S. Government Printing Office, 1970), 331–35, 38–41, 575–78.

men are exempt. I haven't had to brave the sex bias of labor unions and employers, only to see my family subsist on a median salary 40 percent less than the male medial salary.

I hope this committee will hear the personal, daily injustices suffered by many women—professionals and day laborers, women housebound by welfare as well as by suburbia. We have all been silent for too long. But we won't be silent anymore.

The truth is that all our problems stem from the same sex based myths. We may appear before you as white radicals or the middle-aged middle-class or black soul sisters, but we are all sisters in and against these outdated myths. Like racial myths, they have been reflected in our laws. Let me list a few.

That women are biologically inferior to men. In fact, an equally good case can be made for the reverse. Women live longer than men, even when the men are not subject to business pressures. Women survived Nazi concentration camps better, keep cooler heads in emergencies currently studied by disaster-researchers, are protected against heart attacks by their female sex hormones, and are so much more durable at every stage of life that nature must conceive 20 to 50 percent more males in order to keep the balance going.

Man's hunting activities are forever being pointed to as tribal proof of superiority. But while he was hunting, women built houses, tilled the fields, developed animal husbandry, and perfected language. Men, being all alone in the bush, often developed into a creature as strong as women, fleeter of foot, but not very bright.

However, I don't want to prove the superiority of one sex to another. That would only be repeating the male mistake. English scientists once definitely proved, after all, that the English were descended from the angels, while the Irish were descended from the apes; it was the rationale for England's domination of Ireland for more than a century. The point is that science is used to support current myth and economics almost as much as the church was.

What we do know is that the difference between two races or two sexes is much smaller than the difference to be found within each group. Therefore, in spite of the slide show on female inferiorities that I understand was shown to you yesterday, the law makes much more sense when it treats individuals, not groups bundled together by some condition of birth. . . .

Another myth, that women are already treated equally in this society: I am sure there has been ample testimony to prove that equal pay for equal work, equal chance for advancement, and equal training or encouragement is obscenely scarce in every field, even those—like food and fashion industries—that are supposedly "feminine."

A deeper result of social and legal injustice, however, is what sociobiologists refer to as "Internalized Aggression." Victims of aggression absorb the myth of their own inferiority, and come to believe that their group is in fact second class. Even when they themselves realize they are not second class, they may still think their group is, thus the tendency to be the only Jew in the club, the only black woman on the block, the only woman in the office.

Rape, an Act of Terror (1971)

Liberation groups emphasized that a woman's individual encounter with male abuse was more than the random behavior of a violent man. As can be seen from this document, these groups viewed rape as a form of terrorism, the most extreme manifestation of male abuse of women. Liberationists also alleged that cultural norms and laws regarding rape were biased in favor of the rapist. The rape victim needed to prove her innocence by obtaining corroborating evidence, establishing prior virtue, and proving nonprovocative behavior. Why did liberationists argue that rape is "a political act of oppression"? What does the reference to "sexist ideology" mean?[*]

Terror is an integral part of the oppression of women. Its purpose is to ensure, as a final measure, the acceptance by women of the inevitability of male domination. . . . The most important aspect of terrorism is its indiscriminateness with respect to members of the terrorized class. There are no actions or forms of behavior sufficient to avoid this danger. There is no sign that designates a rapist since each male is potentially one. While simple fear is utilitarian, providing the impetus to act for one's safety, the effect of terror is to make all action impossible. . . .

Rape is a punishment without crime or guilt—at least not subjective guilt. It is punishment for the *objective* crime of femaleness. That is why it is indiscriminate. It is primarily a lesson for the whole class of women—a strange lesson, in that it does not teach a form of behavior which will save women from it. *Rape teaches instead the objective, innate, and unchanging subordination of women relative to men.*

Rape supports the male class by projecting its power and aggressiveness on the world. For the individual male, the possibility of rape remains a prerogative of his in-group; its perpetration rekindles his faith in maleness and his own personal worth.

Rape is only slightly forbidden fruit . . . . In New York State, for instance, the law stipulates that the woman must prove she was raped by force, that "penetration" occurred, and that someone witnessed the rapist in the area of the attack. Although the past convictions of the defendant are not admissible evidence in a rape trial, the "reputation" of the rape victim is. The police will refuse to accept charges in many cases, especially if the victim is alone when she comes in to file them. In New York City only certain hospitals will accept rape cases and they are not bound to release their findings to the courts. Finally, the courts consistently refuse to indict men for rape.

---

[*] Excerpted from "Rape: An Act of Terror" by Barbara Merhrhof and Pamela Kearon in *Notes from the Third Year* (1971).

It is clear that women do not come under the law on anything like an equal footing with men—or rather, that women as women do not enjoy the protection of law at all. Women as victims of rape, unlike the general victims of assault, are not assumed to be independent, indistinguishable, and equal citizens. They are viewed by the law as subordinate, dependent, and an always potential hindrance to male action and male prerogative. Rape laws are designed to protect males against the charge of rape. The word of a peer has a special force; the word of a dependent is always suspicious, presumed to be motivated by envy, revenge, or rebellion.

Rape . . . . is not an arbitrary act of violence by one individual on another; it is a political act of *oppression* (never rebellion) exercised by members of a powerful class on members of the powerless class. Rape is supported by a consensus in the male class. It is preached by a male-controlled and all-pervasive media with only a minimum of disguise and restraint. It is communicated to the male population as an act of freedom and strength and a male right never to be denied. . . .

Many women believe that rape is an act of sick men or is provoked by the female. Thus women as a class do not yet have a consensus on a counter-reality which defines the true meaning of rape for us. . . .

The first step toward breaking the debilitating hold on us of the Sexist Ideology is the creation of a counter-reality, a mutually guaranteed support of female experience undistorted by male interpretation. . . . We *must* understand rape as essentially an act of terror against women—whether committed by white men or minority group males. This is the only means of freeing our imagination so that we can act together—or alone if it comes to it—against this most perfect of political crimes.

Chicana Demands (1972)

In search of their own identity and cultural validation, ethnic women organized their own feminist protest groups. During the 1970s, ethnic identity-based groups proliferated. In what ways do these demands express the intersection of class, ethnic, and feminist issues?[*]

We, as *Chicanas*, are a vital part of the *Chicano* community. (We are workers, unemployed women, welfare recipients, housewives, students.) Therefore, we demand that we be heard and that the following resolutions be accepted.

---

[*] From "Chicana Demands" in *Ms.*, December 1972, p.128.

Be it resolved that we, as *Chicanas*, will promote *la hermanidad* [sisterhood] concept in organizing *Chicanas*. As *hermanas*, we have a responsibility to help each other in problems that are common to all of us. . . .

Be it also resolved, that we as *Raza* must not condemn, accept, or transfer the oppression of *La Chicana*.

That all *La Raza* literature should include *Chicana* written articles, poems, and other writings to relate the *Chicana* perspective in the *Chicano* movement.

That *Chicanas* be represented in all levels of *La Raza Unida* party and be run as candidates in all general, primary and local elections.

Jobs

Whereas the *Chicana* on the job is subjected to unbearable inhumane conditions, be it resolved that:

Chicanas receive equal pay for equal work; working conditions, particularly in the garment-factory sweatshops, be improved; *Chicanas* join unions and hold leadership positions within these unions; *Chicanas* be given the opportunity for promotions and be given free training to improve skills; there be maternity leaves with pay.

Prostitution

Whereas prostitution is used by a corrupt few to reap profits for themselves with no human consideration of the needs of *mujeres*, and *whereas* prostitutes are victims of an exploitative economic system and are not criminals, and *whereas* legalized prostitution is used as a means of employing poor women who are on welfare, be it resolved that:

(1) those who reap profits from prostitution be given heavy prison sentences and be made to pay large fines.

(2) that *mujeres* who are forced to prostitution not be condemned to serve prison sentences;

(3) that prostitution not be legalized.

Abortions

Whereas we, as *Chicanas*, have been subjected to illegal, dehumanizing, and unsafe abortions, let it be resolved that we endorse legalized medical abortions in order to protect the human right of self-determination. . . .

Community-Controlled Clinics

We resolve that more *Chicano* clinics (self-supporting) be implemented to service the *Chicano* community. . . .

Child-Care Centers

In order that women may leave their children in the hands of someone they trust and know will understand the cultural ways of their children, be it resolved that *Raza* child-care programs be established in *nuestros barrios.* . . .

National Black Feminist Organization, *Manifesto* (1974)

African-American feminists developed their own agenda and separated themselves from white women's groups. Unlike white women, African-American women found themselves oppressed by both racism and sexism. At the core of black feminist protest is recognition of this dual oppression that also has resulted in keeping most black women poor. What are the "distorted images" of black women referred to in the document? What does the author mean by the remark that black women are the "almost cast aside half of the black race?" Why are black men considered "sexist"?[*]

The distorted male-dominated media image of the Women's Liberation Movement has clouded the vital and revolutionary importance of this movement to Third World women, especially black women. The Movement has been characterized as the exclusive property of so-called white middle-class women and any black women seen involved in this Movement have been seen as "selling out," "dividing the race," and an assortment of nonsensical epithets. Black feminists resent these charges and have therefore established The National Black Feminist Organization, in order to address ourselves to the particular and specific needs of the larger, but almost cast-aside half of the black race in Amerikka, the black woman.

Black women have suffered cruelly in this society from living the phenomenon of being black and female, in a country that is *both* racist and sexist. There has been very little real examination of the damage it has caused in the lives and on the minds of black women. Because we live in a patriarchy, we have allowed a premium to be put on black male suffering. No one of us would minimize the pain or hardship, or the cruel and inhumane treatment experienced by the black man. But history, past or present, rarely deals with the malicious abuse put upon the black woman. We were seen as breeders by the master; despised and historically polarized from/by the master's wife, and looked upon as castrators by our lovers and husbands. The black woman has had to be strong, yet we are persecuted for having survived. We have been

---

[*] From "National Black Feminist Organization Manifesto" in *Ms.*, May 1974, p.99.

called "matriarchs" by white racists and black nationalists; we have virtually no positive self-images to validate our existence. Black women want to be proud, dignified, and free from all those false definitions of beauty and womanhood that are unrealistic and unnatural. *We,* not white men or black men, must define our own self-image as black women, and not fall into the mistake of being placed upon the pedestal, which is even being rejected by white women. It has been hard for black women to emerge from the myriad of distorted images that have portrayed us as grinning Beulahs, castrating Sapphires and pancake-box Jemimas. As black feminists, we realized the need to establish ourselves as an independent black feminist origination. Our aboveground presence will lend enormous credibility to the current Women's Liberation Movement, which unfortunately is not seen as the serious political and economic revolutionary force that it is. We will strengthen the current efforts of the Black Liberation struggle in this country, by encouraging *all* of the talents and creativities of black women to emerge, strong and beautiful, not to feel guilty or divisive, and assume positions of leadership and honor in the black community. We will encourage the black community to stop falling into the trap of the white male left, utilizing women only in terms of domestic or servile needs. We will continue to remind the Black Liberation Movement that there can't be liberation for half the race. We must together, as a people, work to eliminate racism, from without the black community, which is trying to destroy us as an entire people; but we must remember that sexism is destroying and crippling us from within.

Lesbian Feminist Organization, *Constitution* (1973)

Lesbians looked to the feminist movement to address the inequities they faced as women and as lesbians. In this manifesto, lesbian women alleged that even the "liberation of gays" would still leave them oppressed as women. Aside from the controversy surrounding homosexuality, lesbian lifestyles raised the issue of female independence from men in its most extreme form. What is meant by the term "heterosexual chauvinism"?[*]

We, Lesbian Feminist Liberation, dedicate ourselves to promoting our identities as Lesbians and combating sexism as it manifests itself in heterosexual chauvinism and male supremacy.

---

[*] From "Lesbian Feminist Organization Constitution" in Judith Papachriston, ed., *Women Together* (NY: Alfred A. Knopf, Inc., 1976).

We as Lesbian-feminists assert the right of every woman to be a self-defined individual. We declare the necessity for all women to discover and use the potentials and resources which exist in themselves and each other. We assert the right of every woman to express herself with her body, intellect and emotions as the complete human being that society has discouraged her from being. We assert the right of every woman to express her sexuality in any way she chooses as an affirmation of her individuality. We declare our intention to confront and disarm the attitudes and institutions that attempt to limit these rights.

We foresee the day when all individuals are free to define themselves in a non-sexist society. However, our present oppression as Lesbians and as women, makes it imperative that we not content ourselves with this utopian vision. Because the achievement of our liberation as gay people would leave us still oppressed as women, we recognize that our primary strength is in feminism. Feminism is not so much a given set of specific issues, as it is a way of life which considers as primary our identities as women. As Lesbian-feminists the focus of all our thoughts and actions centers on our identities as Lesbian women. Now we must dedicate our energies primarily to discovering ourselves and our special causes, and, acting as our own spokeswomen, to promoting ourselves everywhere, at all times, as Lesbian women. To this end, it is crucial that we function as an organization distinct from both the gay and feminist movements, unique unto ourselves, yet making coalitions with groups on gay and feminist issues, specifically as they relate to our Lesbian identities.

Our feminism and our Lesbianism fuse in our love and respect for women. We are determined to live as we see fit, with other women, in pride and dignity.

National Organization for Women, *General Resolution Lesbian/Gay Rights* (1973)

Initially, NOW's leadership attempted to distance itself from the enormously controversial issue of sexual orientation or preference. However, as the following resolution states, lesbian civil rights issues became a part of NOW's agenda. Has civil rights legislation successfully reduced discrimination against lesbians?*

Whereas, women have the basic right to develop to the maximum their full human sexual potential, and

* From the National Organization for Women's Resolutions of the 1973 National Conference. Reprinted by permission.

Whereas, diversity is richly human, and all women must be able to freely define and to express their own sexuality and to choose their own life style, and

Whereas, NOW's public relations and communications have omitted references to the unified efforts of women of tradition and diverse sexual experience, and

Whereas, Lesbians have formed a caucus in NOW to communicate openly, without fear and hostility, and

Whereas, the threat traditionally felt from Lesbianism must no longer be a barrier to open communication between all people, and

Whereas, we recognize that women are all oppressed by one common oppression, and therefore, surely we must not oppress one another for any reason;

Therefore be it resolved that a statement adopting the sense of this resolution be included in all appropriate NOW publications and policy statements; and,

Be it further resolved that NOW actively introduce and support civil rights legislation designed to end discrimination based on sexual orientation, and to introduce with legislation to end discrimination based on sex, the phrase "sexual orientation" in areas such as, but not limited to, housing, unemployment, credit, finance, child custody and public accommodations.

14

Contested Terrain: Change and Resistance

Feminism played a major role in the transformation of gender norms and the empowerment of women. In response to the resurgence of feminist collective action during the 1970s, Congress passed a variety of gender equity acts and included women in affirmative action guidelines. Women entered nontraditional fields as police and fire *persons*. Even language changed and became, as the preceding job titles illustrate, gender neutral. Gender-designated advertising for employment ended. Women's studies and women's history joined the college curriculum. Texbooks displayed a new sensititvity to the issues of gender bias. New employment opportunities led to an upsurge in the numbers of women in law, medicine, and college teaching. Women entered the formerly male preserve of news and even sports broadcasting. In *Roe* v. *Wade* (1973), the Supreme Court upheld the right of women to choose abortion.

Yet, even as the women's movement gained momentum, victories met with increasing opposition. Right-to-life groups mobilized to repeal *Roe* v. *Wade*. Although Congress passed the ERA in 1972, the requisite number of states did not ratify the amendment. Anti-amendment groups rallied around conservative activist Phyllis Schlafly in a highly effective Stop ERA campaign. Among its multiple meanings, the 1980 Reagan victory expressed a societal retreat from widespread social and cultural change. The Republican party withdrew its support from the ERA, and political leaders spoke out against abortion rights and in favor of traditional family values. Increasingly, conservative critics pitted women's rights against family values and charged the entire women's movement with the increased divorce rate and the destabilization of families. During the 1980s feminist objectives also fostered a gender gap. Caught in the spiral of the national transformation to a post-industrial and global economy, that caused the loss of jobs and downward mobility, some white men lashed out at the women's movement as the cause of their economic and social distress. An electoral gender gap emerged: compared with white women, white men voted in higher numbers for conservative Republican candidates.

Advocates of women's rights also confronted a generation gap. Many younger women did not identify with women's issues, or the need for women as a group to resolve remaining gender inequities. In an manner reminiscent of the 1920s "new style" feminists, they focused on individual achievement. Profiting from greater employment opportunity and increasing social acceptance of changing women's roles, they distanced themselves from the older generation of feminists. Some joined the backlash described by Susan Faludi.

Despite the unsympathetic federal administrations of the 1980s and the growing conservative backlash, the feminist agenda still reponded to the needs of millions of women. The feminist philosophy that the "personal is political" continued to resonate. Issues such as spousal abuse, sexual harassment and abortion rights received grass-roots support and national attention. Activist women continued to campaign for the resolution of persistent workplace inequities, and the provision of adequate and affordable childcare. Even before the organized women's movement, growing numbers of married women with children had been entering the workforce. For many the difficulties involved in combining work and motherhood remained enormous. Single mothers generally faced the greatest hardship. The media publicized their plight the growing "feminization of povery." By the mid-1990s welfare mothers faced the prospect of a roll-back of the entitlements in place since the 1930s.

In significant ways, the formation of domestic policy during the 1980s and the early 1990s, reflected the cultural battles being waged between groups demanding the restoration of traditional family values, and those protecting women's changing gender roles. The contest over women's rights has remained pivotal to the policy debate. It has influenced Supreme Court appointments and helped determine election results. While the election of a Democratic president in 1992 promised greater affirmation of women's rights, the 1994 congressional victories of conservative Republicans signified the potential for retreat. This contested terrain remains central to the nation's cultural battleground.

Roe v. Wade (1973)

This Roe v. Wade Supreme Court decision upheld the right of women to obtain medically safe abortions. To feminists, abortion rights were essential to women's freedom. For abortion opponents, fetal rights took precedence over women's rights. Moreover, the ability of a woman to terminate pregnancy represented the ultimate challenge to what many religious and conservative groups still considered women's God given maternal function. The most divisive of all women's issues, the controversy between the right to abortion and the right to life continues to divide not only women, but the nation in general. How did the court define the right to privacy? *

Mr. Justice Blackmun delivered the opinion of the Court.

It perhaps is not generally appreciated that the restrictive criminal abortion laws in effect in a majority of States today are of relatively recent vintage. Those laws, generally proscribing abortion or its attempt at any time during pregnancy except when necessary to preserve the pregnant woman's life, are not of ancient or even of common-law origin. Instead, they derive from statutory changes effected, for the most part, in the latter half of the 19th century.

Three reasons have been advanced to explain historically the enactment of criminal abortion laws in the 19th century and to justify their continued existence.

It has been argued occasionally that these laws were the product of a Victorian social concern to discourage illicit sexual conduct. Texas, however, does not advance this justification in the present case, and it appears that no court or commentator has taken the argument seriously. . . .

A second reason is concerned with abortion as a medical procedure. When most criminal abortion laws were first enacted, the procedure was a hazardous one for the woman. . . . Thus, it has been argued that a State's real concern in enacting a criminal abortion law was to protect the pregnant woman, that is, to restrain her from submitting to a procedure that placed her life in serious jeopardy.

Modern medical techniques have altered this situation. Appellants and various amici refer to medical data indicating the abortion in early pregnancy, that is, prior to the end of the first trimester, although not without its risk, is now relatively safe. Mortality rates for women undergoing early abortions, where the procedure is legal, appear to be as low or lower than the rates for normal childbirth. Consequently, any interest of the State in protecting the woman from an inherently hazardous procedure, except when it would be equally dangerous for her to undergo it, has largely disappeared. Of course, important state interests in the area of health and medical standards do remain. . . .

The third reason is the State's interest—some phrase it in terms of duty—in protecting prenatal life. Some of the argument for its justification rests on the theory that a new human life is present from the moment of conception. The State's interest and general obligation to protect life then extends, it is argued, to prenatal life. Only when the life of the pregnant mother herself is at stake, balanced against the life she carries within her, should the interest of the embryo or fetus not prevail. Logically, of course, a legitimate state interest in this area need not stand or fall on acceptance of the belief that life begins at conception or at some other point prior to live birth. In assessing the State's interest, recognition may be given to the less rigid claim that as long as at least *potential* life is involved, the State may assert interests beyond the protection of the pregnancy woman alone. . . .

---

*From *Jane Roe* v. *Henry Wade*, Opinion of the Court 410, U.S. 113, L. Ed. 2d 14793. Supreme Court 705, 1973.

The Constitution does not explicitly mention any right of privacy. In a line of decisions, however, the Court has recognized that a right of personal privacy, or a guarantee of certain areas or zones of privacy, does exist under the Constitution. . . .

This right of privacy, whether it be founded in the Fourteenth Amendment's concept of personal liberty and restrictions upon state action, as we feel it is, or, as the District Court determined, in the Ninth Amendment's reservation of right to the people, is broad enough to encompass a woman's decision whether or not to terminate her pregnancy. The detriment that the State would impose upon the pregnant women by denying this choice altogether is apparent. Specific and direct harm medically diagnosable even in early pregnancy may be involved. Maternity, or additional offspring, may force upon the woman a distressful life and future. Psychological harm may be imminent. Mental and physical health may be taxed by child care. There is also the distress, for all concerned, associated with the unwanted child, and there is the problem of bringing a child into a family already unable, psychologically and otherwise, to care for it. In other cases, as in this one, the additional difficulties and continuing stigma of unwed motherhood may be involved. All these are factors the woman and her responsible physician necessarily will consider in consultation.

On the basis of elements such as these, appellant and some amici argue that the woman's right: is absolute, that she is entitled to terminate her pregnancy at whatever time, in whatever way, and for whatever reason she alone chooses. With this we do not agree. Appellant's arguments that Texas either has no valid interest at all in regulating the abortion decision, or no interest strong enough to support any limitation upon the woman's sole determination, is unpersuasive. The Court's decisions recognizing a right of privacy, also acknowledge that some state regulation in areas protected by that right is appropriate. As noted above, a State may properly assert important interests in safeguarding health, in maintaining medical standards, and in protecting potential life. At some point in pregnancy, these respective interests become sufficiently compelling to sustain regulation of the factors that govern the abortion decision. The privacy right involved, therefore, cannot be said to be absolute.
. . .

We, therefore, conclude that the right of personal privacy includes the abortion decision, but that this right is not unqualified and must be considered against important state interests in regulation. . . .

With respect to the State's important and legitimate interest in the health of the mother, the "compelling" point, in the light of present medical knowledge, is at approximately the end of the first trimester. This is so because of the now-established medical fact that until the end of the first trimester mortality in abortion may be less than mortality in normal childbirth. It follows that, from and after this point, a State may regulate the abortion procedure to the extent that the regulation reasonably relates to the preservation and protection of maternal health. . . .

With respect to the State's important and legitimate interest in potential life, the "compelling" point is a viability. This is so because the fetus then presumably has the capability of meaningful life outside the mother's womb. State regulation protective of fetal life after viability thus has both logical and biological justifications. If the State is interested in protecting fetal life after viability, it may go so far as to proscribe abortion during that period, except when it is necessary to preserve the life or health of the mother. . . .

Phyllis Schlafly, *The Positive Woman* (1977)

Politically active in conservative causes since the 1950s, Phyllis Schlafly became well known for her successful mobilization of opposition to the ERA. In this excerpt from her book *The Positive Woman*, Schlafly argued that female attributes are God given and part of the fixed order of nature and the universe. For Schlafly, "positive women" accept their inborn nature, and feminists are unnatural. Gender as a cultural construction that changes over time has no meaning to critics such as Schlafly. What does Schlafy mean by women's "kind of superior strength"? What does she mean by the statement "men are philosophers, women are practical and, was ever thus"? How are her views similar to those of Amelia Barr? *

The first requirement for the acquisition of power by the Positive Woman is to understand the differences between men and women. Your outlook on life, your faith, your behavior, your potential for fulfillment, all are determined by the parameters of your original premise. The Positive Woman starts with the assumption that the world is her oyster. She rejoices in the creative capability within her body and the power potential of her mind and spirit. She understands that men and women are different, and that those very differences provide the key to her success as a person and fulfillment as a woman. The women's liberationist, on the other hand, is imprisoned by her own negative view of herself and of her place in the world around her. This view of women was most succinctly expressed in an advertisement designed by the principal women's liberationist organization, the National Organization for Women (NOW), and run in many magazines and newspapers, and as spot announcements on many television stations. The advertisement showed a darling curlyheaded girl with the caption: "This healthy, normal baby has a handicap. She was born female."

This is the self-articulated dog-in-the-manger, chip-on-the-shoulder, fundamental dogma of the women's liberation movement. Someone—it is not clear who, perhaps God, perhaps the "Establishment," perhaps a conspiracy of male chauvinist pigs—dealt women a foul blow by making them female. It becomes necessary, therefore, for

---

*From Phyllis Schlafly, *The Power of the Positive Woman* (New York: Arlington House, 1977), 11–19. Reprinted by permission of Crown Publishers, Inc. Copyright © 1977 by Phyllis Schlafly.

women to agitate and demonstrate and hurl demands on society, in order to wrest from an oppressive male-dominated social structure the status that has been wrongfully denied to women through the centuries.

By its very name, therefore, the women's liberation movement precipitates a series of conflict situations—in the legislatures, in the courts, in the schools, in industry—with man targeted as the enemy. Confrontation replaces cooperation as the watchwords of all relationships. Women and men become adversaries instead of partners.

The second dogma of the women's liberationists is that, of all the injustices perpetuated upon women through the centuries, the most oppressive is the cruel fact that women have babies and men do not. Within the confines of the women's liberationist ideology, therefore, the abolition of this overriding inequality of women becomes the primary goal. This goal must be achieved at any and all costs—to the woman herself, to the baby, to the family, and to society. Women must be made equal to men in their ability *not* to become pregnant and *not* be expected to care for babies they may bring into the world. . . .

The Positive Woman will never travel that dead-end road. It is self-evident to the Positive Woman that the female body with its baby-producing organs was not designed by a conspiracy of men, but by the Divine Architect of the human race. Those who think it is unfair that women have babies, whereas men cannot, will have to take up their complaint with God because no other power is capable of changing that fundamental fact. . . .

The third basic dogma of the women's liberation movement is that there is no difference between male and female, except the sex organs, and that all those physical, cognitive, and emotional differences you *think* there are, are merely the results of centuries of restraints imposed by male-dominated society and sex-stereotyped schooling. The role imposed on women is, by definition, inferior, according to the women's liberationists.

The Positive Woman knows that, while there are some physical competitions in which women are better (and can command more money) than men, including those that put a premium on grace and beauty, such as figure skating, the superior physical strength of males over females in competitions of strength, speed, and short-term endurance is beyond rational dispute. . . .

Does the physical advantage of men doom women to a life of servility and subservience? The Positive Woman knows that she has a complementary advantage which is at least as great—and, in the hands of a skillful woman, far greater. The Divine Architect who gave men a superior strength to lift weights also gave women a different kind of superior strength.

The women's liberationists and their dupes who try and tell each other that the sexual drive of men and women is really the same, and that it is only societal restraints that inhibit women from an equal desire, and equal enjoyment, and an equal freedom from the consequences, are doomed to frustration forever. It just isn't so, and pretending cannot make it so. The differences are not a woman's weakness but her strength. . . .

The new generation can brag all it wants about the new liberation of the new morality, but it is still the woman who is hurt the most. The new morality isn't just a "fad"—it is a cheat and a thief. It robs the woman of her virtue, her youth, her beauty, and her love—for nothing, just nothing. It has produced a generation of young women searching for their identity, bored with sexual freedom, and despondent from the loneliness of living a life without commitment. They have abandoned the old commandments, but they can't find any new rules that work. . . .

The differences between men and women are also emotional and psychological. Without woman's innate maternal instinct, the human race would have died out centuries ago. There is nothing so helpless in all earthly life as the newborn infant. It will die within hours if not cared for. Even in the most primitive, uneducated societies, women have always cared for their newborn babies. They didn't need any schooling to teach them how. They didn't need any welfare workers to tell them it is their social obligation. Even in societies to whom such concepts as "ought," "social responsibility," and "compassion for the helpless" were unknown, mothers cared for their new babies.

Why? Because caring for a baby serves the natural maternal need of a woman. Although not nearly so total as the baby's need, the woman's need is nonetheless real. The overriding psychological need of a woman is to love something alive. A baby fulfills this need in the lives of most women. If a baby is not available to fill this need, women search for a baby-substitute. This is the reason why women have traditionally gone into teaching and nursing careers. They are doing what comes naturally to the female psyche. The schoolchild or the patient of any age provides an outlet for a woman to express her natural maternal need. . . .

Finally, women are different from men in dealing with the fundamentals of life itself. Men are philosophers, women are practical, and 'twas ever thus. Men may philosophize about how life began and where we are heading; women are concerned about feeding the kids today. No woman would ever, as Karl Marx did, spend years reading political philosophy in the British Museum while her child starved to death. Women don't take naturally to a search for the intangible and the abstract. The Positive Woman knows who she is and where she is going, and she will reach her goal because the longest journey starts with a very practical first step.

A Letter from a Battered Wife (1983)

Feminists made women's private concerns public and connected the personal to the political. They argued that male violence stemmed from inequitable power relationships and society's permissive attitude toward abuse of women. What evidence does the abused wife offer of her relative helplessness? This letter was written in 1983; what gains, if any, have women made in combating violence?[*]

I am in my thirties and so is my husband. I have a high school diploma and am presently attending a local college, trying to obtain the additional education I need. My husband is a college graduate and a professional in his field. We are both attractive and, for the most part, respected and well-liked. We have four children and live in a middle-class home with all the comforts we could possibly want.

I have everything, except a life without fear.

For most of my married life I have been periodically beaten by my husband. What do I mean by "beaten"? I mean that parts of my body have been hit violently and repeatedly, and that painful bruises, swelling, bleeding wounds, unconsciousness, and combinations of these things have resulted.

Beating should be distinguished from all other kinds of physical abuse—including being hit and shoved around. When I say my husband threatens me with abuse I do not mean he warns me that he may lose control. I mean he shakes his fist against my face or nose, makes punching-bag jabs at my shoulder, or makes similar gestures which may quickly turn into a full-fledged beating.

I have had glasses thrown at me. I have been kicked in the abdomen when I was visibly pregnant. I have been kicked off the bed and hit while I was lying on the floor—again, while I was pregnant. I have been whipped, kicked and thrown, picked up again and thrown down again. I have been punched and kicked in the head, chest, face, and abdomen more times than I can count. . . .

Now the first response to this story, which I myself think of, will be "Why didn't you seek help?"

I did. Early on in our marriage I went to a clergyman who, after a few visits, told me that my husband meant no real harm, and he was just confused and felt insecure. I was encouraged to be more tolerant and understanding. Most important, I was told to forgive him the beatings just as Christ had forgiven me from the cross. I did that, too. . . .

I turned to a professional family guidance agency. I was told there that my husband needed help and that I should find a way to control the incidents. I couldn't control the beatings—that was the whole point of my seeking help. At the agency I found I had to defend myself against that suspicion that I wanted to be hit, that I invited the beatings. Good God! Did the Jews invite themselves to be slaughtered in Germany?

I called the police one time. They not only did not respond to the call, they called several hours later to ask if things had "settled down." I could have been dead by then!

---

[*] From Del Martin, *Battered Wives* (New York: Pocket Books, 1983). Reprinted by permission of the Volcano Press.

I have nowhere to go if it happens again. No one wants to take in a woman with four children. Even if there were someone kind enough to care, no one wants to become involved in what is commonly referred to as a "domestic situation."

As a married woman I have no recourse but to remain in the situation which is causing me to be painfully abused. I have suffered physical and emotional battering and spiritual rape because the social structure of my world says I cannot do anything about a man who wants to beat me. . . . But staying with my husband means that my children must be subjected to the emotional battering caused when they see their mother's beaten face or hear her screams in the middle of the night.

I know that I have to get out. But when you have nowhere to go, you know that you must go on your own, and expect no support. I have to be ready for that. I have to be ready to support myself and the children completely, and still provide a decent environment for them. I pray that I can do that before I am murdered in my own home.

I have learned that no one believes me and that I cannot depend upon any outside help. All I have left is the hope that I can get away before it is too late.

I have learned also that the doctors, the police, the clergy, and my friends will excuse my husband for distorting my face, but won't forgive me for looking bruised and broken. The greatest tragedy is that I am still praying, and there is not a human person to listen.

Being beaten is a terrible thing; it is most terrible of all if you are not equipped to fight back. I recall an occasion when I tried to defend myself and actually tore my husband's shirt. Later, he showed it to a relative as proof that I had done something terribly wrong. The fact that at that moment I had several raised spots on my head hidden by my hair, a swollen lip that was bleeding, and a severely damaged cheek with a blood clot that caused a permanent dimple didn't matter to him. What mattered was that I tore his shirt! That I tore it in self-defense didn't mean anything to him.

My situation is so untenable I would guess that anyone who has not experienced one like it would find it incomprehensible. I find it difficult to believe myself. . . .

Kate Shanley, *Thoughts on Indian Feminism* (1984)

Although Kate Shanley identifies with her Native American background, she also shares many of the concerns of mainstream feminism. Her words provide direct testimony to the complexity of dual identities. Why does she feel that white feminists see Indians as "spiritual mascots"? What does she cite as the essential characteristics of Indian feminism?*

Attending the Ohoyo conference in Grand Forks, North Dakota, was a returning home for me in a spiritual sense—taking my place beside other Indian women, and an actual sense—being with my relatives and loved ones after finally finishing my pre-doctoral requirements at the university. Although I have been a full-time student for the past six years, I brought to the academic experience many years in the workaday world as a mother, registered nurse, volunteer tutor, social worker aide, and high school outreach worker. What I am offering in this article are my thoughts as an Indian woman on feminism. Mine is a political perspective that seeks to review the real-life positions of women, in relation to the theories that attempt to address the needs of those women.

Issues such as equal pay for equal work, child health and welfare, and a woman's right to make her own choices regarding contraceptive use, sterilization and abortion—key issues to the majority women's movement—affect Indian women as well; however, equality *per se*, may have a different meaning for Indian women and Indian people. That difference begins with person and tribal sovereignty— the right to be legally recognized as people empowered to determine our own destinies. Thus, the Indian women's movement seeks equality in two ways that do not concern mainstream women: (1) on the individual level, the Indian woman struggles to promote the survival of a social structure, whose organizational principles represent notions of family different from those of the mainstream; and (2) on the societal level, the People seek sovereignty as a people in order to maintain a vital legal and spiritual connection to the land, in order to *survive* as a people.

The nuclear family has little relevance to Indian women; in fact, in many ways, mainstream feminists now are striving to redefine family and community in a way that Indian women have long known. The American lifestyle from which white middle-class women are fighting to free themselves, has not taken hold in Indian communities. Tribal and communal value have survived after four hundred years of colonial oppression.

It may be that the desire on the part of mainstream feminists to include Indian women, however sincere, represents tokenism just now, because too often Indian people, by being thought of as spiritual "mascots" to the American endeavor, are seen more as artifacts than a real people able to speak for ourselves. Given the public's general ignorance about Indian people, in other words, it is possible that Indian people's real-life concerns are not relevant to the mainstream feminist movement in a way that constitutes anything more than a "representative" façade. Charges against the women's movement of heterosexism and racism abound these days; it is not my intention to add them except to stress that we must all be vigilant in examining the underlying assumptions that motivate us. Internalization of negative (that is, sexist

---

* Reprinted from Kate Shanley "Thoughts on Indian Feminism," in Beth Brant, ed., *A Gathering of the Spirit* (Berkley, Ca.: Sinister Wisdom Books, 1984).

and racist) attitudes towards ourselves and others can and quite often does result from colonialist (white patriarchal) oppression. It is more useful to attack the systems that keep us ignorant of each other's histories.

The other way in which the Indian women's movement differs in emphasis from the majority women's movement, lies in the importance Indian people place on tribal sovereignty—it is the single most pressing political issue in the Indian country today. For Indian people to survive culturally as well as materially, many battles must be fought and won in the courts of law, precisely because it is the legal recognition that enables Indian people to govern ourselves according to our own world view—a world view that is antithetical to the *wasicu* (the Lakota term for "takers of the fat") definition of progress. Equality for Indian women within tribal communities, therefore, holds more significance than equality in terms of the general rubric "American."

Up to now I have been referring to the women's movement as though it were a single, well-defined organization. It is not. Perhaps in many ways socialist feminists hold views similar to the views of many Indian people regarding private property and the nuclear family. Certainly there are some Indian people who are capitalistic. The point I would like to stress, however, is that rather than seeing differences according to a hierarchy of oppressions (white over Indian, male over female), we must practice politics that allows for diversity in cultural identity as well as in sexual identity.

The word "feminism" has special meanings to Indian women, including the idea of promoting the continuity of tradition, and consequently, pursuing the recognition of tribal sovereignty. Even so, Indian feminists are united with mainstream feminists in outrage against woman and child battering, sexist employment and educational practices, and in many other social concerns. Just as sovereignty cannot be granted but *must be recognized* as an inherent right to self-determination, so Indian feminism must also be recognized as powerful in its own terms, in its own right.

Feminism becomes an incredibly powerful term when it incorporates diversity—not as a superficial political position, but as a practice. The women's movement and the Indian movement for sovereignty suffer similar trivialization, because narrow factions turn ignorance to their own benefit, so that they can exploit human beings and the lands they live on for corporate profit. The time has come for Indian women and the Indian people to be known on our own terms. This nuclear age demands new terms of communication for all people. Our survival depends on it. Peace.

Anita Hill, *Statement to the Senate Judiciary Committee* (1993)

Anita Hill's (b. 1956) allegation in 1993 that Supreme Court nominee Clarence Thomas, the former head of the Equal Employment Opportunity Commission (EEOC), was guilty of sexual harassment propelled the issue to national attention. As a result of Hill's testimony, many other women filed sexual harassment complaints. Over the centuries African-American women have struggled against the simultaneous oppression of race and gender. The testimony of Hill, an African-American female, against Thomas, an African-American male raised both race and gender issues. What would some of these issues be? [*]

Mr. Chairman, Senator Thurmond, members of the committee:

My name is Anita F. Hill, and I am a professor of law at the University of Oklahoma. I was born on a farm in Okmulgee County, Oklahoma, in 1956. I am the youngest of thirteen children. . . .

For my undergraduate work, I went to Oklahoma State University and graduated from there in 1977. I am attaching to this statement a copy of my resume for further details of my education. . . .

I graduated from the university with academic honors, and proceeded to the Yale Law School, where I received my J.D. degree in 1980.

Upon graduation from law school, I became a practicing lawyer with the Washington, D.C., firm of Wald, Wakrader & Ross. In 1981 I was introduced to now Judge Thomas by a mutual friend.

Judge Thomas told me that he was anticipating a political appointment, and asked if I would be interested in working with him.

He was in fact appointed as assistant secretary of education for civil rights. After he had taken that post, he asked if I would become his assistant, and I accepted that position.

In my early period, there, I had two major projects. First was an article I wrote for Judge Thomas's signature on the education of minority students. The second was the organization of a seminar on high-risk students, which was abandoned because Judge Thomas transferred to the EEOC, where he became the chairman of that office.

[*]From Anita Hill, "Statement to the Senate Judiciary Committee in Hearings before the Committee on the Judiciary," U.S. Senate, 102nd Congress, 1st Session; nomination of Judge Clarence Thomas to be Associate Justice of the Supreme Court of the United States (Washington, D.C.: U.S. Government Printing Office, 1993), part 4, 36–40.

During this period at the Department of Education my working relationship with Judge Thomas was positive. I had a good deal of responsibility and independence. I thought he respected my work, and that he trusted my judgment.

After approximately three months of working there, he asked me to go out socially with him. What happened next, and telling the world about it, are the two most difficult things—experiences of my life.

It is only after a great deal of agonizing consideration, and a number of sleepless nights, that I am able to talk of these unpleasant matters to anyone but my closest friends.

I declined the invitation to go out socially with him, and explained to him that I thought it would jeopardize what at the time I considered to be a very good working relationship. I had a normal social life with men outside the office. I believed then, as now, that having a social relationship with a person who was supervising my work would be ill-advised. I was very uncomfortable with the idea and told him so.

I thought that by saying no and explaining my reasons, my employer would abandon his social suggestions. However, to my regret, in the following few weeks, he continued to ask me out on several occasions.

He pressed me to justify reasons for saying no to him. These incidents took place in his office, or mine. They were in the form of private conversation, which would not have been overheard by anyone else.

My working relationship became even more strained when Judge Thomas began to use work situations to discuss sex. On these occasions he would call me into his office for a course on education issues and projects, or he might suggest that because of the time pressures of his schedule, we go to lunch to a government cafeteria.

After a brief discussion of work, he would turn the conversation to a discussion of sexual matters. His conversations were very vivid. He spoke about acts that he had seen in pornographic films involving such matters as women having sex with animals, and films showing group sex or rape scenes.

He talked about pornographic materials depicting individuals with large penises or large breasts, involving various sex acts. . . .

Throughout the period of these conversations, he also from time to time asked me for social engagements. My reaction to these conversations was to avoid them by limiting opportunities for us to engage in extended conversations.

This was difficult because, at the time, I was his only assistant at the office of education—or the office for civil rights. During the latter part of my time at the Department of Education, the social pressures, and any conversation of his offensive behavior, ended. I began both to believe and hope that our relationship could be a proper, cordial, and professional one.

When Judge Thomas was made chair of the EEOC, I needed to face the question of whether to go with him. I was asked to do so, and I did.

The work itself was interesting, and at the time it appeared that the sexual overtures which had so troubled me had ended.

I also faced the realistic fact that I had no alternative job. While I might have gone back to private practice, perhaps in my old firm or another, I was dedicated to civil rights work and my first choice was to be in that field. Moreover, at that time, the Department of Education itself was a dubious venture. President Reagan was seeking to abolish the entire department.

For my first months at the EEOC, where I continued to be an assistant to Judge Thomas, there were no sexual conversations or overtures. However, during the fall and winter of 1982, these began again. The comments were random and ranged from pressing me about why I didn't go out with him, to remarks about my personal appearance. I remember his saying that some day I would have to tell him the real reason that I wouldn't go out with him.

He began to show displeasure in his tone and voice, and his demeanor and his continued pressure for an explanation. He commented on what I was wearing in terms of whether it made me more or less sexually attractive. He incidents occurred in his inner office at the EEOC.

One of the oddest episodes I remember was an occasion in which Thomas was drinking a Coke in his office. He got up from the table at which we were working, went over to his desk, looked at the can, and asked, "Who has put pubic hair on my Coke?"

On other occasions, he referred to the size of his own penis as being larger than normal, and he also spoke on some occasions of the pleasures he had given to women with oral sex. At this point, late in 1982, I began to be concerned that Clarence Thomas might take out his anger with me by degrading me, or not giving me important assignments. I also thought that he might find an excuse for dismissing me.

In January of 1983, I began looking for another job. I was handicapped because I feared that if he found out, he might make it difficult for me to find other employment and I might be dismissed from the job I had. Another factor that made my search more difficult was that this was during a period of a hiring freeze in the government. . . .

On, as I recall, the last day of my employment at the EEOC in the summer of 1983, I did have dinner with Clarence Thomas. We went directly from work to a restaurant near the office. We talked about the work I had done, both at Education and at the EEOC. He told me that he was pleased with all of it, except for an article and speech that I had done for him while we were at the Office for Civil Rights. Finally he made a comment that I will vividly remember. He said that if I ever told anyone of his behavior it would ruin his career. This was not an apology; nor was it an explanation. That was his last remark about the possibility of our going out or reference to his behavior.

In July of 1983 I left the Washington, D.C., area and I've had minimal contacts with Judge Clarence Thomas since. . . .

It would have been more comfortable to remain silent. I took no initiative to inform anyone. But when I was asked by a representative of this committee to report my experience, I felt that I had to tell the truth. I could not keep silent.

Ruth Bader Ginsburg, *On Being Nominated to the Supreme Court* (1993)

Judge Ruth Bader Ginsburg's nomination to the Supreme Court reflected the Clinton Administration's decision to appoint women to the highest-level national positions. A nationally known advocate for gender equity, Ginsburg (b. 1933) joined Sandra Day O'Connor, the first woman appointed to the Supreme Court, on the bench. What changes have occurred for women in the law profession between the late 1950s and the present? *

The announcement the President just made is significant, I believe, because it contributes to the end of the days when women, at least half the talent pool in our society, appear in high places only as one-at-a-time performers. Recall that when President Carter took office in 1976, no woman had ever served on the Supreme Court, and only one woman . . . then served at the next Federal court level, the United States Court of Appeals.

Today Justice Sandra Day O'Connor graces the Supreme Court bench, and close to twenty-five women serve at the Federal Court of Appeals level, two as chief judges. I am confident that more will soon join them. That seems to me inevitable, given the change in law school enrollment.

My law school class in the late 1950s numbered over 500. That class included less than 10 women. . . . Not a law firm in the entire city of New York bid for my employment as a lawyer when I earned my degree. Today few law schools have female enrollment under 40 percent, and several have passed the 50 percent mark. And thanks to Title VII, no entry doors are barred. . . .

I am indebted to so many in for this extraordinary chance and challenge: to a revived women's movement in the 1970s that opened doors for people like me, to the Civil Rights movement of the 1960s from which the women's movement drew inspiration. . . .

I have a last thank you. It is to my mother, Celia Amster Bader, the bravest and strongest person I have ever known, who was taken from me much too soon. I pray that I may be all that she would have been had she lived in an age when women could aspire and achieve, and daughters are cherished as much as sons. I look forward to stimulating weeks this summer and, if I am confirmed, to working at a neighboring court to the best of my ability for the advancement of the law in the service of society. Thank you.

---

*From Ruth Bader Ginsburg, "On Being Nominated to the Supreme Court," in White House Press Release, June 14, 1993.

Susan Faludi, *Backlash* (1992)

Susan Faludi wrote that the "backlash" against women involved media distortions of feminism, as well as governmental denial of vital support necessary to sustain working mothers. In this excerpt from her book, she describes the 1980 election in terms of a gender gap over women's rights. Why does Faludi believe that some white men "feared and reviled feminism"?*

But what exactly is it about women's equality that even its slightest shadow threatens to erase male identity? What is it about the way we frame manhood that, even today, it still depends so on "feminine" dependence for its survival? A little-noted finding by the Yankelovich Monitor survey, a large nationwide poll that has tracked social attitudes for the last two decades, takes us a good way toward a possible answer. For twenty years, the Monitor's pollsters have asked its subjects to define masculinity. And for twenty years, the leading definition, ahead by a huge margin, has never changed. It isn't being a leader, athlete, lothario, decision maker, or even just being "born male." It is simply this: being a "good provider for his family."

If establishing masculinity depends most of all on succeeding as the prime breadwinner, then it is hard to imagine a force more directly threatening to fragile American manhood than the feminist drive for economic equality. And if supporting a family epitomizes what it means to be a man, then it is little wonder that the backlash erupted when it did—against the backdrop of the '80s economy. In this period, the "traditional" man's real wage shrank dramatically (a 22 percent free-fall in households where white men were the sole breadwinners), and the traditional male breadwinner himself became an endangered species (representing less than 8 percent of all households). That the ruling definition of masculinity remains so economically based helps to explain, too, why the backlash has been voiced most bitterly by two groups of men: blue-collar workers, devastated by the shift to a service economy, and younger baby boomers, denied the comparative riches their fathers and elder brothers enjoyed. The '80s was the decade in which plant closings put blue-collar men out of work by the millions, and only 60 percent found new jobs—about half at lower pay. It was a time when, of all men losing earning power, the younger baby boom men were losing the most. The average man under thirty was earning 25 to 30 percent less than his counterpart in the early '70s. Worst off was the average young man with only a high-school education: he was making only $18,000, half the earnings of his counterpart a decade earlier. As pollster Louis Harris observed, economic polarization spawned the most dramatic attitudinal change recorded in the last decade and a half: a spectacular doubling in the proportion of Americans who describe themselves as feeling "powerless."

When analysts at Yankelovich reviewed the Monitor survey's annual attitudinal data in 1986, they had to create a new category to describe a large segment of the population that had suddenly emerged, espousing a distinct set of values. This segment, now representing a remarkable one-fifth of the study's national sample, was dominated by young men, median age thirty-three, disproportionately single, who were slipping down the income ladder—and furious about it. They were the younger, poorer brothers of the baby boomers, the ones who weren't so celebrated in '80s media and advertising tributes to that generation. The Yankelovich report assigned the angry young men the euphemistic label of "the Contenders."

The men who belonged to this group had one other distinguishing trait: they feared and reviled feminism. "It's these downscale men, the ones who can't earn as much as their fathers, who we find are the most threatened by the women's movement," Susan Hayward, senior vice president at Yankelovich, observes. They represent 20 percent of the population that cannot handle the changes in women's roles. They were not well employed, they were the first ones laid off, they had no savings and not very much in the way of prospects for the future. By the late '80s, the American Male Opinion Index found that the *largest* of its seven demographic groups was now the "Change Resisters," a 24-percent segment of the population that was disproportionately underemployed, "resentful," convinced that they were "being left behind" by a changing society, and most hostile to feminism.

To single out these men alone for blame, however, would be unfair. The backlash's public agenda has been framed and promoted by men of far more affluence and influence than the Contenders, men at the helm in the media, business, and politics. Poorer or less-educated men have not so much been the creators of the antifeminist thesis as its receptors. Most vulnerable to its message, they have picked up and played back the backlash at distortingly high volume. The Contenders have dominated the ranks of the militant wing of the '80s antiabortion movement, the list of plaintiffs filing reverse-discrimination and "men's rights" lawsuits, the steadily mounting police rolls of rapists and sexual assailants. They are men like the notorious Charles Stuart, the struggling fur salesman in Boston who murdered his pregnant wife, a lawyer, because he feared that she—better educated, more successful—was gaining the "upper hand."